Just Passing Through
On My Way To Heaven

Just Passing Through
On My Way To Heaven

Marci Zollinger

ISBN: 9798550489574
Independently Published

Dedication

This book is dedicated to my hero, my best friend, my dad and savior who from beyond the veil held my hand and rescued me through the darkest days of my life. This book wouldn't be what it is without my amazing editor Christina Whitecar who always believed in me and pushed me to be a better writer. Robert Boyd who was the talent on the illustration of the book.

My beautiful mom always believed in my writing from when I was a small child. She inspired me to write a book someday. She supported me and shared words of wisdom to make my dreams now be realized. When she told me she was proud of me I was in tears.

Many people have given me loving support to write this book after my near-death experiences, where I went to heaven and met the Savior. Jim Graham who is like a big brother to me and his wife Alice Graham who took me under their wing when I became deadly ill. My mission president Marsden Blanch and his wife Lynette Blanch who were like my second parents since my dad's passing. They have been my rock through some of my most challenging days. My closest friends, my Facebook family, immediate, extended family. They showed me charity and love through my tears and suffering enduring the worst three years of my life on my deathbed.

Lastly to my hero and best friend my Savior Jesus Christ who taught me that suffering is a part of life. Suffering gives us compassion to others, patience, humility, forgiveness. It develops empathy within us. It brings us closer to Christ and who we are meant to be. We don't have to suffer alone. If we ask him to help us he will send his angels to help us endure our mountains of trials.

Synopsis

After 8 surgeries, including a devastating hysterectomy, Marci was left struggling with both physical and emotional pain as she faced the reality that she would never conceive a child. As her health declined, she lost her faith in God and in religion. After her loving father passes on, she feels alone and hopeless. In despair she determines the only solution to end her pain and suffering is to take her own life. Through a series of miracles and angelic visitations from her father from beyond the veil, she is rescued each time her life comes crashing down.

This is only the beginning of a life and death struggle for Marci as she is diagnosed with gastroparesis following a botched appendectomy. Her body can no longer tolerate food and drink. She is forced to go to the ER weekly for IV fluids to stay alive as the covid-19 pandemic makes healthcare nearly impossible for her. Unable to physically work and support herself, she turns back to God and faith. Twice she nearly dies, and while unconscious she visits the other side where she meets the Savior. She wants to stay in heaven with him, but He tells her that she needs to return and finish writing her book Just Passing Through On the Way to Heaven.

As her body continues to shut down she enters hospice care. At death's door she is saved by Divine Intervention and becomes what many call a "Walking Miracle".

In this true inspiring, miracle story you will see how time and again God intervened in Marci's life as she fought her way through a trial that most wouldn't survive. It is a story of hope as Marci renews her faith in mankind, family, and in her Savior, Jesus Christ.

Chapter 1

Losing My Greatest Gift

"Always remember God will never take anything away from you without the intention of replacing it with something much better"-Via Curiano

I was sitting uncomfortably on the exam table. I could hear the crackle of paper under my legs as they kicked back and forth anxiously. I stared at the medical diagrams on the walls and nervously picked at my cuticles. The door swung open and in walked Dr. Wally. "It's not in the cards for you," he said softly.

My mind raced back to my childhood to my happiest memories. When I was two years old, I carried my cherished doll in my arms like she was my own beautiful baby. My doll matched the colorful plaid pajamas I wore every night.

Later in my teen years, I loved taking care of my younger brothers and younger sister like they were my own treasured doll. I adored changing their stinky diapers. I played peek-a-boo with them. When I heard them cry out in the middle of the night, I would slowly tiptoe into their rooms and walk over to their cribs. I would reach out to comfort them, hold them in my arms and rock them back to sleep with a soothing lullaby.

When my mom had arrived home from the hospital after giving birth to my youngest brother, Levi, I had raced excitedly home from school to see my new baby brother. I ran up the wooden stairs and hurriedly opened the door to my home. I could smell fresh baked bread in the kitchen as I hurried to the living room. I could

1

feel the grimy dirt in between my toes as I flung my socks and shoes on the living room carpet.

The living room had a modern design, with family pictures hanging on the green walls. My mom, a beautiful woman, was sitting on our red sofa. As I ran up to her she held out a beautiful baby boy. She said, "Welcome home, honey. Do you want to hold your new baby brother?"

I held my brother in my arms. He smelled like fresh baby powder, and he stared at me with his blue eyes and his contagious smile. I cupped his tiny hand in my fingers and looked into his eyes with the biggest smile on my face. I said to myself, "I can't wait to be a mom!"

When I was a young child, I would fantasize about my Prince Charming-- tall, dark and handsome man, whisking me away to our beautiful, white modern home. Our four children--two boys and two girls --would be playing in the yard. I could almost hear them giggling while they would sing and dance. Each child would run towards me and wrap their arms around me and give me a gentle kiss, whispering in my ear, "Mommy, I love you."

My beautiful childhood memories were abruptly interrupted by Dr. Wally's voice, relaying the horrific news, "Marci, you need a full hysterectomy."

I thought to myself in sheer horror, How could this be? I had already suffered five long years of laparoscopic surgeries, eight in total. Surgery after surgery, it drained me physically and mentally. I sweat blood and tears in the operating room and emergency room, hoping to finally be fully healed. I endured unspeakable pain in the hopes of one day conceiving my own child.

Now the dream is over. Thoughts raced through my head. Why God? Why don't you love me? How could you do this to me?

What have I done to deserve this? All I had ever wanted since I was a small child was to be a loving, devoted mom. I felt as though God was tearing and ripping away this beautiful dream from me.

Subconsciously, I held on to the hope that maybe God would create a huge miracle. That God would heal me. That God would save me from this disease that plagued my body for so many years. I was too young to give up my dream of being a mom. I was only in my early thirties. My youthful olive skin, brown eyes, athletic physique and wavy caramel hair gave me the resemblance of being in my early twenties. But it didn't matter-- the fight was over. I had lost. I was going to lose the only precious thing I held sacred to myself, my womanhood.

Still unmarried, I was waiting for Mr. Right." Who would want me now?" I thought to myself.

It was then that I began to lose faith in God, in miracles. I thought to myself, If God really loved me, then why would he take from me the only thing that I ever wanted to be? A mom.

I wandered sadly out of Dr. Wally's office with my head held low. As I pushed open the steel doors to go outside, I could smell newly cut grass and feel the warm sun kissing my cheeks as tears continuously flowed down my chin.

Breaking the terrible news to my parents was like breaking the news to a parent that their child's cancer had returned. Endometriosis affects a large percentage of women. It's a devastating condition where endometrial tissue grows outside of the uterus which causes symptoms like pain, bleeding and irritation. Eventually scar tissue develops in the affected areas. This can lead to infertility and life-long pain. It was like a cancer that afflicted my body. I was diagnosed with endometriosis when I was twenty-nine years old, and my loving parents were

3

supportive. They had said, "We are going to beat this. You will have your own children one day. We know it."

But the fight was over. Now, I had to break the devastating news to my parents that children simply weren't in the cards for me.

The sun was fading into the gray clouds. I felt a heavy darkness wash over me as I walked into my parent's condo. I could smell fresh baked rhubarb pie in the kitchen, my mom and dad were eating dinner. I sat down next to my parents, tears streaming down my cheeks. I could barely choke out the words, "I need a hysterectomy. Dr. Wally told me today children are not in my future."

A parent's love for a child is deeper than the heart of the ocean. My parents both gasped in devastation at the unsettling news. My mom said with a concerned look, "Are you sure? There is nothing more they can do to save your uterus?"

I replied, sobbing in my mom's inviting arms, "No."

I was in a blinding haze. It was like I was in a diabolical nightmare, still hoping my brave hero would save me from this ferocious beast that spread throughout my body. I was in encompassing denial. I couldn't accept this frightful fate. I fought the alarming news for a week until my pain was so severe, I could barely stand. I finally gave up the struggle. My poor body was finished physically. I immediately scheduled the hysterectomy surgery for two weeks later with Dr. Wally.

Having a hysterectomy felt like I was in a graveyard with buried hopes. The day of my surgery, I was in a trance. I was enveloped by my own murky despair, and everyone around me felt like they were moving in slow motion. My deep thoughts raced to all I would miss being a mom. I would never experience carrying a beautiful baby in my womb and feeling a small kick for the first time. I would never experience feeling the joy of giving birth to my new baby, whose DNA was composed of both me and my devoted husband. Maybe our baby would have had my brown eyes, light brown hair and my husband's cute nose. I would never feel the joy of bringing my baby home for the first time and rocking him to sleep on my warm chest. My heart ached with sadness so deep I thought I would drown in it.

My thoughts were interrupted by a pleasant voice, "Marci, are you ready to go back for surgery?"

My worst nightmare had begun. It felt like I was in a dark black hole and suddenly large dirt clumps were falling on top of me, burying me into the ground. I was gasping, but the piles of dirt continued to fall on me like hail in a rain storm hitting me, cutting me, bruising me and almost suffocating me. That's how I felt enduring this horrible event-- like I was suffocating. My dream of being a mom was my reason for living. What reason did I have to keep breathing now?

My dreadful terror continued. A lady wearing blue scrubs led me down a dark abyss. She said nicely with a warm smile, "Get undressed and into the surgery gown. I will be back to start an IV."

She closed the white curtain, and I was surrounded by bare white walls resembling my bare empty soul. I felt like a shackled prisoner waiting to lose her identity by being tortured with sharp objects. I scanned the dark room for comfort from my troubled mind, but all I saw was a plaid nightgown laying on a drafty bed sheet. It felt as if it were announcing my eternal doom. I slipped into the night gown and sat patiently on the bed with my knees bent. I covered my watery eyes, dreading this gruesome day.

The room felt as if it was closing in on me. I could feel a dark shadow lurking nearby, and the curtain swung open. A young lady entered but I couldn't see her face in the shadows. Frightened, I

5

pulled the covers over my head to hide my quivering lip. I heard a piercing voice say, "I'm here to start your IV."

The nurse seemed kind enough, but she was like a torturous villain who smiled sweetly as she pricked my veins with a sharp needle. I shivered in my own skin as I looked at the dreaded needle piercing my body. To me, this symbolized never being able to bear my own children.

Ten minutes later, my ordeal worsened as a tall young man with dark brown hair and brown eyes walked toward me. He wore a surgical cap covering his forehead. He seemed to be an evil surgeon coming to steal from me the only thing I held precious to my heart--my womanhood. I glanced at his name tag hanging from his neck. Anesthesiologist Mark. He said with a kind voice, "Are you ready for surgery?" I nodded, reluctantly holding my covers with my trembling fingers, petrified by the thought of what would transpire next.

A twilight shadow dangled over me, haunting me like a thief in the night. The anesthesiologist wheeled me down a long hallway with more naked walls, my parents holding my jittery hand. But not even my loving parents could save me from the jaws of death that awaited me in the operating room. I felt like I was in a scene from the Twilight Zone, and I was terrified of who else might appear in the scene of my dreadful nightmare.

I saw a nice tall man with captivating blue eyes and a surgical cap over his bald head. He welcomed me with a warm smile. My heart raced. I thought to myself, "Dr. Wally has come to rescue me from this horror film."

I heard my concerned father say with a pleading voice, "Does this absolutely need to be done?"

Dr. Wally replied, "If she is going to have any quality of life, yes."

I screamed inside, "No, Dr. Wally! You are supposed to rescue me, not lead me to my bleak reality. "My parents waved goodbye and kissed me softly on my sweaty forehead. I felt like a whimpering, abandoned puppy. Was there no one to rescue me from this terrifying vision?"

The operating room smelled like a dank dungeon. I saw sharp instruments laying on a cold steel table in the middle of the room being prepared for me. I saw vast machines hooked to other machines. I was shaking and trembling with undeniable fear. I pleaded with the anesthesiologist to give me something to numb me from this terrifying ordeal. I screamed out, "I can't handle this! I'm going to freak out."

The anesthesiologist quickly administered an intravenous drug through my veins to make me sleepy, but I was still aware of what was going on around me. I felt a huge rush going into my veins. I immediately tasted and smelled the effects of the loopy drug in my mouth. I felt my body slowly drifting, my eyes becoming heavy and droopy. My terrifying tribulation was slowly fading into a realm of serenity.

I felt my body floating in a beautiful heavenly paradise. I felt only happiness and glee. The anesthesiologist placed a tight breathing mask on my face. He instructed me to count to ten and breathe in. I took a deep breath, smelling and tasting the smoky gas from the mask. I counted one, two, three... my eyes drifted slowly into a deep, peaceful sleep

I awoke in a puny hospital bed. I looked at the disrobed walls surrounding me. I was feeling dizzy and blurry. I was experiencing excruciating pain. My parents were beside my hospital bed. They asked me, "How do you feel?"

I replied groggily, "Ten pounds lighter. Just extreme pain from surgery. But I do not feel the endometriosis pain anymore."

Dr. Wally walked past my runty room and overheard me talking to my parents. He walked into the room, "I'm so relieved to hear you say that. Your endometriosis was stuck like honey inside your uterus. You would have never had a chance to conceive."

I felt some relief by Dr. Wally's unexpected news. But a part of me yelled inside, "What have you done?"

When Dr. Wally released me to go home the same day as the surgery I was happy but as frightened as a little kitten snatched from her mother. Dr. Wally had become like a father figure to me, truly concerned about my welfare and well-being. He prescribed a high dose of strong pain pills, and he had thoughtfully arranged for the pharmacist to come to my room to bring me my prescription before I left the hospital.

Going outside to face the world again after a hysterectomy was like sending a house pet to live in the wild. I wasn't ready to face the world and introduce them to my hopeless feeling of despair. I tried to put on a happy face like the old me, but inside I was feeling like a small child whose security blanket was ripped and stolen from her trembling hands. The ride home to my apartment was a misty haze. I could smell the leather seats and vanilla freshener hanging from the rear-view mirror in my parent's brown Cadillac. I was still feeling the aftereffects of the anesthesia and was nauseated, so I rolled the window down. I could feel the fresh air softly brushing my cheeks with a cool breeze.

But soon the night's curtain drew upon me. Going into my small apartment in my tidy room with my comfy bed gave me a feeling of warmth and security. I could smell fresh pledge from my oak shelves in my room. I could feel the fluffy carpet under my feet as I slipped off my sandals. My parents tucked me into my warm bed. I was sore and witless from surgery, and I just wanted to rest. My parents kissed me on my forehead and said, "We love you! Call if you need anything and sleep tight." My parents left me alone in my room with a feeling of despair.

Inviting my friends into my new world made me feel like I was a baby, entering an unfamiliar world for the first time. I awoke to loud knocking at the door. I opened the brass doorknob to the door of my apartment. My friends, two guys and two girls, were standing outside my door. They grabbed me and hugged me, saying joyfully, "Where have you been?

I graciously invited my friends into my apartment and said with an indifferent look on my face, "I just had surgery."

I wouldn't dare tell them I had a hysterectomy.

They said in unison with concerned looks, "I'm sorry. If we had known, we would have visited you in the hospital."

I said smiling, "It was only a same day surgery."

My friends are good, loyal friends. I met them at church in my ward six months previously. They also lived in my complex. The two girls were beautiful, athletic and comical. The two guys had dark hair. They were tall and very handsome. I watched my friends laughing and talking. But I felt like I was an outsider. I was aching inside, physically and mentally. Having a hysterectomy was one of the most difficult things I had endured. I was healing physically from the pain of surgery. However, trying to heal emotionally and mentally was a different story.

I asked my guy friends, "Would you ever adopt children?"

They answered like a choir singing together in unison. "No way. I want my own children."

I sat there in a trance of sadness. I couldn't shake the feeling of hopelessness. I had lost my womanhood. Who would want me now?

After my friends left me and went back to their own happy lives, I sat in my room and wallowed in a puddle of tears. I was at my lowest. I couldn't endure the emotional pain any longer. The thought of never conceiving my own children was too difficult to endure. I thought to myself, Who will ever want me?

I texted my brother, Todd with tears flooding down my cheeks. "I'm ending my life. I can't do this anymore."

Sharing the painful news with my brother that I was about to commit suicide was like telling my brother there is an evil intruder in my house ready to end my life. Unbeknownst to me, Todd received my suicidal text and called my sister, Chantelle, frantic. My older brother, Brian, who received a frantic call from Chantelle about my suicidal text, raced from the other side of town trying desperately to save me.

After thirty minutes of desperate sobbing, I thought to myself, I don't want to die. But this was the only way to be free from the loss of never having the ability to bare my own children. I sat on the edge of my cushy bed. I slowly gathered the bottle of pain pills that Dr. Wally had prescribed. With my quivering hands, I opened the lid to the pain bottle. I opened my mouth slowly to try to swallow each pill in one big gulp. The room was spinning in a fog of despondency.

Suddenly, my bedroom door swung open and my brother, his eyes moving quickly like a cat, snatched the pain pills from my quivering hand. He embraced me tightly. I fell deep into my brother's arms. I sobbed uncontrollably on Brian's shoulders. I said sadly, "Why did you do that? No one will want me. I want to die!"

Brian replied with concerned eyes, "We love you. We care about you. We don't want to lose you. I'm calling mom and dad."

My brother's call to my parents to tell them I almost committed suicide was like telling my parents I had almost been murdered. When my dad and mom got the news of my suicide attempt, they cried out in fright. "We could have lost her. Our baby girl almost left us."

Chapter 2

A Dr.Jekyll and Mr. Hyde

"Cheaters often accuse you of cheating. Liars often accuse you of lying. Insecure people often crumble your security. Behavior speaks . . . How someone treats you may have nothing to do with you; but can be a reflection of who they are." Steve Mariboli

When a child attempts suicide, a parent is like a mother kitten protecting her baby kittens. She doesn't dare leave them for one second. After my frantic suicide scare, my parents didn't want to leave me alone. I moved in with my parents in Roy, Utah. My parents and I weren't close growing up as a child but living with them in my thirties was a very healing experience.

My parents lovingly took me under their wing. They cared for me like I was their only child. We stayed up watching movies together, reminiscing about my glorious childhood. My dad and I were as close as two peas in a pod. We spent so much time together. I remember smelling and tasting the delicious Mexican food we ate at our favorite restaurant, Rubios. I remember the feeling of the cement on my feet as I ran in a nearby park with my dad following close beside me. I loved my special time together on my daddy daughter dates.

At home, I remember waking up to a card sitting on the green stem of a red rose inside a beautiful vase sitting on my oak dresser in my room. The card read: I wish I would have known you in your tender years like I know you now. You are a special daughter to me. Love, Dad."

I wiped away the tears as I read the card. Feeling my dad's tender affection for me began to heal my broken heart. My dad had read a book to me as a small child called Jonathan Living Seagull. He always told me, "You are like a seagull: strong, courageous and kind."

My dad's faith in me made me feel like an eagle soaring into the night. Spreading its wings to soar above the mountains to find his place in the universe. My dad always said, "Time heals all wounds, and this too shall pass."

Over time, I slowly began getting my life back together after my painful ordeal of getting a hysterectomy. My dad encouraged me to go back to school to get my RN. He said, "You would be a great nurse because of what you have been through. You can empathize with others going through their own trauma."

I listened to my dad's advice and talked to an academic counselor at a local college about their Nursing Program. The counselor gave me the courses needed to obtain my registered nursing license in four years. The counselor also encouraged me to obtain my certified nursing

license and put myself through nursing school. I enrolled in school next semester. I took a 30-day Certified Nursing assistant day class in Murray, Utah, and I graduated with my certified nursing assistant license.

I interviewed at a home health care facility as a Certified Nursing Assistant and was hired on the same day I interviewed. I felt confident with my choices. I could feel the green grass under my feet and smell the clean air as I walked to class each morning. I loved being back in school again and working in Home Health. I was making new friends at school and work. I felt like my life had purpose again. But I was sad that I had no one in my life to share my hopes and dreams with. I longed to be married to someone who would whisper sweet nothings in my ear. Someone whom I could share my life with.

I felt like I had just won the lottery when I received a call from my good friend Amber inviting me to Huntington Beach, California to attend an event for my church, The Church of Jesus Christ of Latter-day Saints. It was a mid-singles conference, where singles 30 and older would gather to learn more about our church and have fun activities together. I jumped for glee like a small child who was given a new toy. A weekend vacation in sunny California sounded like the ticket to enjoy my life again and maybe meet a special guy!

Amber and I were invited to stay at her friend, Bill's, beach house for the weekend. After arriving we dropped off our luggage at Bill's and immediately drove to the conference in Huntington Beach.

At the conference, I could feel the ocean air brushing my cheeks. The waves crashed together. I felt the warm sand etching between my toes. I dove into the air, my stomach pounding the sand trying to hit the round volleyball over the net. I could wiff the ocean breeze as the waves rushed together over my head as I dove like a surfer trying to catch its first wave. I could smell barbecue hotdogs and hamburgers grilling on an open fire pit on the beach. I was in heaven. This was life. This was my happy place.

Suddenly the brisk night began falling upon me. I felt like a giddy school girl in junior high school at the 80's dance that night, scoping the dance for a cute guy to talk to. Rocking out to oldies music like "Danger Zone", "Take my Breath Away," and Cindy Lauper's "Girls Just Wanna Have Fun."

I noticed a cute guy standing by himself in the dark. I could see his shadow standing next to me. I thought to myself, "Should I go talk to him?"

I saw the perfect opportunity when he pulled out a stick of gum from his pocket. I walked over to him slowly and asked, "Can I have a stick of gum?"

He smiled and handed me gum and replied, "Hi! I'm Troy."

I answered nervously, with my hands in my back pocket, "Hi, I'm Marci."

He gave me a warm smile, "Where are you from?"

I replied, smiling, "I am from Utah."

Troy answered with a surprised expression. "I am from Utah! I moved to California a few years ago to do pest-control."

Meeting Troy was like meeting my Prince Charming. We talked for a while at the 80's dance. He was so charming, so easy to talk to and he made me laugh. Suddenly, the lights turned on and I could see more clearly the most beautiful man standing in front of me with dark blonde hair, ocean-blue eyes and a dreamy smile.

Troy asked me confidently, with a huge smile on his face, "Can I get your number?"

Happily, I gave Troy my number. Troy quickly entered my number into his flip-phone, and the rest is history. Falling in love with Troy was puppy love at first, but I knew after a few months I was head over heels crazy for this guy. With me living in Utah and Troy living in California, the distance was strenuous on our relationship, but we were determined to make it work. We talked on the phone for hours and hours every night. He would often text me sweet messages in the mornings, "Good morning sunshine. Just thinking of you."

After two weeks of talking on the phone every night with Troy, we decided we needed to see each other again in person. My mom was so excited I had met someone special that she offered to fly me out to California to see Troy for ten days.

The anticipation of seeing Troy after two weeks made me feel like a young child who was nervous and excited to open her Christmas presents. Will I have the same feelings for him? Will he have the same feelings for me?

When Troy picked me up at the Los Angeles airport, he walked towards me and his smile melted my heart. He took me into his arms and he gave me a bear hug and said, "Hey babe. So good to see you. I've missed you."

I felt safe and loved in Troy's tender arms.

Did he just call me babe? Does that mean I'm his girlfriend?

The next ten days with Troy were the happiest days of my life. I felt like I was in a sensual romantic movie that would never end. Troy took me out to Disneyland on our first date for my birthday. We held hands in between the rides, and we screamed with delight when we rode scary rides together like Indiana Jones. When the dark night was falling upon us, Troy drove us back to his house in his shiny car. I loved riding in Troy's car; it smelled like a summer breeze at the beach.

I had never been in love with a guy before who I felt like I could spend the rest of my life with and be happy with until I met

Troy. When we walked into Troy's living room, Troy set up a large blanket in the living room. I could feel the fuzzy blanket under my feet laying down next to Troy. I could smell his intoxicating cologne. He nestled me close to his chest. This was the first time we had been this close. I felt my heart race when I felt Troy's sensual lips touch mine.

After Troy and I kissed, he held my hand. He whispered in my ear, "I love you. You are beautiful on the inside and outside. You make me so happy."

I embraced Troy tighter and thought to myself, Is this really happening? Did he just tell me he loves me? This guy is charming and handsome, and he wants me!

The following days and nights I spent with Troy made me feel like a nonsensical schoolgirl, with the cutest football player paying attention to me. Troy wooed me and made me feel like a princess who had just met her Prince Charming. I could feel the slimy seaweed in between my toes on the hot sandy beach, Troy's arms tight around me as we dove into the waves. To end the perfect day together, we watched the alluring sunset as the ocean waves collided together. Our toes were buried in the cold sand, sitting on a blanket, huddled together for warmth. Troy had wrapped his arms tightly around me, whispering in my ear, "I love you."

Troy and I were crazy about each other. We were seriously talking about getting married. But I felt I owed it to Troy to divulge the dreaded news that I couldn't have my own children. The last night of my visit with Troy I told Troy, trembling, "I can't have my own children. I had to have a hysterectomy."

Troy took me into his arms and said with a warm smile, "That's OK, babe. I love you. We can adopt children."

I couldn't believe my ears. Could this be true? All my worries of never being a mom were washed away by hope. Has my Prince Charming finally arrived?

Troy and I dated for three glorious months. At first we were deeply in love. He treated me like a queen. One day he bought me beautiful red roses while I was in his apartment making him a delicious candlelight dinner. He walked in the door and handed me the roses declaring his feelings for me, "You are so beautiful. I can't wait to marry you. ``I love you."

I pinched myself to see if I was dreaming. But my dream was about to become my worst nightmare. I had flown out to see Troy at his place in California. We hadn't seen each other in two weeks. But my visit was not as I had anticipated it would be. The first night I arrived at Troy's house, he shared with me his dark side. He admitted to me that he wasn't living according to the belief system of the Church of Jesus Christ of Latter-day Saints like I was. He was not living the law of chastity required to attend the temple of our LDS faith.

Now Troy was pressuring me to lose my virtue to him. I told Troy how important the church was to me. I desired to be married in the temple to my forever sweetheart. The temple is a sacred place only worthy members of the Church of Jesus Christ of Latter-day Saints attend to make covenants to God.

Troy reassured me that he wanted to be married in the temple to me. He promised me he would clean up his life and become a better man. But it was all a facade. It seemed the more determined I was to keep the law of chastity, the more Troy pressured me to cave in to his wants and desires. We started to mess up. I almost gave myself to him. I was devastated and it drew us apart. I was beginning to think that Troy may not be the best man for me and I questioned our relationship.

Our last night together, I remember sitting with Troy at the table in a nice restaurant and I noticed a text on his phone from a girl.

I inquired, bewildered, "Who is that?"

Troy replied nonchalantly, "Just a friend."

But I could see the text as clear as day. I shrank into my seat in the booth we were sitting in. It said: I miss you. I know you have a girlfriend now, but I want to see you.

I replied with a hurt look, "That is no friend. Who is she?"

Troy replied softly, "It's my ex-girlfriend."

I replied in shock, "Why are you in contact with your ex-girlfriend?"

Troy replied, defensively, "We are just friends. She is having a difficult time right now. She needs me. We were together for three years, and we were best friends when we were dating."

I sadly replied, "I need you. You are my boyfriend now, not hers. She clearly wants you back. I don't want you talking to her anymore. It's her or me."

He replied with a smile, "Of course I choose you."

He hugged me tightly and reassured me, "You are my only girl. ``I love you."

19

Troy was like a Dr. Jekyll and Mr. Hyde. He appeared to be trustworthy but inside he was a deceitful snake. I couldn't shake the feeling that Troy was cheating on me with his ex-girlfriend. I flew home to Utah the next morning. When I arrived at the Salt Lake airport, I sent him a text: Just arrived at the airport. Miss you. Love you. But he did not respond. I texted him a few times again, and still no response. When my mom picked me up at the airport I told my mom, "I think Troy is cheating on me. I caught him texting his ex- girlfriend and he told me he is still in contact with her. I tried to text him when I landed, but he didn't respond."

My mom said, concerned, "Oh no! That's terrible. What are you going to do?"

I replied, still unsure of myself, "I don't know. I love Troy. But for some reason I don't trust him. I don't know why?"

My mom replied firmly, "That is a red flag if you can't trust him."

I finally heard back from Troy four hours later. He exclaimed on the phone, "I fell asleep and missed your text."

I didn't believe his story. Scared of the response, I asked him, "Are you still talking to your ex-girlfriend?"

He was silent on the phone. He said quietly, "Yes."

I replied, almost crying, "I can't trust you. You obviously still want to be with your ex-girlfriend and not me. It's clear to me now that we want different things. You aren't changing like you promised me that you were. You are breaking my heart. I thought you were my dream guy. But I guess it was all a façade."

He replied angrily, "Why are you so insecure about me talking to my ex-girlfriend?"

I replied sadly, "She is your first choice. I am sloppy seconds. You should be with her. I'm breaking up with you. I'm sorry. I love you. But you obviously don't love me or you would change."

I hung up the phone. I wept and wept. I thought to myself, I thought he was my dream guy. Who will want me now?

Breaking up with Troy was the right thing to do, but it left a hole in my heart. I knew I couldn't trust him or be with him when we were going down different paths. But my heart was aching and breaking for Troy. It was the longest week of my life not talking or seeing him. I thought to myself, I have made the biggest mistake of my life. Why did I let Troy go? Who would want me now?

Later, I was at a co-ed party with some of my good friends from church, still missing Troy. All of the guys around me were cute and fun, but I knew in my heart they would never accept me, broken as I was. I could never give them what they wanted--their own offspring. I received a text from Troy as I was walking out the door from the party with my friends: I miss you. How are you?

My heart sank. All the old feelings for Troy came rushing back into my mind. I couldn't let him go. I called him after his text. He told me, "I don't want to get back together. I want to be friends."

I told Troy, "That is fine. We can be friends. I miss you. I just want to see you."

When we were dating, Troy and I had planned to attend my family reunion that summer together. He still wanted to go when we broke up. Why? I will never know.

21

Staying friends with my ex after we broke up is one of the most awkward things I've ever done. I was anticipating our relationship to be somewhat of the same. But I was in for a big surprise. Troy treated me unkindly--like I was someone he no longer cared for. I soon discovered how nasty Troy was as I peeled back his outer exterior. On the inside, there was a rotten interior.

Troy drove down from California to Utah to pick me up at my parent's home for my family reunion. It was being held in Spokane, Washington, where my brother lived. I had already missed two days of the reunion waiting for Troy to pick me up. When Troy arrived at my parent's home, I was excited to see him. I rushed to hug him. But he was aloof. He barely hugged me back and said rudely, "Hurry up, let's go."

We barely spoke on the drive to Spokane. We stayed in a hotel overnight. I was exhausted from the long drive. I felt like an abused puppy because of the cold, callous way Troy was treating me. Troy and I arrived in Spokane later the next night. Being around my family brought me happy smiles and joyous laughter. My family was excited to see me and ran to hug me when I arrived. I introduced my family to Troy. My brother, Levi, was acting strange when he met Troy.

He told me later, "I don't like him. I don't like the way he talks to you. You aren't yourself around him."

I wish I would've listened to my brother's intuition and ended it with Troy. But I was broken. I had no hope of finding or being with anyone else.

The next morning the sun glazed over the gray clouds in the vast sky like a thin brush stroke. It was a perfect day to go boating. Levi invited our family to go on his boat that sunny morning. The speed boat took us on the glassy blue lake. It was perfect for tubing. I could feel the cool water splashing in my face and over my body as we raced on the lake. The sun's rays were beaming, leaving me with a glistening dark tan as we tubed all day.

My family is extremely competitive with each other, and we had a contest to see who could stay on the tube the longest without falling off. Of course, I was talking smack that I could win. Levi, Troy, and I stayed on the tube the longest; fifteen minutes passed and no wipe out. Total victory. My sisters were unhappy I had beat them and instructed the boat driver to speed up the boat. I felt the jerk of the boat going faster and faster. I lost my balance on the tube. I crashed hard, hitting my head with a sharp blow on the water. I felt like I was paralyzed from the waist down. My leg cramped, my neck throbbed and my body tingled all over. I was frightened when I could barely move my body to get back into the boat.

I felt my brothers and brother-in-law rescuing me from the water. They lifted my limp body onto the boat, carrying me to safety. I could smell the salty lake on my swimsuit. The boat rushed me to the grassy area offshore to my towel lying on the wet grass. Troy did not stay with me to comfort me in my time of need. He selfishly went on another boat ride with my family. He left me alone with Chantelle. She was upset and said angrily, "My husband would never leave me. I can't believe he left you."

That night, I broke the news to my family that Troy and I had broken up. Levi said, "I don't care. I don't like the way he treats you. Or the way he speaks to you."

Levi was right. Troy was no prize like I had thought. I spent the entire night in neck pain. I hurt my neck badly from the boating accident. I could feel the ice pack on my aching neck. I felt the ibuprofen start to numb the pain. My mom nursed me back to health. Troy only checked on me once the entire time I was injured. He said to me unkindly, "I think you should ride back with your family."

I wish I could turn back the clock and make a better decision than I made on that dreary night. I wonder how different my life would have been. But I was broken and holding on to love or what I thought was love. Deep down I knew if I continued to spend time with Troy that I would one day need to choose between my commitment to God and Troy. Even though, until then, I had held onto my beliefs with Troy, I was heartbroken and vulnerable after losing my ability to bare my own children. I felt like God had abandoned me. I was now in my early thirties and still not married. I just wanted to share my life and love with someone. I was lonely and desperate for male affection.

I decided to try to make it work with Troy. I was still in love with him, and I wasn't ready to say goodbye to him. I encouraged Troy to ride back together to California with me. The plan was for Troy to move to Utah that week. I would help him move his personal belongings to his parents' home in Park City. I wanted to stick to the plan. I thought, "Maybe if we spend a few more days alone, we can work on our relationship and be a happy couple again." I was dead wrong.

Chapter 3

A Father's Love For His Beloved Daughter Transcends Even Death

"Sometimes the veil between this life and the life beyond becomes very thin. Our loved ones who have passed on are not far from us." Ezra Taft Benson

The time finally came to help Troy move. As I helped him pack, I felt like I had run up two flights of stairs from the effort. I wiped drops of sweat from my forehead as I packed his personal things in his room. I was exhausted from the two day drive from Spokane to California. Troy's deadline was to be in Park City by Saturday, so we had to hurry. We only had the rest of the night to pack up his things for his move

I felt like a confused mouse in a maze trying to find his belongings in his unkempt room. I smelled fresh oak as I opened Troy's walk-in to collect more of his mess of belongings. I gasped when I saw a Playboy centerfold tucked underneath some t-shirts at the top of his shelf.

The breeze coming from the bedroom window sent chills up my spine as I sank motionless on Troy's dirty carpet. A tall dark figure was prowling in the shadows. As he approached me, I asked him, bewildered, "Why do you have porn in your closet?"

Troy responded smiling as though surprised, "Oh. That must belong to the guy who used to live here."

25

I angrily shook my head in disbelief, "Do you think I'm an idiot?"

Troy lowered his head and replied, humiliated, "I'm not perfect. But neither are you. I've been addicted to porn since I was ten years old. I didn't look at porn while we were dating. But when you broke up with me, I was lonely and sad. I started looking at porn again for comfort."

I looked at Troy. He looked like a small child who had been scolded by his mother for his poor behavior. His head was hanging low, and his lip quivered like he was going to cry. I felt sorry for him. I felt responsible for breaking up with him. He was right, I was broken too. I was a wounded bird that needed someone to mend my broken wings as well. Maybe Troy just needed a kind, understanding friend.

I said to Troy, with my arms wrapped around his shoulder, "I think you just need a friend right now. Let's just be friends."

Troy said happily, "Sure, we can be friends."

Troy was as patient as a snake with a rat in a cage. Troy knew if he occupied most of my time I would not have a chance to meet other guys to date. Troy maliciously and affectionately pretended that he was into me like he was when we were dating. Troy took me out on dates, but he labeled us as just friends. We loved to ride go-carts together at theme parks, split savory chocolate cake that melted in our mouths at our favorite restaurants and indulge in a bag of salty popcorn at the cinema.

We sat up for hours talking in a large booth in restaurants huddled close together, reminiscing about our childhood memories and sharing our hopes and dreams. We playfully joked around with each other and teased each other like a boy and girl playfully act when they first meet in a playground. Troy would tease me with just enough affection like touching me on my knee or grabbing me playfully and wrapping his arms around me tight to physically arouse me. Then whisper in my ear, "I love being with you. I could see myself with you someday."

Troy was grooming me like a predator. He slowly wore me down for a year to do what he wanted when he wanted it. I was very physically attracted to Troy. He used this knowledge to lure me in.

The night was beautifully lit by the shimmering moon. Troy went in for the kill. He squawked and clawed me like a vicious eagle scooping up his innocent prey. Troy picked me up at my parent's house to take me out for a nice dinner at Chili's. Troy looked handsome, his blonde hair was gelled up in front and he was clean-shaven. He was wearing new blue jeans he had just bought and a black short sleeve shirt. Troy gave me a hug when I came to the door. I could smell his cologne that made me woozy and my heart flutter. In the car on the way to dinner Troy flirted with me, teasing me in a playful way and touched my knee.

I jokingly said to Troy laughing, "Should we start being friends with benefits?"

To my surprise, Troy smiled devilishly and said, "Let's do it."

I replied with a shocked look on my face, "Really? Are you serious?"

Troy replied, a gleam in his eye that he had finally conquered his prey, "Lets just have fun. Let's just be friends with benefits."

He softly kissed my neck. Feeling his soft kisses again gave me butterflies in my stomach. But I wanted to be sure he was only with me physically and no one else. I told Troy with a stern look, "We have to make a pact we will only be with each other physically."

Troy was a masterful charmer; he knew just what to say and how to reel me in to take the bait. He nodded his head and smirked, "Agreed. Let's skip going to dinner. Get a motel for the night and order in dinner. We will go buy some alcohol, get really drunk and fall passionately into each other's arms."

I smiled willingly, "Let's do it."

The rest of the night was like an insane dream. I had dreamt of being physical with Troy for so long. Now it is finally happening. My anticipation but reservation for the night was high. Troy cornered his car like it was on wheels to the liquor store. He grabbed my hand and whisked me out of the car to a room filled with alcohol like vodka, beer, and wine. I thought to myself, "This is it. I'm going to give myself to Troy tonight. If I choose to do this, I am choosing between God and Troy."

I hesitated for a brief second about following through with my decision to be with Troy tonight. I felt Troy's arms wrap around me and he said, kissing me softly on the neck, "I want you."

Troy grabbed a case of beer and a bottle of vodka from the middle shelf. I said to myself, "I can't resist Troy. He's so dreamy. He wants me. A cute guy wants me? And I want him. What good is God in my life? He stole my womanhood. God doesn't want me to be happy. Troy is my only ticket to be a mom. I'm going for it."

Nightfall had beckoned us, and the moon had disappeared into the dark silhouette. Troy sped like a racing car driver to the closest vacant motel. We walked into a tawdry motel office and Troy said handing the clerk his credit card with a smile of glee, "One single bedroom, non-smoking please."

The clerk handed Troy a hotel card. Troy grabbed me like a brave lion holding on to its baby cub. He acted like he was protective of me, but he was luring me into his seductive trap. He led me into a cozy room with a single bed and brass furniture. I nervously sat on the white bedspread. Troy could sense my apprehension but excitement about being with him physically that night. He knew if he could lower my inhibitions, I would definitely give myself to him that night.

Troy opened the bottle of vodka and poured it in a crystal glass next to the nightstand by the bed. He handed me a glass of vodka and said with an evil smile, "Drink up."

I could smell the alcohol as I cupped the glass in my fingers and drank its contents in two gulps. Immediately, I felt the room spinning like a merry go round at a theme park. I dropped the empty glass to my side feeling loopy and slowly fell onto the bed on my back in a dizzy gaze. The vodka lowered my sensibility.

Troy grabbed a bottle of beer sitting on the nightstand and drank it in one gulp. He laid down next to me and he wrapped his arms tightly around my waist. I could barely see Troy's face amongst the haze. Troy kissed me softly on my neck. I was like a limp rag doll. I could barely move my body. Troy ravished me that night.

The sheer curtains were blinded by the sun's rays early the next morning. I awoke with Troy's arms wrapped around me. I thought to myself, "This is nice. I don't want this to end. I want to be with Troy."

He awoke when I moved his hand closer to my waist. He moved his hand away and coldly said, "Well, we better get going."

As we walked outside, I could smell the fresh pine trees and feel the breeze kissing my face, like a giant hug. I thought to myself this is going to be a good day.

I asked Troy with a smile on my face, "Do you want to go get some breakfast? I'm hungry."

Troy coldly replied with a stern look on his face, "No I need to get home."

Troy had won his prize like a star athlete who won the race and claimed his trophy. I was his trophy girl now and he had won me over then tossed me aside like cheap jewelry. Troy raced me home with no touching, no emotion, just cold silence in the car. He left me standing in the dust after he coldly hugged me in his car saying, "It was fun. See ya."

Troy was playing me like a fiddle. He knew I wanted to be with him now that we had been together physically. He let it ride. He made me work for him. All week long, not one text or call from Troy. I finally texted him, "How are you? Do you want to hang out this weekend?"

Troy took a day to reply to my text. He was toying with me. He finally texted me back, "Sorry, I've been busy. Yeah, let's hang out Saturday."

Troy arrived at my house like a hungry shark ready to devour his kill. He flirted with me in the car and touched me in places he knew would arouse me. Then he whispered in my ear, "Let's go up to the beautiful mountains for a nice, scenic drive."

Troy drove up to the mountains and stopped to look at the gorgeous view at the top of the mountain. He grabbed me roughly and started to kiss me all over. He motioned me to go in the backseat of the car with him. I hopped over the front seat to the backseat of the car. Troy forcefully grabbed me and ravished me in the backseat of his car. Then he climbed back into the front seat of his car and said harshly, "Come on, hurry up."

Troy treated me roughly like I was a stubborn horse to be trained by his cruel master. Over time, Troy's porn addiction worsened. He was like a small child who gets a piece of candy and craves more and more. Troy was now obsessed by the naked images and violent acts he was viewing on a daily basis. He needed to act out on me what he was watching on his computer and phone screens. I was now an object to Troy. He was charming and sweet to me until he got what he wanted. Then he was cruel and nasty to me. He played with me when he wanted me and discarded me when he had no use for me. He abused me in the most vilest of ways mentally and sexually. He criticized me, screaming at me for the smallest things I did. Frightened, when I asked, "Why are you yelling at me?"

He would reply angrily. "In my house, we yell to be heard. I am not going to change. Live with it."

Troy's twisted mind was like a corkscrew, slowly manipulating the cork. He always made me drink vodka during our physical encounters. He wanted my inhibitions lowered so he could do whatever he wanted to me. The last night we were together he almost raped me. He was extremely sexually rough with me. I told him to stop. He wouldn't stop. He violently held down my hands and continued to be sexually vicious with me.

I screamed at the top of my lungs, "Stop it. You're hurting me."

He finally stopped and said, "You're such a wimp."

31

As he lay next to me that night, I was shivering. Not because I felt cold, but because Troy's heart was cold. I went into the bathroom and wept uncontrollably. What have I become? I was his porn toy. I was like a robot. No feelings. No emotion. I was humiliated the way Troy treated me and I didn't want my family or parents to know Troy was using me. I told my parents I was going out with Troy as friends. But my family soon caught on that I was friends with benefits with him. Levi confronted me about it when he was visiting me and my parents for a week at my parent's condo. He asked me, "Are you friends with benefits with Troy? And don't lie to me because I know you are. I'm not stupid. You sneak off with him at night and stay out all night."

I replied, "Yes."

Levi replied, "He is just using you."

I couldn't admit the humiliation to my brother that Troy was using me. I said, "No, he's not using me. We only are physical with each other. We made a pact."

Levi replied chuckling, "I guarantee you he is cheating on you. That guy is a deceitful snake."

My brother was like a courageous jaguar protecting his youngling. Levi always looked out for me. I thought to myself, "Is Troy cheating on me? He texts me to tell me he's with other girls when I ask him why he hadn't replied to my texts."

I listened to my brother and I confronted Troy on the phone immediately about cheating on me. I called him and asked, "Troy, are you sleeping with other women?

Troy acted hurt. "Why would you think that?"

Then he asked, "Are you cheating on me?"

I was so far into Troy's control and abuse that I actually defended myself that I was being faithful to Troy. I would never cheat on him. He always turned the focus back on me so I wouldn't question his deception and lies.

My family was worried about me being with Troy, especially my dad. He noticed how my sweet disposition had changed being with him. I was moody and barely smiled anymore around my family. My dad detested Troy like a leech sucking on human blood. My dad sat me down and looked straight into my eyes and asked, concerned, "Why are you with this boy who doesn't appreciate you? Who doesn't respect you? Why can't you see yourself the way I see you?"

I thought to myself, maybe my dad is right. Who have I become from staying with an abusive guy who is just using me? To Troy, I was a shattered vase that is only good in the trash and that's how I felt with him-- like trash. I no longer wanted to feel this way. I knew I needed to end it with Troy.

It was a cold dark night. I was like a chained coyote howling for my freedom from Troy. I had just seen him a week ago, but I knew that if I asked him to meet me for dinner, he would take the bait. Troy knew that he would get what he wanted that night, me.

When I saw him walking into the restaurant to meet me for dinner, I was shaking like a leaf. But I knew I needed to permanently cut off all connection with Troy. When he sat next to me in the booth, he welcomed me with a warm hug and a nice smile. I was anticipating waiting until after dinner to break the news to him, but I felt brave so I said, a stern look on my face, "I think it's best we aren't friends anymore I need to move on from you. I am breaking off contact with you. Please don't text me anymore or call me anymore."

33

Troy knew how to play me. He used sulking and manipulation to lure me back, and he replied sadly, "OK, if that's what you want. I am not keeping you from moving on. Move on if you want. If you don't want to be friends with me, then don't be my friend."

He sulked, lowering his head like a spoiled little child who doesn't get his own way. I felt sorry for him and I ended up consoling him. I put my own feelings aside to meet his needs. Once again, I was back in his trap of total control. Troy knew what to say and when to say it to keep me from leaving him. Troy said with a huge smile hugging me tight, "I love being with you. I can see myself with you one day."

I was too broken to let Troy go. Who else would want me? I continued to deal with Troy's abuse for six long terrible years. Being captive to Troy's control felt like I was living on a witness stand required to excuse myself, defend myself, to beg for forgiveness and to plead for mercy. With each passing day, I was losing my confidence, my self-respect, and any hope of being free from a porn-addicted man who imprisoned my sweet soul.

Then lightning struck. My dad became extremely ill with a brain disease called aphasia. I was still living with my parents when my dad was ill. I helped my mom take care of my dad for six months. I wasn't able to see Troy as often. But we were still friends with benefits when Troy wanted me.

Taking care of my Dad when he got sick drew my dad and I closer. We spent almost every day together. I remember smelling his favorite breakfast; a spinach omelet I cooked for him. I could feel myself sinking into the soft couch cushion watching his favorite TV program with him, NCIS. I could feel my running shoes pounding the pavement on our runs together at the park. I could feel my dad's arms around me as we snuggled together sharing stories of our favorite memories together as daughter and father. He said, "I love you."

My dad became my best friend. My buddy. My confidante. He loved me unconditionally. My dad didn't want anything from me like Troy did, just my companionship and love. Slowly, each day I was with my dad, I didn't want to be with Troy as much. My dad was slowly replacing Troy. I now had positive male companionship. I loved being with my dad.

But my dad was wrestling with the thought of dying. He didn't want to leave his beloved wife and children he adored. My dad was faithful to God his whole life. He never wavered in his faith even when he got sick. He loved the Savior. It broke my dad's heart when I stopped going to church. When I stopped believing in God, he could sense how lost and miserable I was without God in my life.

Later the crisp evening smelled like summer in a bowl. I could smell the beautiful flowers my dad had picked in our garden and placed in a blue vase on the kitchen table. I could feel the soft rose petals against my warm skin. I was in the kitchen eating dinner at the table when my dad sat down next to me and said in a concerned voice, "If I have to die and leave this world, then I'm going to haunt you and make you come back to church."

I replied with a hearty laugh, "Oh, Dad, you are so funny."

My dad somehow knew that his health was declining and that he was about to leave this world. Within a few weeks, his health started to dwindle rapidly. My dad could barely speak and couldn't walk after a month. My mom had help from hospice aids to give my dad a bed bath and help feed him in bed.

A week later, I was in the middle of finals at school when Levi called to warn me, "Dad is not doing well. He is having a difficult time breathing. You need to come see him now."

Levi and his family had driven from Spokane all night to be with my dad. My mom had called my brother the night before and told my brother, "Your dad is dying. I can feel it."

When I got the troubled news from my brother, I was on my last final. I couldn't concentrate. I told my teacher, "My dad is dying. I can't concentrate on my final."

My teacher released me from my finals to go be with my dad during his last hours on this earth. I raced home to my parent's home in Roy. When I walked into their home, the living room was filled with family members. I could smell fresh pot roast and baked potatoes cooking in the oven. My siblings and their families had gathered to see my dad.

I was sobbing when I entered my dad's room and saw him lying helpless on the bed. It felt like my heart was shattering into a million pieces. My dad glanced at me immediately when I walked into the room and mouthed the words, "Marci." It was a tender moment between daughter and father because he had not spoken in months.

Watching my dad slowly die made me feel like a young child who loses his father to a bloodthirsty bear. My father was being ripped and clawed from my life and there was nothing I could do about it. I was terrified watching his breathing becoming more shallow, fighting to catch every breath. I held his gentle hands. I felt his fingers caressing my quivering hand. He was slowly passing on to the other side. Tears rolled down my cheeks and I screamed inside angrily, "How can this be happening? I am finally close to my dad. Now he is leaving me? How is that fair?"

36

But my dad was like a bull warrior, and he pawed relentlessly, fighting his way until the end. He was not going to pass until he said goodbye to all of his eight beloved children and wife of fifty years. Each child called or was present and wept tears when they said goodbye to their hero. When the last child, my brother, called to sing my dad's favorite lullaby, "God Be With You Until We Meet Again," He gently closed his eyes, dropped a single tear from his cheek to his chin, and slipped into a deep coma.

Before my dad passed, I gently clasped his hands in mine and whispered in his ear, "Dad, I am lost right now. Please help me find my way."

My dad squeezed my hand and he took a deep breath. His blood pressure and saturation dropped rapidly. My mother held his hand and asked to be alone with her loving husband. I sadly left the room, gently kissing my dad on his forehead. My mother was the last person in the room to say goodbye to her husband. My dad took his last breath and passed beyond the veil that afternoon.

Later when my mother entered the crowded living room of the family to share the dreaded news that my dad had passed on, I began sobbing like a child who lost his favorite doll or train. I had just lost my best friend. I was so distraught over my father's death that I couldn't sleep for days. I texted Troy to try to receive some comfort in my time of distress. I said in the text: My dad just passed away. Can you come with me to his funeral for support? I would really appreciate it.

But there was no response from Troy. I thought about my dad. I thought of how much he loved me. How he disliked this narcissist I was dating. I realized, this selfish guy doesn't care about me. He is using me. My dad cares about me. My dad loves me, not Troy.

Later that week, my dad's funeral was like a hollow gorge that sucked me into its shadow of death. I looked around the chapel and saw my relatives, family and loved ones all dressed in black, sitting on the pew with their heads low, sobbing for the loss of my beloved father. My dad was loved by so many people in this world, and each one came to pay their respects to our family and to my father.

As I walked outside after the funeral, I could smell the dirty farm air that my dad had been raised on as a small child. I could smell the cattle on the grassy meadows next to the funeral home. I could feel the wet grass in my open-toed shoes as I walked to the plot my dad was being buried in. This was my dad's home, where he had loved to spend time with his siblings on hayrides and playing gleefully in the green grass.

I felt like this was a dream. I was sure I was going to wake up and my dad would still be alive. A text on my phone woke me from my trance. I looked at the text in horror. Every word pierced my mind. Troy. "Just got your text. Let's get together."

When I received his text, I sank to the grassy ground. My father just passed away. This guy just wants to use me. I screamed out, "Please, Dad! Help me get away from this abusive man who doesn't care about me. I'm not strong enough to do it alone."

A father's love for his beloved daughter transcends even death. My dad rescued me. For the next week, I felt my dad close by. I don't know how to describe it, but there was a presence around me all the time. I knew it was my dad. I cried out loud, "Dad, I feel you. What do you want?"

No answer from my dad, But I continued to feel his presence around me. I texted my niece Kenna, "I'm feeling my dad hovering around me. He won't leave me alone. What do you think he wants?"

Kenna replied, "I think Grandpa is telling you if you don't clean up your life and come back to church, you may not be with him."

Kenna's text hit me hard. That night, I was talking to my cousin, Mickey, on the phone. She asked me, "Are you still dating Troy?"

I replied, "Yes."

She scolded me kindly, "Marci, my ex-husband, was addicted to porn. He was cheating on me. Troy is cheating on you. Deep down, you know it's true. I saw you at the funeral. You didn't look good. Troy is sucking the life out of you."

I told Mickey, "Troy almost raped me one night. It was so scary. I feel my dad hovering around me like he's trying to tell me something. But it's like he can't tell me."

Mickey replied, "How do you know the next time you're with Troy he won't rape you? Your dad is trying to tell you something. To warn you. Pray to know what it is."

I got chills when Mickey told me this about Troy. I replied, "Okay, I will pray."

I hung up the phone. I thought, "How can I pray after six years?"

I stopped praying when I made the decision to be physical with Troy. I was so angry at God for taking away my ability to bare my own children. In my heart, I was never coming back to God. I stopped believing in miracles. I stopped believing in God. But I desperately wanted to know what message my dad wanted to share with me.

I got on my knees. I prayed sincerely for the first time in six years. "Please help me to know what my dad is trying to tell me. To know if Troy is cheating on me."

I got off my knees. Immediately, I heard my dad's voice, "You know this to be true. Text him and end it now."

I knew without a shadow of a doubt. I had heard my dad's voice. I picked up my iPhone. I ended it with Troy. I texted him: I don't want to be with you. I don't want to marry you. You are just using me. You are keeping me from the person I am meant to be with. I am blocking all your texts and calls. Don't contact me again.

I immediately blocked Troy's number giving him no chance to reply. With a huge smile on my face, I then realized that my dad was watching over me from beyond the veil. He wants me to be happy. To be free of Troy. My dad rescued me.

Troy attempted to contact me again a week later. I had bought a new phone and when I downloaded my new contacts to my phone, I forgot to block Troy's number. I later received an unexpected text from him: I miss my friend Marci.

When I received his text, I shivered with disgust. I knew I was done with Troy for good. The healing process of moving on and becoming happy again slowly transpired over time.

Chapter 4

God is for Real

"Human history is the long terrible story of man trying to find something other than God which will make him happy."
C.S. Lewis

I had this recurring nightmare. I was in a dark oubliette I couldn't escape. Someone had tricked me and lured me into slavery. Demonic laughter echoed in my ears, "Ha Ha." I would wake up screaming and trying to escape. When I cut off contact with Troy, the torment stopped. I realized my soul had been in shackles dating Troy. But now my soul was free. I vowed to never lose myself to a guy again.

Soon after I ended it with Troy, I heard my dad's voice: "Church. Church."

I laughed. I spoke aloud, "Dad, just because you saved me from Troy doesn't mean I'm going back to church."

I awoke the next morning, the dew smelled like an assortment of fruit. I could feel the damp rain trickling on my face. I had taken a job caring for an elderly woman who lived in a lovely white-paned house at the end of the street. I knocked on the door. A kind gentleman with dark black hair answered. He was dressed in nice black slacks and a black long sleeve shirt. He opened the screen door to let me in. The man said with a smile, "My mother is in her bedroom. I will be home around 8:00 from work. Thank you for coming to take care of her today."

41

I smiled as he left, a black umbrella covering his head from the wet pouring rain. I briskly walked into a tidy room. I could smell wet wipes and Johnson baby oil sitting on top of the silver dresser. The woman I was caring for was an elderly woman with white hair, flawless skin laying on a sheeted bed. I smiled and said, "Hi Virgina! My agency sent me to take care of you today. My name is Marci."

Virginia replied, shaking her finger, "Don't come near me or I will shoot you!"

Virginia was a sweet but spunky lady in her late nineties. She had short term memory loss due to Alzheimer's. She was bedridden and dying.

I replied softly, "Virginia, it's okay. I won't hurt you. Your son asked me to take care of you."

Virginia replied, "Well, come in honey. Tell me about yourself. Are you married? Do you have children?"

I replied sadly, "No, I haven't found the right person yet. I'm not able to conceive my own children. I had a hysterectomy. But I want to adopt children someday, if I ever get married."

It was during my visit with Virginia that I realized that when someone starts to pass to the other side, they see and hear things incomprehensible to us mere mortals. Virginia began experiencing visions of spirits beyond the veil; their glory undefined.

Virginia replied, bewildered, "Why are there little children in the room?"

I was puzzled. "I don't see little children."

She replied confidently, "Yes, there are little children in the room. Can't you see them?"

A feeling of warmth swept over me like a gust of wind. I thought to myself, "Is Virginia seeing my children from the other side? Are those my adopted children that are supposed to come down to me? Is that possible?"

I yearned to know more of this light that Virgina could see. But I couldn't. It was like a white veil was blinding my eyes. But as the veil was lifting from Virginia's eyes, she was seeing heavenly angels. Virginia asked me kindly, "Are you a religious person? Do you believe in God?"

I replied sadly, "I was active in the Church of Jesus Christ of Latter-day Saints, But now I'm inactive. I lost faith in God. In miracles. I lost my dad recently to a brain disease. I miss him."

Virginia smiled. "I'm a member too. How sweet it is. The room is surrounded with people in white. Can't you see them?"

Suddenly, I could feel a heavenly presence around me as if I was lifted into another element of a striking light reflecting love and tranquility. I couldn't see the heavenly realm around me, but I felt the entire room crowded with spirits from beyond the veil. I felt my good friend, Kiersten, who had died from ovarian cancer a few years ago. I felt my cousin, Ryan, who had died in a car accident ten years ago. I felt my Grandpa and Grandma Zollinger who had passed on five years ago. I felt something lightly touch my shoulder. Like the heavenly being wanted to hold me in his arms; I felt my dad.

The feeling intensified. My heart felt like it could burst. I felt myself sailing in the air traveling to a bright light of welcoming arms. The light shined brighter. It lightly touched me. Encircling the heavenly angels and myself. It was the Savior, Jesus Christ. My tears flooded the room. I felt an intense love and peace that I hadn't felt in years.

I had felt heavenly messengers. I knew this sweet lady was passing to a mystical world of endless possibilities. The body is like a hard shell covering a radiant soul waiting to be called home to his creator. Virginia was being called home. She cried out with a pleading voice, "Heavenly Father! How do I get out of this body? You need to send someone to help me out of my body."

After spending six sublime hours with my new friend, I said my goodbyes with a smile. "When you get to the other side. Please tell my dad I love him. I miss him."

I showed Virginia a picture of my dad. She replied, "I see your daddy here in the room. He is smiling."

An overwhelming feeling of love pierced my heart. I broke down and sobbed. I kissed this sweet lady on the forehead slowly exiting her room. I told her son, who I had called earlier, standing at the door, "I had the most spiritual experience with your mom today. I have been inactive in the LDS church for six years. But tonight I felt my dad and others who have passed through the veil through your mom. My incredible experience has woken up my soul, "I'm going back to church."

The son replied, "Did you know she had a blessing a week ago that it was her time to go. But she would go on with her time."

I replied, "I feel like she was meant to save me. Now she can pass on."

44

Later, I received a call from work she had passed on that night. After being in the dark for so long, when a bright light turns on and shines love and harmony, it's like the soul is reborn. After the unbelievable spiritual experience with this lady, I knew without a shadow of a doubt there was a God who loved me. He had created miracles to bring me back to the Savior.

I called my bishop from the local ward I lived in. I told him I was ready to come back to church. The bishop was like a pastor. He watched over his little flock of sheep like a shepherd. He received me with open arms.

When I left the church, I had slowly lost the knowledge I had learned since I was a small child. I was like a preschooler entering a new world of books, pictures and illustrations.

I knew in my heart the two missionaries from my ward, Elder Mitchell and Elder Jones were messengers sent to me from God. They were two of the most Christlike Elders I had ever met. But it was not an easy road coming back to church. Learning to have faith in God again was the easy part; putting it into action was the difficult factor. I always had a difficult time trusting God. Now I had to rely on his strength to carry me through.

I climbed over roadblocks, enduring bumps and scrapes along the way. But after a year of perseverance, I put my life back in order to enter God's holy house again. I went back to the temple a year from the day that my dad had passed. It was a glorious and wonderful day for my family and friends when I re-entered the temple.

Aside from attending the temple I found my true passion in life. Caring for hospice patients. I felt like God was sharing with me a little piece of heaven through caring for them. When my agency assigned me to a hospice patient in Murray I gladly

45

accepted the position. I took care of my new patient, Darin, for three months. He was slowly moving beyond this world. I received a call from the hospice nurse one morning that Darin wasn't doing well. I knew it was his time to go.

When I arrived on shift, Darin was unresponsive with a high fever. He was having a difficult time breathing. I placed cold rags on his face, chest and legs. I gave him Tylenol to bring his fever down. I knew he was in pain, because he was laying on his back on his raw tailbone. Darin's fever came down after a few hours. His breathing stabilized. He opened his eyes a few times during the night. He couldn't speak because he was in a semi-coma.

I sat by his bedside all night. I took care of his every need. Family members arrived throughout the night. Each one of them was tearful because their loved one was dying. There were certain people, like his handicapped brother Alan I knew Darin wanted to say goodbye to. When Alan arrived and saw Darrin lying helpless on the bed. He fell down on top of his chest sobbing. "Oh, my brother Darin. I love you."

I had contained my composure until now, But when Alan was sobbing, my heart broke. Darin opened his eyes a few times to say goodbye to members of his family.

Jenny, his sister, told me, "Darrin said he had a dream last week that all his relatives who had passed were at the foot of the bed. He said our mom touched his shoulder and asked him, "Are you ready to come home now."

Darin's family had requested the Chaplain to see Darin before he passed. His family were devout Christians. Darin was a pastor for their church before he got sick.

The nights I sat up with Darin he had shared with me his love for Jesus. He said smiling, "Jesus is my best friend. He has led me through some tough times in my life like when I lost my mother. He held my hand when I got ill with neuropathy. Jesus strengthens me. He wipes my tears when I have dark days."

Darin was a kind man with a heart of gold. Suddenly a tall, dark haired man with brown eyes and a black suit entered the room. Jenny greeted him with loving arms and said, "Thanks for coming Chaplin. Would you say some comforting words to help us say goodbye to Darin?"

The Chaplain smiled and said, "It's like Darin is on a ship leaving the port. He is saying goodbye to all of us. But he is moving towards others who are welcoming him home. There are people from the other side who are in this room welcoming him home. His mother and father who have passed are some of them. Each person who passes as we watch them go to the shadows of death gives us a message of what the other side is like."

As Darin started to slip on to the next life to join his loved ones I whispered in his ear, "I loved taking care of you. When you get up there look up my dad, Doug Zollinger. Tell him his daughter Marci loves him. She misses him deeply."

I cried, saying my goodbyes to my buddy. My friend, Darin. The hospice nurse arrived thirty minutes later. We dressed him in his favorite Coca-Cola pajamas. The mortuary came thirty minutes later, wrapped Darin in a white sheet. They placed him on a gurney. The family and I said our last goodbyes. I held Jenny as we broke down and uncontrollably wept.

That night, I left at 4:00 a.m. and broke down and cried. I lost my buddy and a special friend. Darin was such a big part of my life for three months. He was always cracking jokes and making me laugh, even when he was bed bound. He could not walk or turn over without my help.

47

His legs and tailbone were causing him unbearable pain, being bed bound for so long. I prepared his meals. I gave him liquids to drink. I changed his soiled briefs. I cared for him for three months. He was my buddy. But I was happy he could now walk, run and be pain-free in heaven.

The experience with Darin when he passed was the same experience I had with my dad before he passed. The experience made me miss my dad. I mourned the loss of my dad and Darrin.

I loved being a certified nursing assistant. I couldn't wait to be a nurse. I had such a great love for hospice patients. They warmed my heart. God be with you, my sweet friend Darin. Until we meet again.

Chapter 5

Fighting the Good Fight

"Our destiny is not determined by the number of times we stumble but by the number of times we rise up, dust ourselves off and move forward." Dieter F. Uchtdorf

Working with hospice patients increased my desire to earn my degree as a registered nurse. I had been in school for two years and I was ready. But I needed to save money for nursing school. When Chantelle offered for me to live with her and her sweet family, I happily accepted. I instantly connected with Chantelle's family, especially her three red- headed, beautiful, bright, energetic girls. We laughed and talked until the wee hours of the night. I supported them in their sporting events and watched their soccer games. I remember smelling baked pizza and Italian pasta in our favorite restaurants we ate at together after watching their games. They treated me like I was a part of their family. I thought of those three angels like they were my own kids.

But now that I was living in Cedar Hills with Chantelle I needed to find a job closer to where I lived. A few months after moving in I interviewed and landed a great job with a local hospital, as a full time Certified Nursing Assistant. Working at the hospital was a whole new world for me. I was now responsible for taking care of ten patients on my shift --unlike Home Health where I was only responsible for one patient a shift.

My responsibilities for my patients included: taking their vitals, transferring them from the restroom to their bed, catheter care, giving them bed baths and discontinuing their intravenous. I reported their results verbally through medical charting to the nurse and doctor.

I felt in control of my own life. It was like I was the captain of my own destiny, sailing the rocky waves in a magnificent boat. I was happy and very satisfied with the direction my life was going for an entire year.

Then one day it was like a firebolt hit my world. As part of my job description, I was also required to take care of patients that were confused or combative and needed one-on-one attention. I remember working early in the morning, assigned to take care of an autistic patient. He was a smart boy, fit and strong with blonde hair and blue eyes in his early thirties. The doctor had ordered him to be in restraints for violent behavior.

The day I took care of him, the doctor felt it was appropriate to remove his restraints. But his behavior was still inappropriate. His restraints should have never been removed. The morning of my shift I remember feeling an object hit my face. I looked up to see where the object was coming from. I saw Mark whipping spoons at me, laughing in glee. Suddenly the spoons stopped striking me when a lady in scrubs with long dark hair walked in the room. I immediately took the nurse aside and whispered in her ear, "Mark is throwing spoons at me."

She was uncaring in her reply, "Let me know if his behavior continues. Just make sure you get his vitals every four hours. He is due for a vital check now."

She abruptly left the room, leaving me alone with Mark. I walked over to Mark. I told him nicely, "I'm going to take your vitals, okay?"

I slowly lifted his arm to take his blood pressure. Like a vicious mountain lion pouncing on his prey, he grabbed me by my neck with his firm hands. At first, I thought he was kidding around. I asked him nicely, "Let go."

He tightened his grip and laughed. He swung my head around like a tetherball to tighten his grip more firmly. I struggled to free myself, but he gripped harder. It now felt like a tug-of-war between a mountain lion and myself. The more I struggled, the tighter he gripped. I thought to myself I'm going to pass out. One more tight grip. He could break my neck. I screamed for help for ten minutes. No one came to rescue me. I finally prayed for help. I felt I should scream bloody murder one more time. I screamed at the top of my lungs, "Help!"

Finally, just as I was ready to pass out, three medical staff came charging into the room to try to release me from his clutches. But they couldn't loosen his chokehold on my neck. I felt like he was strangling me to death. I felt the room spinning. My body was getting weaker as I tried to fight him off. Suddenly, the strong bind around my neck lessened. I was taken to safety. I heard a kind voice ask, "Are you okay?"

Immediately, my neck ached like I had terrible whiplash. I replied to the charge nurse holding my neck in pain, "No, I can barely move my neck."

In a panicked voice she replied, "Go to the emergency room and get checked out to make sure you are okay."

Ten minutes later, I walked into the emergency room. I was supporting my neck with my hand in excruciating pain. The nurse at the front desk saw me. She immediately checked me in. She wheeled me back to an exam room where I was greeted by a nice group of medical staff, who took good care of me. A tall gentleman with blonde hair and green eyes examined me. He

51

ordered x-rays. An hour later the medical doctor informed me of my condition. "You sprained your spine. You definitely will need physical therapy. Apply heat and ice every twenty minutes and take ibuprofen as needed for the pain."

Later that night, the pain enhanced. I could barely get out of bed to eat dinner. Chantelle nursed me back to health. I remember smelling hot chicken noodle soup cooking on the stove. I could taste the noodles in my mouth as I would slurp the broth. Chantelle made me delicious home cooked meals. She brought them to me in bed. She checked up on me during the late nights to make sure I was okay. She unselfishly attended to my every need.

I visited the employee health doctor. He referred me to work with a physical therapist. I remember laying on a heating towel on a leather massage table in a tiny room. I smelled lavender body lotion. I felt its warmth absorbed in my skin. The knots in my neck and back felt as hard as granite. The physical therapist had to knead them out like tough bread dough. The treatments twice a week were unbelievably painful. I laid in bed for weeks applying ice and heat to my injured spine.

Weeks and weeks had passed. My boss was understanding that I was hurt at work and that I needed time to heal, but he was also anxious for my return. After intense physical therapy for six weeks, the employee health doctor finally released me back to work. But the thought of going back to work filled me with trepidation. I had healed physically. But healing emotionally and mentally was a whole other ball game.

The hospital that I had loved working in was creating a feeling of anxiety and danger. All day I would try to block the vicious attack from my mind. But when I walked past the room Mark had assaulted me in, I would start to shudder with fear. I couldn't shake the feeling of the heinous trauma I had experienced.

On one of my shifts, I was instructed by a nurse to take my patient's vitals every four hours, as part of my work routine. I walked into my first patient's room, I felt drops of sweat dripping down my face. I lifted my patient's arm to put on his blood pressure cuff, I started shaking with a deja vu feeling. I thought, "What if he attacks me and breaks my neck?"

Luckily, he didn't assault me, but I was scared to death that he, or any of my patients, could or would. After a week of enduring the flashbacks of the attack, I sadly realized I needed to leave this unsafe environment. I decided to apply online at another hospital, a cancer treatment center. I had always dreamt of working with cancer patients.

A week after applying, I was called in for a mock interview. I interviewed with ten other Certified Nursing Assistants. I confidently and enthusiastically answered the interview questions to the medical team that consisted of four people.

They were nicely dressed, friendly and knowledgeable in their professional fields. They told us kindly after the interview, "We are interviewing fifty qualified Certified Nursing Assistants to fill four positions to join our medical surgical floor. We will get back to you in a few weeks to announce if you got the job or not."

My anticipation was high. I prayed I would get the job. But I soon forgot about it when I was at work the next day and came down with all the symptoms of a stomach flu. I had a high fever; I was sweating profusely. My body ached all over. I had been vomiting all day. It felt like a thousand knives were stabbing me in my upper abdomen. I could barely get through my shift at work. I decided to go to the emergency room after work when my fever and stomach pain continued to get consistently worse.

In the emergency room, a nice nurse with kind green eyes noticed me doubled over in stomach pain. She immediately checked me in. She rushed me back to the examination room.

When the medical doctor entered my room, I was curled up in the fetus position holding my stomach in arduous pain. The doctor immediately rushed to my aid and ordered blood work, intravenous fluids, intravenous nausea meds and intravenous pain meds.

I remembered looking at the confined room I was in. The curtain was closed, and medical instruments surrounded me like they were announcing my heinous fortune. My thoughts were interrupted by the doctor's haunting words, "Your lipase is four hundred. You have pancreatitis. We need to admit you to the hospital."

I thought to myself, "I just got attacked at work and now I'm being admitted to the hospital for pancreatitis. How many more hits can I take?"

When I was admitted to the hospital, they wheeled me from the emergency room to the third floor of the hospital. I remember looking at the bare walls thinking, "Is this how my life is going to be? A series of nightmare after nightmare of trauma?"

My pancreas was not digesting fats and protein. I needed to fast to allow healing. The doctor ordered an intravenous drip to prevent dehydration. He ordered intravenous meds for my pain. I was required to stay in the hospital on intravenous fluids and meds until I could keep liquids down again.

Meanwhile, Chantelle had just moved into a new, million-dollar house in Highland. It was her dream house. She had designed it herself, for her and her family. She owned, Diviine Modestee. Her own company where she sold glamorous, high end, modest bathing suits. After eight long years of hard work, she was finally seeing the fruit of her labors. I had always admired Chantelle for her amazing talent of design and for her passion to bring modesty to the world.

54

She had graciously allowed me to keep living in her old house in Cedar Hills. She wanted me to house sit until she sold it. When the doctor finally released me from the hospital Chantelle picked me up from the hospital. She dropped me off at her old house. I felt content having my own place to live in. But when I entered the house a feeling of loneliness swept over me.

I remembered sitting on her red silk bedspread in her old room. The brass chest of drawers were hand-carved with exquisite writings. The gray carpet led to a huge adjoining bathroom with a vast tub. I climbed into the bathtub. I could feel the warm water on my body. I watched the white bubbles as they floated to the top of the tub. I slowly sank my body into a pool of bubbles. I didn't want to come up for air. I thought to myself, sadly, "When will I have a life like this? No worries or pain, only experiencing joy?"

I slowly raised myself up out of the tub. I wrapped a fluffy towel around me. I could feel my damp feet on the squishy mat on the floor. I fell to the floor in sobs. I felt like I was off my rope physically, mentally, and emotionally. I couldn't take the emotional pain any longer. I decided I was going to take my life that night, but the thought of leaving my loved ones behind without saying goodbye made my heart ache. I decided to text my brother Brian, "I can't do this anymore. I love all of you. Bye."

I felt he would be too busy to get the text to stop me. But at least he could pass on the text to my loved ones to say my final goodbyes. I glanced at the two bottles of pills sitting on my dresser. I quickly snatched them up in my quivering hands. I swallowed each pill, one by one, like they were candy. I laid on my soft bed in a puddle of tears. I waited to leave this miserable world once and for all. I felt my body meandering off to sleep. My mind raced to an imagined wonderland of peace and love. I imagined a world of no pain and suffering. I imagined seeing my dad standing before me embracing me in his loving arms. I imagined seeing the Savior, Jesus Christ, and kneeling down to him in awe of his glory.

My beautiful imaginations were abruptly interrupted by a loud pounding at the door. I was reluctant to open the door. But the thumping grew louder and louder. I opened the brass handle of the door and my sister and three nieces rushed to hug me crying, "We are so relieved and happy that you are still here. We were so scared."

My sister told me with a frantic voice, "We got Brian's text. I am not leaving you alone tonight. You are coming to stay at my house."

My sister is like a mother hen. She has always taken care of me in my time of need. She helped me pack my things and we drove to her house. She wanted to take me to the emergency room but I told her, "No, I'm fine. I'm not going to the emergency room."

She wasn't convinced. She stayed by my side all night. Later that night, I finally felt the effects of the overdose. I felt as light as a feather. I slowly slipped off of the leather coach downstairs in my sister's new house. Chantelle freaked out. She rushed me to the emergency room. I confessed to the medical doctor that I had a drug overdose. He immediately ordered for me an intravenous drug and an intravenous drip to counteract the overdose.

A nice lady dressed in a white lab coat entered my room a few hours later. She questioned, "Do you want to kill yourself?"

In a flood of tears, I replied, "Yes, I want to die."

She gave me a puzzled look. "Why?"

I relayed to her all I had been through in my life with constant illness, being attacked at work, my abusive relationship with Troy, not being married, losing my ability to have my own children, losing my dad, being a burden on my family, and the list seemed to go on and on.

I broke down into uncontrollable tears. Finally, I had someone to talk to about the trauma I experienced in my life. The therapist gave me advice. "You need help. You need a support group. A therapist to talk to. I am sending you to a psych ward here at the hospital."

Immediately after the therapist's visit, my sister made calls to my family informing them of my suicide attempt. My family was devastated and concerned by the news. Later that night, two tall dark-haired men with black beards arrived at my room with a yellow stretcher. They helped me onto the stretcher and tied down my arms and legs with a thick black strap. They wheeled me to a red ambulance van parked outside. Chantelle took a picture of them wheeling me to the ambulance. She told me later, "You had no hope in your eyes. You had given up on life. It scared me to death."

Chapter 6

Overcoming Great Obstacles

"Instead of being ashamed of what you've been through, be proud of what you've overcome." Dr. Phillip McGraw

Statistics show that after someone leaves the hospital after a suicide attempt, they have a ninety percent chance of trying it again within ninety days. I am not going to lie. I hated being confined to a psych ward. I thought to myself, "Why can't these people just let me die? I don't want to be alive anymore. Nothing they can do or say will change my mind." I was not a happy camper and I complained to my family on the phone, "I hate this dungeon."

When I first arrived at the psych ward, a lady forced me to strip my clothes like they do in prison. She demanded I put on a gaudy gray gown. She took away my phone. She removed the ties in my sweats and sweatshirts. I wasn't allowed a razor to shave my legs. They started looking like an amazon jungle.

My stomach felt like a huge semi-truck had run over it from the drug overdose. I just wanted to rest. But they didn't allow me to be alone. I had a roommate in my cold room. I was stuck with her even if she snored. Everything in the building was locked down. I felt like a caged animal ready to growl at anyone who crossed my path.

One good thing, to me, about this prison cell was the wonderful drugs. When I made a big scene, they would give me a sedative to calm me down. I snarled at the nurse, "I feel like a caged animal. I hate it here, I feel claustrophobic. I need something for my twisting stomach pain. I can't take this anymore."

The nurse willingly gave me anxiety meds and meds for my stomach pain. The medication made me feel numb and happy. I felt like I was floating into a nether world, and I longed to live there.

A few days later, I was finally allowed visitors. Chantelle and Brian came to visit me. I was indifferent to seeing them. My sister told me with kind eyes, "God is watching over you. He loves you."

I replied with a disgusted look, "What God? He just wants me to suffer. He doesn't love me."

I was miserable. I just wanted to die. After a few days in what felt like a guard house, I realized the secret to leave. All I had to do was fake like I was getting better and no longer suicidal. I started to fake acting happy. In my individual daily therapy sessions the therapist asked me, "Are you suicidal?"

I replied, fake happy, "Nope!"

But a strange thing happened when I changed my sour behavior. I started to warm up to the other residents. We became close friends. I participated in groups. I soon learned "Wow, I am not alone. All these people have had trauma too."

I started to enjoy my therapy sessions. I let go of feelings I had repressed for years. The more I let go, I began to empathize with my fellow residents. I thought to myself, These people aren't crazy, not all of them. Most are like me--suffering from trauma. They feel hopelessness and want their emotional pain to end. They

59

feel like suicide is the only way to end their heart-breaking pain, just like me"

I was surprised that some of these patients were nurses, pharmacists, lawyers and other well-respected people in society. I remember one nice lady I met. She had told me that she had lost her father, her best friend and was having trouble sleeping. She couldn't deal with the pain anymore. She wanted to take her own life. Another kind lady who had tried to end her life was a nurse. She told me that her recent divorce was so painful that even her kids weren't enough to keep her around. I listened to story after story of the pain that these people had endured. I shared with them my pain, my trauma. They said, "Wow, you've been through so much, maybe we don't have it so bad?"

I was slowly making friends in my new environment. I felt joy, especially when I befriended a cute young blonde girl. Christine was fair skinned and had friendly blue eyes. When she shared her story and said to me, "I was kicked out of the house at sixteen. I was forced to live on the streets. I turned to drugs and alcohol to numb my pain. But when I tried to get sober, I failed and overdosed on drugs, almost killing myself. Even though my parents abandoned me, my younger brother has always been there for me throughout my life. He has helped me through some painful days."

I thought about Chantelle, Brian, Levi who had always been there for me, and I sobbed. My mind raced back to the good memories with them. Levi was like a brave lion protecting me like I was his vulnerable cub. Brian watched over me like a hawk and always saved me from danger. Chantelle always took care of me like a mother tending to her baby chicks. I remembered the kind text I had received from Levi after I overdosed, "I would step in front of a bus for you. I love you and my heart would ache if anything happened to you."

I will never forget the day when I experienced true tragedy. Christine and I were walking in the hallway back from lunch. One of the nurses dressed in pink scrubs approached Christine and said nicely, "Christine, you have a phone call."

A few minutes later, I saw Christine holding the phone in her hands, sobbing. I saw her fall on the floor in tears. I ran to her. "What's wrong, Christine?"

She was a puddle of tears, "My brother just committed suicide. My dad came home and found him unresponsive. My dad called 911. The paramedics couldn't revive him from the drug overdose. It's all my fault. He tried to call me a week ago, but I was too busy to talk to him. He told me he had just lost his job. He was depressed. Now he's gone. My little brother is gone."

I watched my friend grieve the loss of her brother, it did something to me inside. I imagined my loved ones reaction if they had received the unimaginable news that I had taken my own life. I remembered my brother, Brian, telling me when he came to visit me, "It's like a loss. Like it really happened. I'm trying to push past the fear of you not doing it again, but, most people who attempt suicide do it again. I don't know what I would do if you took your own life."

My thoughts were interrupted by Christine vocalizing her thoughts to her deceased brother, "I'm so sorry little brother. I should have been there for you."

I had never seen the other side of the coin. I had never witnessed the suffering of the loss of a loved one to suicide. It affected me gravely. I thought to myself, "I could never put my family through the pain of me taking my own life."

61

I decided I would fight for my life and survive. After a few more days of intense individual therapy and group therapy, my therapist asked me are you suicidal. I replied, "No,"

I meant it. My therapist felt it was safe and released me to go home. I could finally be unleashed to experience life again. I was happy. But I was sad to leave my new friends. We exchanged numbers and promised to stay in touch

When I left the psych hospital that afternoon. I anticipated feeling excitement. But instead I felt sadness. For five days, I had been given a gift to escape the world. To focus on only healing emotionally and mentally. Now, I was stepping back into the world. It shocked me like a lost, baby kitten torn from the security and safety of its mother.

I remember feeling like I was living in a shattered world. I had to pick up the pieces one by one. It felt like the more I tried to survive, a hurricane kept knocking me down over and over again. Making it impossible to live. Chantelle had so much on her own plate with her own family. She couldn't take care of me anymore. I understood. I moved back in with my mom in Roy a few days later. But I felt like a yo-yo being tossed from one family house to another. I felt like a burden on my family.

Living with my mom was pleasant at first. We got along great, sharing stories and reminiscing about my dad. But, as time passed, it all fell apart. My mom had a difficult time dealing with my father's passing. My dad had been her rock. I felt she was not in a good place to take care of me. I missed my dad. His good advice. How he always made me laugh when I wanted to cry. Brian and Levi tried to take my dad's place. They would call me almost every night to check in with me. But it wasn't the same.

I had no idea I was about to experience the most grueling year of my life. One of the biggest pieces of advice the psychiatrist gave me before he released me was, "Don't make any life altering decisions. Don't start a new job and focus on yourself and on healing. You don't need stress right now, you need to just heal."

I wish I had listened to his good advice. But I received an unexpected call a week later. It was from the cancer center I had applied at. "We would like to offer you a job as a certified nursing assistant on the medical surgical floor."

I thought to myself, "I made the cut out of 50 other people they interviewed! I am so happy, I am finally being offered my dream job. Maybe things are finally looking up for me?"

Everyone and anyone in the medical field wanted to work at this facility. It was a coveted job for a certified nursing assistant because it was higher pay than any other hospital in Utah. The patient population was only cancer patients. I officially accepted their offer and was hired to start training in two weeks with a three month probation period. I submitted my two weeks' notice to my boss at my old job that same week.

My last day of work, I hugged my cherished employees and boss goodbye. I was excited for a new adventure that awaited me. Working at the cancer hospital was like a dream come true. The building was one of the most lovely interior hospitals I had ever seen. The patients' rooms looked like hotel suites with brass wooden chest of drawers and colossal televisions. The patient bathrooms were as ornate as the inside front entrance of the hospital. The patients were a joy to care for and they rarely complained about their cancer treatments. I was given more responsibilities assisting the nurses with more critical care than my previous job.

I adored my job. But it was frustrating because I was forced to park far from the building. I had to take the bus to come to work on my morning shifts. One of the female managers, Lori, who wasn't fond of me as an employee reprimanded me for being late a few times.

I remember driving to work one morning in the damp snow. Snowflakes were falling on the outside of my front car window. My outside window wipers swiftly wiped off the frosty flakes from my front window. I saw cars skidding off the freeway into five feet snowbanks on the side of the road. I felt a sharp pain in my upper abdomen. The agony was so severe it stopped me from being able to drive to work. I raced to the emergency room at a hospital in Ogden. I called work and told the charge nurse, "I'm going to the emergency room for abdominal pain. I can't drive. I'm in so much pain."

The charge nurse replied, "You are expected at work in thirty minutes. This isn't good but if you need to go to the emergency room, then go."

When I arrived at the hospital ten minutes later, the charge nurse saw me cradling my stomach in stabbing pain. She immediately checked me in. She wheeled me in a wheelchair to an examination room. A nice man in green scrubs saw me doubled over in pain sitting upright in bed crying. He immediately ordered a CT scan, a blood panel, and intravenous pain meds. It felt like hours before the results came back. Finally, the doctor entered my room and said nicely, "We aren't sure what caused your abdominal pain, but you can go home now. Just come back if the pain gets worse."

It was like the doctor's pronouncement was a foreshadowing of what was to come. The pain definitely got worse. I ended up calling out sick again because the pain was so intense. I braved going to work the day after, and Lori called me into her office. One of the Human Resources employees was also in the room with us. Lori told me cruelly, "We are going to terminate your employment with us."

I was in shock, "Why?" I asked, bewildered.

She replied, "You have only been with us for two weeks. You haven't finished your training days because of sick calls. You were on probation for three months. We won't be extending you a permanent position."

I pleaded with Lori, "I have doctor notes of my absences. I had to go to the emergency room. It was life or death."

She told me, "This isn't the right fit for you right now. I'm sorry."

I slowly walked out to the parking lot. I opened my car door and slid into the driver's seat. I forcefully grabbed and hit my head against the steering wheel. I cried out, screaming, "Are you kidding me, God? I have just lost my dream job!"

But the suffering didn't stop there. Within a week, I was back in the emergency room. My abdominal pain had substantially increased. I went back to the hospital in the middle of the night. I was immediately wheeled back to a room to be examined. But a cruel man entered my room. He refused to give me any pain meds until he diagnosed me. The medical doctor was uncompassionate. I was writhing in unbearable pain, crying for relief. I begged him, "I'm not leaving this hospital until you figure out what is wrong with me. I've had a CT done. Do an ultrasound. Something is wrong with me."

The doctor finally listened to me and ordered an ultrasound. During the ultrasound the tech told me, "Something is wrong. Your gallbladder is sledged and collapsing."

He immediately wheeled me back to the emergency room. The doctor entered the room with his head down in shame, "Your gallbladder is collapsing. You need emergency surgery. Would you like some pain meds?"

I was screaming in pain. "Yes, please!"

The nurse finally gave me intravenous meds for the pain. I finally felt some relief.

Chapter 7

Beyond the Veil

"I believe we need to speak of and believe in and bear testimony to the ministering of angels more than we sometimes do. They constitute one of God's greatest methods of witnessing through the veil." Jeffrey R. Holland

The doctor at the hospital referred me to a surgeon to perform the emergency surgery to remove my gallbladder. I met with the surgeon on Monday, a day after I arrived at the hospital. The surgeon informed me, "Your gallbladder is collapsing. It's causing pancreatitis. I need to wait until your pancreas settles to do the surgery. Your pancreas is inflamed in the ultrasound picture."

I was so angry. I thought to myself, "All this time! Not once did they do an ultrasound! They would have caught my malfunctioning gallbladder. Then it wouldn't have scarred my pancreas. No wonder I keep getting pancreatitis and ending up back in the hospital so much."

The surgeon, dressed in surgical scrubs with glasses on his face, looked like a smart professor. He seemed to be confident in what he was doing. He reassured me that the surgery would stop the pancreatitis. I trusted the surgeon's judgment and agreed that the surgery needed to be done.

A week later, I went in for my tenth abdominal surgery - cholecystectomy. Post-surgery, I had no appetite and everything I ate came out the other end. I could barely stomach liquids. I was in intense pain because I had undergone so many surgeries. My poor abdomen wasn't healing properly. One of the scars ripped open. I had to go back to the emergency room to be treated. But my scars healed eventually. In six weeks I recovered from surgery.

However, now I was unemployed. I needed to find work immediately. Luckily, a week later a medical staffing agency in Murray discovered my resume online. They called me in for an interview. I happily interviewed. I was hired per diem to float to hospitals in Utah--Salt Lake City, Midvale and Jordan Valley. One of the hospitals loved my work so much they bought me out from medical staffing. I signed a contract with them. The pay wasn't as good as the cancer research center, but it was better than other jobs I had previously. I accepted their offer to be a full-time certified nursing assistant with benefits.

My new boss adored me. I was healthy for eight months. I was living life again. I felt like my life was finally on the road to success to a full recovery.

Little did I know, I was about to endure the worst pain of my life. I was at work on the medical surgical floor when I felt upper abdominal pain. It twisted and turned inside my upper abdomen. I was crunched over and unable to stand. The pain went on for an entire week. I immediately rushed myself to the emergency room in indescribable pain. A thoughtful nurse saw me in tears, almost collapsed on the floor. I was clutching my stomach in pain. She raced me to an exam room. The doctor was very nice and sympathetic to my condition. He was handsome, with dark brown hair and heavenly blue eyes. He ordered blood work and intravenous pain meds. He came back into my room a half hour later and sadly announced, "You have pancreatitis. I'm going to admit you to the hospital."

"How could I have pancreatitis again after gallbladder surgery?" I asked the doctor, in shock of the bad news.

The doctor told me nicely, "The gallbladder almost collapsing scarred your pancreas. You now have chronic pancreatitis."

I couldn't believe what awful news I heard. I was admitted to the hospital that evening. I was in the hospital for five long days that felt like five months. The hospital staff took good care of me, especially since I was an employee at the facility. But I was on strict doctors orders of nothing by mouth during my hospital stay. I was given an intravenous drip to prevent dehydration.

I remember the hopeless feeling I felt in the hospital. I never felt more disconnected from the world. A few of my siblings called me to see how I was doing. I tried to put on a happy face, but inside I was falling apart seam by seam.

One dark night, my intravenous line blew. The nurse had to stick me seven times to try to poke my vein. I finally threw up my hands and said, "Enough! I can't take this pain anymore. Please put in a picc line."

The nurse listened to my request. The next morning, two young gentlemen entered my room to put in a picc line. They sterilized the whole room. They were dressed in a blue gown over their blue scrubs. They covered the steel table with a blue shield-like material. They laid medical supplies on the material. They covered my upper right arm with the same blue covering. They numbed the outside of my arm with a large needle. They proceeded to thread in a large 12 foot picc line in my artery. When they were done with the procedure they left me alone. Closing the door behind them.

I laid in my hospital bed, dressed in a green gown. A large PICC line in my arm and sobbed. I thought, "Is this my life now, PICC lines and constant hospital stays?"

69

The doctor finally discharged me after a week when I could keep liquids down again. I slowly started to pick up the pieces of my shattered life. But Christmas was approaching. I was missing my father. I had no one special to share my life with through the holidays. I shared my feelings of hopelessness with my mom. I told her I was suicidal. My mom was overwhelmed with my depression and constant thoughts of suicide. She told me that she couldn't handle the stress anymore without my father to help her. She went to Mexico with my brother's family on a long trip.

I never felt more alone and scared to survive. I later forgave my mother for not being there for me through the most trying times of my life. I understood that without my dad as her rock to help her with my suicide attempts it was too overwhelming for her to handle.

Christmas Day I was alone. I felt a wind of hopelessness wash over me. I was supposed to work that day at the hospital but got called off because the hospital didn't need me. I remember sitting in the living room- a blank stare. I no longer had the energy to survive another day. I was done. I got on my knees and prayed for forgiveness for my next actions, "I can't do it anymore. I am off my rope. I don't want to be here anymore. Please forgive me. I am taking my own life. You have given me more than I can handle."

I felt like I was in irredeemable despair. I was only thinking of the emotional and physical pain I was enduring. I said to myself, "This is the only way to escape my suffering and pain."

I went into the family room. I sat on the red coach in a cloud of daze. I decided this time that I needed to do it right. I could have no slip ups. I decided to refrain from texting a loved one to say goodbye. But to leave them with an empty void. I wasn't concerned about anyone else but myself. I desperately wanted to end my pain.

I slowly opened a bottle of pain pills. I swallowed each pill one by one. I don't remember how much time had passed. I just remember I felt my spirit floating from my body to another enchanted world of feeling only peace and equanimity. I saw a bright light approaching me, I felt it was my dad inviting me to his illustrious world. The blinding reflection got closer and closer, I felt my dad nearer than I had ever felt him before. I heard my dad softly whisper, "Please don't."

My euphoric feeling was abruptly interrupted by a text on my phone from Chantelle: I love you. How are you? Just want to make sure you are okay?

I started to cry. I don't know how or why? But somehow my dad's plea to stay, followed by Chantelle's text, gave me the motivation to call 911 to try to save myself. But I had ingested several pain pills. I was quickly leaving this world and moving to the other side when the ambulance arrived at my house.

I remember being rushed to the emergency room on a yellow stretcher. Two guys, wearing blue and red jackets, announced to the emergency room staff, "She overdosed on pain pills."

The emergency staff immediately administered intravenous fluids and a drug to counteract the overdose. My oxygen saturation was dropping rapidly. They pumped oxygen through my face mask. My blood pressure was relinquishing. I was sweating and convulsing. I heard the nurse and doctor speaking. It felt like an out of body experience. I wasn't aware of my ambience. I slowly could feel myself vanishing into a new world of eternal hope and everlasting love. I felt angels all around me lifting me up to greater heights than I had ever experienced. I felt like I was being led to a bright light. I remember thinking, Will I see Jesus?

I imagined in my mind what it would be like to see Jesus. My mind raced back to the beautiful lyrics to a song I loved by MercyMe, "I Can Only Imagine"

I can only imagine what it will be like

When I walk by your side

I can only imagine what my eyes will see.

When your face is before me.

I can only imagine..

I can only imagine..

Surrounded by your glory

What will my heart feel?

Will I dance for you Jesus?

Or in awe of you be still?

Will I stand in your presence?

Or to my knees will I fall?

Well I sing hallelujah?

Or will I speak at all?

I can only imagine...

I can only imagine...

I can only imagine when that day comes

When I find myself

Standing in the Son

I can only imagine when all I would do is forever Forever worship you

I can only imagine.

My tranquil world disappeared. I woke up later in a foggy mist with tubes up my nose and an intravenous drip in my upper arm. I heard a comforting voice, "We saved you just in the nick of time."

But my fiendish reality continued. Soon after my release from the hospital, I shared my suicide attempt with Chantelle. My mother got word. She was not happy that I had overdosed again. She was upset she had to come home early from her trip to take care of me.

To make matters worse I was experiencing persistent lower abdominal pain. The pain worsened with every step I took. It felt like blood curdling endometriosis pain. I knew this pain all too well. It was not like pancreatitis pain. It was a sharp, throbbing pain in my lower abdomen. It radiated into my lower back.

I immediately made a visit to see Dr. Wally. He was the same doctor who had performed my hysterectomy ten years previously. He had moved his practice to the hospital I worked at a few years ago. During my visit, Dr. Wally examined me. I almost went through the roof in agonizing pain. He said nicely, "I think your endometriosis has returned. We need to schedule you for another laparoscopy."

I was relieved. I was going to be released from this pain. But I couldn't believe my endometriosis had returned after a full hysterectomy. Dr. Wally scheduled me for surgery for two weeks later on his surgical calendar.

I was in unimaginable discomfort. Dr. Wally had given me pain meds. They weren't touching my distress. I would lay in the bathtub, unable to move, or even want to move. I just wanted to be free from this pain. I thought to myself, "How much more can I take?"

My endometriosis, returning after ten years remission, was like cancer returning again. I survived surgery after surgery. Emergency visit after an emergency visit, curled in the fetal position and screaming in torment. Breaking down when I went under the knife to lose my womanhood. And for what? The awful demon had returned? It can't be possible. I felt I was living someone else's nightmare life and I begged for someone to wake me.

I went under the knife again for the eleventh time. Before Dr. Wally opened me up, I prayed and pleaded to God, "Please let me die during surgery. I can't handle one more surgery. I'm done."

I later awoke to a pleasant voice, "Are you in any pain?"

My endless trial continued. I felt bandages on my abdomen. The pain was horrendous. I replied, "Yes, please, I need something strong for the pain."

The nurse administered intravenous pain meds. The tenderness subsided. I felt doltish. I didn't want this feeling to leave. Later when I was released to go home, I was jolted back to reality. While recovering from the surgery, I developed a nasty staph infection, and I couldn't move or bend my right leg.

I called Dr. Wally. He told me to go to the emergency room immediately. I was instantly checked in and wheeled to an examining room in triage. The doctor entered my room within ten minutes and examined me. Afterward, he left my room and called Dr. Wally. They both agreed that I needed intravenous antibiotics and intravenous pain meds for my staph infection in my leg.

Luckily, the staph infection cleared up in seven days. But this surgery was, by far, the worst surgery of my life. It took eight weeks to recover. I tried to return to work in six weeks. But my first day back to work I was lifting a patient and tore the inside stitches in my abdomen. I was out of work for another two weeks.

When I returned to work the next week, my whole world turned upside down. My old boss had moved to a new position in the hospital. My new boss, Bethany, was nasty and she didn't like me. She looked as tall as a giant and treated employees like they were beneath her. The day I came back, she found every reason to get rid of me.

All day at work, I wasn't feeling well. I was vomiting. I had severe diarrhea. I didn't want to lose my job. I powered through. But I couldn't focus on work. I felt sicker than a dog. I had a high fever, chills and upper abdominal pain. When my shift finished, I forgot to give a report to the new certified nursing assistant coming on shift.

Within ten minutes, Bethany came storming down the hallway and demanded me to follow her to Human Resources. I followed her down a red carpet hallway into a tidy room, and Bethany closed the door. My heart was in my throat. A short lady with brown hair, sitting at a black desk in the room, said with a stern look, "We are letting you go. You left a unit without reporting."

I tried to explain myself but both the Human Resources representative and Bethany had daggers out for me. I felt like I was being bulldozed with sharp steel razors, and there was nothing I could do to save myself. I walked out of the Human Resources office and opened the glass doors to go outside. I could feel the gentle wind brushing my cheeks. I hurriedly ran to the garbage can and vomited. I was too sick to care about anything.

The next four months were insufferable. I couldn't keep anything down. Everything that went in my mouth came out the other end. I had intolerable upper abdominal pain, and my pancreas was inflamed again. I was admitted back to the hospital again. The doctor who took care of me in the hospital was baffled why I was ill for so long. He ordered an endoscopy. They found nothing. He ordered a colonoscopy. They found nothing. He finally ordered an ultrasound endoscopy, looking for signs of pancreatic cancer. Luckily, they found nothing.

I was released from the hospital seven days later. I was on doctor's orders for a liquid diet. But I couldn't keep liquids down or from it running right through me. I was sick, weak and dehydrated from vomiting so much that I visited a primary care doctor in Salt Lake City. When I met Dr. Chang, I was comforted by his good bedside manner and his willingness to help me get better.

He was Asian, dark- haired with a kind smile and warm blue eyes. He ordered a full panel of blood work to try to discover what was wrong with me? The blood work came back showing that my pancreas was slightly inflamed but it didn't explain why I wasn't getting better.

Doctor Chang arranged for me to go to an infusion clinic to have infusions twice a week. He ordered intravenous nausea meds and intravenous fluids for my severe dehydration through a PICC line. My veins were now permanently scarred from multiple intravenous lines.

I remember the PICC line being in my arm for weeks and weeks on end. I felt like it was becoming like my blood line. I was dehydrated all week until the day of my infusions. I don't remember what was worse --the insufferable abdominal pain or the constant nausea I felt every waking hour of the day before my infusions.

I felt like I was permanently attached to my intravenous pole. The infusions took two hours to complete and the nice nurse at the infusion clinic, dressed in animal printed pink scrubs, administered intravenous fluids and intravenous nausea meds through my PICC lines. I felt loopy and my nausea finally subsided for most of the day afterwards.

But improvement was slow. I would try to drink something, and within five minutes I would vomit and vomit. The diarrhea returned, making it impossible for me to stay hydrated. One afternoon, I felt so dizzy. I felt like I was going to pass out from the vomiting and constant diarrhea. I was hopelessly wanting to leave this world. I thought to myself, "No one can figure out what is wrong with me. I have been sick for a whole year. I'm done. I can't live like this anymore."

At home I was alone. My mother had left to take care of my sister, Carlie in Provo who was having severe abdominal pain. She had missed my doctor's appointment to take care of Carlie and her children for four days. I thought to myself, "Carlie has a husband to take care of her, and I have no one to take care of me. I felt like a burden on my mom and family. I decided that I was done."

I walked to the garage door, stumbled and lost my balance. I pressed the white button on the wall and closed the heavy garage door. I walked a few feet to my car in the garage. I opened my car door slowly. I slid into the soft, cushioned passenger seat, slowly closed my car door and turned on the car ignition. I could immediately taste the carbon monoxide exhaust fumes from my car. I sat in a daze waiting for death's door to take me to the other side.

Thirty minutes passed. I felt like I was delirious in a misty haze. The carbon monoxide had infiltrated my car. I could smell the smoky gas. I suddenly heard a soft voice, "Hold on. Don't give up. It's almost over."

I felt my dad with me in the car sitting right next to me. I cried out in sobs, "Dad, I can't do this anymore."

I felt a soft tap on my shoulder, like my dad wanted to hug me to tell me everything is going to be okay. My dad from the other side had given me the fortitude to go on. I turned off the car's ignition. I opened the car door. I almost tripped while opening the garage door. I took two steps and turned the doorknob. I jerked open the door to the house. I crawled on my hands and knees. I slid slowly onto the red coach in the family room, weak from the poison I had inhaled.

Chapter 8

The Sun Keeps Rising

"Never give up. Today is hard, tomorrow will be worse, but the day after tomorrow will be sunshine." Jack Ma

I never shared with anyone of my fourth suicide attempt and that my father from beyond the veil had rescued me. The Lord gave me a light at the end of the tunnel from my rigorous trial when he referred me to Dr. Chang, a GI specialist from my Primary Care Doctor. I was impressed by his intelligence. He had a skill of thinking outside the box. He decided to order an MRI- the only test that hadn't been ordered. He immediately sent me to radiology in order to figure out why I had been ill for so long.

A few days later, I had a follow up appointment with Dr. Chang for the MRI results. The day of my appointment, I was sitting in the exam room waiting for Dr. Chang. I was nervously flinging my legs back and forth as I looked at the medical diagrams on the white wall. I thought to myself, "I need some good news. I need hope today to survive."

Suddenly, the door swung open. Dr. Chang walked in and said with a smile, "The MRI scan shows you have colitis and that is why you have been so sick for so long. I'm going to prescribe you antibiotics and it should be cleared up within a week."

Dr. Chang was a miracle worker. Exactly within a week I got better, and I could keep fluids down. Another week passed and I could finally stomach solids again. I was slowly becoming stronger physically. But being sick a whole year took a toll on me emotionally and mentally. I was depressed living at home at age 47, unemployed, not married, and having no semblance of a normal life.

That night, I got on my knees and pleaded with God. "I can't do this anymore. You need to give me something to hold on to. I have no hope for a better tomorrow."

When I got off my knees, I saw a Facebook post on my phone by Jeffrey R. Holland, one of my favorites of the twelve apostles of my church. "When you're feeling low and your days are difficult, remember the Savior hears your songs you can't sing. Don't give up on yourself."

I then saw another Facebook post from my friend Cari; it was a photo with her family. Cari lived in San Diego, and I remembered how much fun I had in California. My thoughts raced back to when I felt joy at the sandy beach-diving into the ocean waves, smelling the warm ocean air, and feeling the grainy sand in between my toes.

I decided to contact Cari on Facebook messenger and asked her excitedly, "I'm thinking of moving to California, but I need a place to stay for a week. I need to find a place to live, and to find a job in San Diego."

She replied to my Facebook message immediately and said kindly, "Sure! Come on down to San Diego. You would love it here."

That same week, I excitedly bought a plane ticket to San Diego and arranged for Cari to pick me up at the San Diego airport. The day before I flew, I couldn't sleep. I was so excited to be going back to sunny California. I looked out my window, felt the chilly frost and glanced at the snow falling on the wet, dirty ground. I was over the freezing weather and driving in four feet of snow. I needed a drastic change to feel alive again.

I remember the day I walked off the plane to San Diego; I felt the warm sun on my face and could taste the ocean air. The palm trees were blooming and the leaves were shifting in the warm wind. I thought to myself, "This is my happy place."

Cari picked me up at the airport. She was a good host and she drove me to the places I needed to go. I had already sent my resume online to hospitals in San Diego. I heard back from one of them before I left and had an interview set up for me during the week I was in San Diego.

It was a miracle how quickly I found a job. The manager from one of the hospitals, Amy, was impressed with my work experience and references. She hired me as a full-time Certified Nursing Assistant on the oncology floor. I was expected to report to work in two weeks for training.

I was also referred by Cari's friend from her ward for a room to rent in her neighborhood. The kind lady, Shari, had lost her husband to cancer a few years ago, and needed renters to help pay her mortgage. Within a week, I had solidified a job and a place to stay in Chula Vista.

I called my mom to let her know I was coming home to Utah to pick up my stuff to move.

When I arrived in Utah the next morning, it was snowing. I could feel the icy, wet ground on my feet as I walked outside the airport to my mom's brown Cadillac. I was certain that it was time to move to tropical sunny California.

The next morning, I hugged my mom goodbye and hurriedly hopped into my white Nissan Versa. My car was packed full of all my belongings. I headed for San Diego, California. I drove ten hours straight, listened to music, and played movies on my iPhone. The drive was pleasant. I loved passing through Las Vegas. The speed limit was 80 MPH on the freeway. I cruise controlled with a huge smile on my face, my windows down and my hair blowing in the wind.

I arrived in San Diego later that night. I had traveled miles to a new state in hopes of starting a new life. When I arrived at the home I was renting, I unpacked my car, climbed a flight of stairs to my new room, carrying my belongings behind me. My new, furnished room was now covered with boxes and garbage bags filled to the brim with my personal belongings. I was exhausted from the move, and when I finished unpacking my stuff, I slipped into the covers of my new bed and happily fell fast asleep.

My new world in San Diego brought me joy and fulfillment. I remember feeling the hot air on my face as I would go on my daily jog, my running shoes hitting the cement. I would spend my weekends at the sandy beach-laying on a large beach towel, basking in the sun, watching the ocean waves dash together. I would inhale the tropical ocean air and think to myself, "I am finally happy."

But, sadly, after a few months working at my new job, I wasn't enjoying it like I had expected to. I was required to give bed baths to every one of my thirteen patients. I felt like a glorified bed bath aid. I had minimal responsibilities. I wasn't allowed to take vitals on my patients like I had in other hospitals I worked at in Utah. Most of the staff at my new job were friendly, but some of the upper management were unkind and micromanaged me. I felt like I was in the army being drilled and reprimanded for every move I made.

I especially didn't like working in the overflow unit. There they placed psychiatric patients that were confused, violent and not easy to work with. Working on that unit brought back horrific memories of when I was attacked by my autistic patient.

One morning, I was working on the overflow unit taking care of a patient who was very confused, violent and not cooperating with staff. One of the nurses asked me to help her change the patient's dressing. He had bed sores from being bed bound so long. During the dressing change, I was closest to the patient on his left side and the other nurse was safely on his right side. The patient didn't want his dressing changed, and he screamed out in pain when the nurse tore off his bandage on his bed- sore.

The patient punched me, three hard blows to my ribs, in frustration. It felt like someone had beaten me in the ribs with a giant club. I was screaming, holding my ribs in pain. The charge nurse heard my cry for help and came rushing into the room. She saw me hunched over in pain, fighting to catch my breath and she asked me, surprised, "What happened?"

I replied, "The patient punched me three times in the ribs. I can barely breathe"

With a concerned look, the charge nurse asked one of the nearby Certified Nursing Assistants passing by, "Get a wheelchair and take Marci to the emergency room."

A few minutes later, the Certified Nursing Assistant entered the room with a wheelchair. She hurriedly wheeled me to the emergency room. The nurse sitting at the front desk saw me battling to catch my breath and immediately came to my aid. She wheeled me back into one of the exam rooms to be checked by a doctor. A young, good-looking man with blonde, sun kissed hair entered the room and checked me over and said, "You bruised your ribs. You have a rib contusion."

Later at home that night, in my comfortable bed, each time I attempted to breathe it felt like a ton of bricks was on my chest. The doctor had released me from work for two weeks with strict orders to apply ice on my injured ribs and take ibuprofen as needed for the pain.

When it came time to go back to work, I remember I was not happy because the charge nurse, Sammy, yelled when she got upset. She had cruel eyes and a dark, black complexion. She had assigned me on the same floor with the same patient who had assaulted me. I tried to reason with her and said sternly, "I was just attacked by this patient. Now I am with him again. I need time to emotionally heal from the assault."

She rudely replied, "Okay, fine. We will take you off the floor for a few weeks. But you can't avoid the floor forever. You are required to work on this floor when we need you. It's your job."

I thought to myself, "I can't believe it! You show me no empathy or sympathy that I have been injured at work."

My frightful realism continued. A week later I was assigned to the psychiatric floor again, to the same violent patient, Tony, who had attacked me. One of the lead nurses, Jody, asked me to assist her with Tony's skin breakdown assessment. He had skin tears all over his body and the nurse was very rough with him during the skin assessment.

Tony screamed out, "Stop hurting me!"

Jody was uncaring, "Sorry, sir," she replied, and continued her harsh assessment.

He was angry and almost took a swing at me again out of frustration. No way was I going to be punched again. I defended myself and grabbed his fist to block his blow and said firmly, "Do not punch me."

Tony backed down and Jody finished her harsh skin assessment. Thirty minutes later, my boss called me into her office. In her office was the lead nurse, my boss and a lady from skin check services. All three of them ganged up on me. My boss asked me, "What happened when the nurse skin-checked the patient?"

I relayed to her the story. My boss replied, "Jody told us that you held the patient down and said, "Don't punch me." Then you continued to hold him down, causing his skin to tear."

I replied, "That's false. His skin- tear bled because Jody was rough with him during the skin assessment."

The three women were like three Siamese black cats and glared at me with their savage eyes. They stuck to each other like adhesive glue and threw me under the bus, Amy replied, "You are suspended. We are going to talk to Human Resources about this. We will decide what to do."

I left the office with my head hanging down. I thought to myself, "What happened?"

Immediately, I went to Human Resources and relayed what had happened. I asked, "What are my options?"

The Human Resources representative, Donna, was very nice. She was sitting in a roll out chair amongst stacks of papers laid on her desk. She said kindly, "This incident has not been reported yet. But if it is reported you could lose your Certified Nursing Assistant license."

I couldn't believe my ears. I replied, in shock, "If I quit, can I leave on good terms?"

Donna replied kindly, "Yes, you could be rehired again. You have no prior infractions on your record."

I rolled my eyes, "This is the worst hospital I have worked at. I definitely will not be coming back."

She handed me the papers, and I signed my termination with the hospital. I thanked her for her time and walked outside to my car and immediately contacted a Medical Staffing agency in San Diego. I learned after conversing with Medical Staffing that they were scouting for qualified nurses and skillful certified nursing assistants to work for them. The pay was double what I had made at the previous hospital. Medical staffing rehired me instantly over the phone and assigned me to their San Diego office.

I experienced thirty days of exhausting training to work at a trauma hospital in San Diego, but I fought the good fight and I finished the race. I passed my training final and I started work per diem in the float pool.

Chapter 9

Prayerful Tears

"What is the weight of a tear? The single tear falls when the buckets have stopped, when dry eyes and a slightly raised chin sometimes let it slip, like a prayer. It carries the weight of a lifetime." Wendy Murray

The trauma hospital was unlike any other hospital I had worked for. They treated their employees like precious gems. There was always a form of unity and teamwork amongst the staff. I felt appreciated and wanted. I felt like I had finally found my niche. Within six months, I was an employee of the month. The intensive care unit and emergency room requested me often from the float pool. The medical staff complimented me and said, "You are a hard worker and you are reliable. Please don't ever leave."

I felt like I was living in heaven on cloud nine. I loved to go to work each morning. I was living on my own in beautiful sunny California. I could run outside every day and enjoy the lovely palm trees and smell the ocean air. I thought to myself, "Life can't get much better than this!"

Unfortunately, a sudden earthquake soon shocked my world. I started having painful migraines-so severe that I was in agony for hours at a time, with no relief. I took ibuprofen to try to numb the pain. After work one day, I was walking out to my car in the parking lot and the left side of my body went numb. My face felt droopy, and my fingers and toes were tingling. I thought to myself, Am I having a stroke?

I decided to walk back to the hospital and go to the emergency room to get checked out. I waited in the waiting room for five hours. When they finally took me back to the examination room, the whole left side of my body was completely numb. I remember a dark blonde man entered the room, and I felt very confused about my surroundings. He asked me nicely, "Can you touch my finger?"

I couldn't feel or touch his finger. I heard the doctor say, "Code her for a stroke."

Within five minutes, the room was crowded with people touching me all over my body. I remember feeling like I was in a dark hallucination, and all around me were medical people dressed in scrubs, poking and prodding me for hours. I could immediately smell and taste gas when the respiratory therapist placed an oxygen mask on my face. A man with kind blue eyes stuck heart rate stickers on me that were connected to a machine on the wall. Another dark haired man tried to start an IV. He was unsuccessful, and he had to stick me seven times in the most painful places: my thumb, my knuckle, and my wrist; all the places on the human body most sensitive to pain.

The intravenous team came in a few minutes later to do an ultrasound to try to poke a larger vein. I felt like I had been almost tortured to death before they finally got an IV in my upper deltoid. Although I could feel the pain, I didn't have a sense of awareness. I thought to myself, "Was I really having a stroke? Am I going to die? I feel so scared and alone."

I felt something lightly touch me on my shoulder and heard a soft voice, "I'm here."

I felt my dad on the other side close to me. An overwhelming feeling of love and peace surrounded me. My dad's heavenly presence calmed me. I thought to myself, "Its okay now. My daddy is here."

Meanwhile, the doctor ordered an MRI. I couldn't handle feeling claustrophobic in small confined spaces, so I begged the doctor to give me something to relax me during the MRI. I remember feeling like the confinement was too much to bear. I heard a loud, blaring noise in my ears from the MRI machine. I was too nervous to relax. I felt so happy when the scan was finally done. Forty minutes later, the doctor came into my room with good news and happily said, "The MRI scan showed no brain damage and no stroke. You can go home now."

I was so happy I didn't have a stroke. I thought to myself, Maybe I'm out of the woods. However, my misery had just begun. Soon after my stroke scare, I had the stomach flu and was vomiting for an entire week. I was pale, white, weak, and nauseated. I was having severe upper abdominal pain.

I decided to go to the emergency room after work one day, when my abdominal pain was relentless. Each step I took to walk to the emergency room was like knives stabbing and jabbing me in my stomach. I almost collapsed to the floor and could barely stand.

A nice nurse saw me grimacing in pain and took me back to an exam room. A young man with blonde hair and blue eyes came to my rescue and ordered an IV for fluids, blood work, and pain medication. I finally felt the medication a while later, flowing through my veins, giving me relief from my torturous pain. I remember feeling like I was in a magnificent dream I didn't want to descend from. I was on a steady wave in the ocean in a tropical paradise, and I couldn't feel my body. I had been given a gift of total insensibility.

But my wonderful dream was soon interrupted by a soft voice. "Your lipase is 480 and you have pancreatitis. We need to admit you to the hospital."

I thought, "Another pancreatitis attack? Another hospital stay? When will this torturous existence ever end?"

My hospital stays for chronic pancreatitis seemed to be lengthening. I was at the trauma hospital with severe pancreatitis for two weeks. I felt pools of perspiration all over my body. I was burning up. My stomach pain increased, so the doctor ordered for me to be on intravenous fluids for my entire hospital stay. I needed to fast my body to try to heal my pancreatitis.

I suffered for days in the hospital. This time, the doctor's orders of nothing by mouth wasn't healing my pancreas. I still had unsettling pain, and still couldn't stomach even fluids. The doctor wanted to start tube feedings. I told him, "I would rather die. I've seen how those feeding tubes are placed and I would gag. No thanks."

I thought, "If it comes to a feeding tube, then I no longer want to prevail, let me die."

I felt like my life had become a series of nightmares of tubes up my nose and pushing drug after drug through an IV in my scarred veins. People dressed in scrubs circling around me like vultures. It felt like I was on a frightful merry-go-round, spinning and spinning, never escaping, off this insane ride that had become my reality.

Meanwhile, my good friends and a few of my siblings tried to reach out to me in the hospital. I stayed in close contact with Chantelle, Brian and Levi. They called me and asked me, "How are you doing?'

I told them sadly, "Not well. I don't know how much more of this I can take."

My brother Lymster was also concerned by my distress of my pain management during my stay in the hospital. He spoke to the doctor about it on the phone and encouraged the doctor to administer more pain meds. The doctor listened to my brother's plea. That same day, the doctor was on his morning rounds to see me and my vein blew again for the fourth time. I pleaded with him, sobbing, "I want to go home. I just can't take this anymore. I feel like I will get better quicker at home than in the hospital."

The doctor realized I couldn't take much more pain, especially from the intravenous treatments. He released me to go home on a liquid diet that day. I was delighted I was finally going home. I remember eagerly walking out to the parking lot to find my car. But I couldn't locate my car at the hospital parking lot where I had parked it. I frantically scoped everywhere for my car. After two hours of searching for my car, I was afraid maybe someone had stolen it. I ran to the security office in a panic and said, "My car is missing. I can't find my car."

The security office tried to help me locate my car. They called the hospital parking lot and with a sad look told me, "Your car has been towed."

I panicked and almost fainted, "What?"

The security office guard gave me the towing company's number. I called them and the man on the phone said firmly, "Your car has been towed by the hospital. Call them to find out why."

I frantically called them to inquire why my car had been towed. The man on the phone replied unkindly, "You got a parking ticket and didn't pay. We towed your car."

I said surprised, "I got the ticket because the meter only takes credit cards. I only had cash on me that day. I got a parking ticket the day before I was admitted to the hospital. How much do I owe and will I pay for it."

He replied, "The parking ticket has tripled, and there are now towing and storage fees for the car. $1600."

I was shocked. I pleaded, "I don't have that kind of money. I haven't worked in two months. I've been sick in the hospital."

He replied rudely, "You have to pay us. There is nothing we can do."

I sank to the carpeted floor in the security office and cried out, "I can't believe I have lost my car, my baby. How am I going to get to work now? I live in Chula Vista and work is an hour drive from where I live. Why is this happening to me?"

Security nicely arranged for a taxi service to take me home since I had no transportation. I remember after the taxi dropped me off at home, I walked into my house, and I slowly climbed the gray carpeted stairs to my bedroom. I fell on my bed, head first, on my pillow and screamed at the top of my lungs, "God, what do you want from me? Why don't you love me? Do you want me to suffer my whole life? I don't want to hurt anymore."

My thoughts were interrupted when my phone rang. Chantelle was calling, and asked me nicely, "How are you?"

I replied in tears, "Crappy! They just towed my car. I can't afford to pay the fees to get it back. It's $1600. I can't work. I'm still sick. The doctor released me on fluids. But I'm too ill to eat or drink anything. I am in constant stomach pain. I can't pay my rent. I am done. I can't do this anymore."

My sister replied, "I'm sorry. What can I do?"

I said, "Nothing. I'm done. I got to go."

I hung up the phone and cried. I started researching on the internet how to find the best way to commit suicide with a drug overdose. I wanted to do it right. No more psych hospitals to heal. I didn't want to exist. I was so depressed, I couldn't breathe. I couldn't think about anything but the pain. I was not of sound mind, and I was in a state of complete and utter hopelessness.

I looked at the three bottles of pills the doctor had prescribed for me, sitting on my oak dresser. I glanced over at the clock. It was 10:00 PM. I picked up the three bottles of pills. I opened each one and sat on my bed in a daze. I was swimming in tears. I thought to myself, "This is the only way to end this nightmare. I can't take any more hospital stays and no quality of life. Now I've lost my car. Who will ever want me when I'm sick all the time?"

I felt so much despair. I was alone. I just wanted my emotional pain and suffering to be gone. Suddenly, I received a text from my landlord on my phone. "Your family just called me. They paid your rent, six hundred dollars total. Fifty dollars is missing. I will make up the difference this month because I know you've been in the hospital."

I immediately picked up the phone, and I called my sister Chantelle in a frenzy. I asked her surprised, "What happened? Who paid my rent? I want to know the names so I can call and thank them personally."

My sister replied, "Levi, Brian, Todd, and me."

I started to tear up, "Thank you. You four angels literally saved my life."

My sister replied, "I know. I could hear the desperation in your voice. It scared me. I knew you were done. I called Levi and we sent out a family text to ask for help to pay your rent. Four siblings offered to help."

I thought to myself, "Four angels rescued me and saved my life. I witnessed a true miracle tonight. Maybe God does love me and care about me."

Now that I had seen that four of my siblings truly cared about me, it gave me the strength to endure my rigorous trial. But it was a long road ahead to get back on my feet. Living without transportation was not easy. I faced great challenges. I was compelled to use taxi services. It cost me a fortune to travel to work and home. I was attempting to work my usual four days of shifts per week at the trauma hospital. But I only had the financial means for taxi services twice a week, still cutting my income in half.

I had been shy obtaining health insurance through work for one month before I was admitted to the hospital. I was $200,000 in medical debt. I had already cleaned out my savings entirely. I experienced days and nights without food. I was more destitute than I had ever been in my life. I was living a sad life in poverty.

I remember crying out to God one day, "I can't take another day of this. Please help me."

God answered my heartfelt prayers. I received $50 in the mail from Chantelle for food. I was thankful to receive anything. I was scraping by the bottom of the barrel.

Hope arrived. I received a call from my good friend Molly in my ward, and she said, "I have a friend in La Jolla close to your work. She has agreed to let you stay with her and pay rent each month. You can take public transportation to work. You don't have to use taxi services anymore. You can save that money to pay rent now."

I was overjoyed. I had been rescued by another angel. Or so I thought . . .I remember being so overjoyed when I met Molly's friend, Becky, after work the following night. I felt like my luck had finally turned around. Becky was short with blonde hair. She was an intelligent neuroscientist who traveled the world for her work. I was fascinated by her glamorous life. She had beautiful paintings from exotic lands: Paris, Italy, Spain and all over Europe. I thought to myself, "I have hit the jackpot."

After a long night of talking and laughing with Becky, I felt like a giddy teenager hanging out with my best friend. We decided we would get along great as roommates. I could no longer afford commuting to work taking taxi services, so we agreed I would move in the following morning on Saturday. The verbal agreement was that I would pay Becky in two weeks for rent. I informed Becky of my unfortunate situation and she was content with the terms.

I remembered I felt a weird feeling when I awoke Saturday morning and my contact ripped. I was practically blind, moving my belongings to Becky's. When I arrived at her house, I could smell the aroma of vanilla candles. I could taste the salty sweat dripping from my forehead to my chin as I climbed up the wooden brown stairs to my new bedroom. I began unloading my prized belongings. After that, I went to unpack my food and could feel the cold food items between my fingers as I crammed them into a small opening in the corner of her fridge. After a full day of moving, I hopped onto my new hard mattress, pulled my soft covers over my head and fell into a dreamy sleep.

The next morning I felt a gruesome, exorcist feeling at Becky's home. I felt like I was living in a warlock's home. I could feel the coldness under my socks that sent shivers up my spine when I was walking on the wooden floors. The furniture was nice, but old fashioned. The red, translucent drapes hung over the chilly windowsills. I could smell a group of scented candles burning on the round wooden table in the center of the living room.

Later that evening, I decided to cook hot soup for dinner. Becky had no heat in the house, and I was freezing to my bones. I felt the black, sharp knife handle in between my fingers as I was cutting fresh potatoes and squash to mix in a black pot on the stove to make soup. I could smell the delicious hot soup cooking on the stove.

I suddenly saw a dark shadow creep by, I heard a loud voice scolding me. I saw Becky there, with cruel blooded eyes. "Why are you turning lights on in the kitchen?"

I was bewildered by Becky's tone and replied, "I need lights on to cook and clean up."

She left in a huff and stormed up the creaky stairs into the darkness. I cleaned the kitchen and did a load of laundry in her cold, spider-infested laundry room. I found it odd she had a sign on the door of her laundry room that said: Abandon hope all ye enter here. I figured it was a joke and shrugged it off. But I soon discovered it was real, and my days and nights of horror had only just begun.

Becky was not at all what she appeared to be. She had a devilish side. I was about to experience a Norman Bates Hotel type of horror where I meet his psychotic sister, Becky.

A black cat was lurking outside my bedroom window that night, like it was an ominous sign of my bleak experience to come.

I heard a noise in the bathroom. It had startled me. I thought maybe someone was breaking into the house. I slowly walked out of my freezing, darkened room. I tiptoed over to the tall bathroom door, slowly opening it, fearful of what I may see. I gasped in dismay at the vision I beheld. The wooden drawers in the bathroom were labeled: Not accessible. Becky had removed my personal things from my drawers in the bathroom and set my belongings in a dirty, small drawer.

The horrifying experience continued. I walked down the dim, rigid wooden stairs to the kitchen. It shared the same grotesque theme of horror. She had labeled each drawer: Not accessible. I thought I had entered the door to the Twilight Zone. Is this really happening? I thought to myself. I pinched myself to make sure I wasn't dreaming. Suddenly, a small fragile lady was in the shadows, staring at me with demonic eyes. She scolded me again, "You are wasteful. You filled the trash bag with food."

I was astonished and replied, "That is scraps from cooking last night."

Her voice raised higher, "You don't waste. The planet earth is suffering because of careless people like you. The scraps go in the white jar on the counter."

My head was in a daze. Her next words pierced my confused mind, "When you shower, open the window in the bathroom. I don't want mold and steam ruining my shower. You did your laundry last night. You do laundry once a month like I do."

I stood there as she continued to abuse my very existence. I was like an annoying bug to her, ready to be squashed. The deranged abuse continued each morning. I awoke before work to a nonsensical, nasty note, belittling me. I felt an evil being staring at me, as if she was memorizing my every move. I cried out, "I want to leave this psycho house of horrors.

I was living in a house of horrors. Evil

had become my life. I was forced to stay in Norman Bates' sister's asylum for thirteen days and thirteen nights of my life. I had no place to go until I got paid the following Friday. But I was counting the days when I could leave the house of filth and unspeakable horror.

I worked as much as I could to avoid this psycho lady I called "landlord," but I had a meltdown seven days into my stay, so I contemplated checking out for good. I thought to myself in a puddle of tears, "My landlord is psychotic. I can't do it anymore. I need to move out again by next Friday. Where am I going to go? I am living in a diabolical horror house. My very soul is being tortured by this abusive, cruel lady. She scolds me like I'm a little child for the stupidest things. I feel like I'm back with Troy in an abusive relationship."

I walked to work the next morning, puzzled and distraught. I was in a trance of living someone else's nightmarish life. I prayed a car would hit me or a blunt object would crush me leaving me helpless in the street. Saving me from my misery. I felt like I had smacked the bottom of the barrel headfirst; I was lying there motionless to move or want to move.

Later that night in the house of despair I glanced at the sleeping pill bottle sitting next to me on my desk. I eagerly wanted to snatch it up and consume its contents to end the madness. This was the reality of my shattered pathetic life. I wanted to be hopeful and happy again. But life kept kicking me down again and again. I just wanted to be numb, even for a night. I took a few pills. I felt very drowsy from taking more than the required dose.

I groggily awoke late afternoon. I remember staring outside at the rain striking the windowsill. My thoughts imagined a glamorous life of me sitting by a warm cozy fireplace, nestled next to my significant other, drinking hot cocoa and watching our favorite show on television. Our sweet children, four of them total, huddled close together in cozy blankets for warmth.

My sweet fantasy was interrupted by a car door slamming outside my window. The blood thirsty vampire of the night had returned. I desperately desired to escape her torturous sanctuary.

I called work to sign up for a shift to work that night. But I was having problems with the taxi service picking me up at my residence. I finally caught a taxi across the street. Thankfully, the taxi driver lady was pleasant.

But she was dropping off other riders instead of me. After her second drop off, we discovered I wasn't in the taxi system. It was like I truly didn't exist. I thought to myself, Then why exist?

The taxi service felt displeased that I was late for work and she called her boss to correct the error. I called work to inform them of my unpleasant situation. When the taxi finally dropped me off at work, I was happy. I worked all night with a burn victim on the patient care burns unit. A cute two year old had her mother "accidentally" leave a boiling pot on the floor. This sweet child had "accidentally" burned herself leaving third-degree burns on her arm. She had been in the intensive care burn unit for two months. Now we were caring for her.

I remember I felt livid inside as I watched this child struggle as she moved her bandaged arm and leg, because of the vile acts of her abusive mother. The surgeon had removed a skin graft from her leg to cover the burn on her arm. I angrily thought to myself, "I can't have my own children, but this deranged mother can. How is that fair? I would give anything to be a mom. It's the only dream I've ever wanted. But it was never a reality."

I spent all night playing and cuddling with her. I was happy this beautiful child of God was going to the state's custody when she was finally discharged. She would no longer be in the clutches of the evils of her abusive mother.

I prayed, "Please send her to a good home. With a kind loving family. One who will love and cherish her every day as I would, if she were my own child."

It was for a brief time I felt joy. The little girl I was nurturing and caring for that long night at the hospital was caring for my broken heart. I thought, tears rolling down my cheeks, "I wish this feeling and night would never end."

After work, I lingered. I didn't want to go back to the house of dread. The sun was beaming in my eyes and the birds were singing in perfect harmony as I walked downtown through the homeless streets of San Diego. I felt like I was in a creepy nightmare as I walked aimlessly through the dirty estranged streets. I was carrying my bags and my coat over my shoulder like I was a hobo myself. I remembered smelling a nasty odor and seeing a dirty down-and-out guy lying on the filthy curb, panhandling. I comically laughed, "Oh buddy. I am just as fair off as you. If I don't get my life back together soon, I may be joining you."

I contemplated my life and all that had transpired. Shaking my head in disbelief, I thought to myself, I have hit the bottom of the barrel. I feel like I'm trying to climb out of the dirty mud, but as I climb I dig further into a pit of filth. Is this how the other half lives?

All this time, I envied those who were well off with their fancy cars and sporty clothes. Driving with not a care in the world. Pulling into their three car garages, with their outdoor pools in the backyard. Now I find myself turning back the clock to when I was driving in my white Nissan Versa, pulling into my humble place of residence with no garage, and parking on the side of the street. But I felt safe and wanted to be in a welcomed place. I could freely converse and giggle with close roommates that were sane, lively to be around, and who enjoyed being around me.

My happy thoughts were interrupted by the horror of my reality. Back at my dungeon, I opened the brown wooden door and walked into a place I considered a prison rather than a home. I stayed night after night in the glacial, terror- stricken oubliette. Filled with trepidation, I felt like the beast would emerge with her mammoth claws and tusks of death. I stayed under my covers on the creaky bed with the door closed tightly shut. I dared not come out from my hiding place until she was fast asleep. I wouldn't dream of waking the sleeping beast.

I awoke in the morning to another nasty note lying on the bathroom sink. It was staring at me like it was announcing my eternal demise. The note demanded money for utilities and other fees for staying in the asylum of horrors. She had closed off the laundry so I didn't have access to it. A black chair was guarding the white door like an evil general waiting to strike its next victim.

A small white sign was taped to the door: Keep out. I contemplated. "She doesn't want me to enter in fear of revealing her deep, dark, filthy secret. Dead skulls buried in small boxes amongst the spiderwebs nearby."

A scene from a real horror movie. But this is my reality . . .no movie director yells "cut!" Could I handle this frightful nightmare anymore? Would I be her next victim? I shivered inside to the thriller of my reality. Only three more days left in psycho land.

Chapter 10

I Keep Going

"I always tell my kids if you lay down, people will step over you. But if you keep scrambling, if you keep going, someone will always, always give you a hand. Always. But you gotta keep dancing, you gotta keep your feet moving." Morgan Freeman

Saturday couldn't come quick enough. I was so ready to leave the murky den of terror. It was Friday and I had the whole day off. I decided to go to prepare my taxes hoping for a sizable refund. I needed money like I needed air to breathe. I walked outside and I could feel the rain drops hitting my face. I was wearing my blue scrubs, the only clean clothes I had and my black tennis shoes trekking in the cold damp rain. The rain was pouring down flooding the sidewalks. Cars were splashing me with huge dirty puddles of water as they speedily drove by.

I finally arrived at the tax place an hour later soaking wet from the rainstorm. I was happy to be indoors and warm. The lady at the front desk offered me a hot beverage. I could smell the peppermint tea and feel the warm cup in my hands as I sipped the tea until the cup was empty. My body was drenched in water and I felt drops of water falling onto the gray carpet. The tax accountant, Laura, greeted me at the door. She walked me back to her tiny cubicle office. She was a nice older lady from Brazil. She was stunningly beautiful and kind. After she prepared my taxes she said smiling, "You will receive a thousand dollars refund in a few weeks on your Emerald Card."

I almost fell off my chair in shock at the good news. I thanked her for her time. I stepped back outside into the cold rain and walked to the bank. I thought to myself, "I just need to get through the next few weeks until I get my refund."

But the dusky night was summoning me. It felt like hours before I arrived at the bank. I was mortified at the sign on the door that read: closed. I only had $17 in my bank account. I couldn't access it with my ATM card that only released $20 bills. My stomach growled like a hungry bear. I was famished and hadn't eaten or drank anything all day.

I called Chantelle and said in a panicked voice, "I can't do this anymore. I am sitting at the bank. It's dark outside. I've been walking in the pouring rain all day. I can't take one more hit."

My sister reasoned with me, "Go Home. Get some food. Get a good night's sleep. You get paid tomorrow. Move out. Get a hotel. Call the bishop in the ward where you move to help you."

I trekked home in the pitch-black darkness. When I finally arrived, I was physically debilitated. I clumsily fumbled for my keys. I tried to turn the small key in the lower keyhole but it wouldn't budge. I pounded and pounded on the door and no one answered. I called my sister frantically and said, "That psycho has locked me out."

My sister was in awe and replied, "No way. You have got to be kidding me?

I replied frantically, "I'm serious I am locked out in the rain,"

My sister said, "Call the police. Get your stuff and go to a hotel."

I panicked and called the San Diego police. "What's your status?" the dispatcher asked.

I replied crying, "My landlord has locked me out of the house. She has all of my stuff. I need the police to help me."

The dispatcher replied nicely, "I have two police on their way."

Two men wearing black uniforms and holsters around their waists arrived ten minutes later. They asked kindly, "What seems to be the problem ma' am?"

I relayed to them the whole story. The police told me nicely, "We can bang on the door and help you get your stuff. But the situation is not ideal to live under. I would get your stuff and leave. I wouldn't stay here tonight."

The police banged and banged on the door to the Norman Bates hotel yelling, "Open up. It's the San Diego police."

A small frail lady finally came to the door acting innocent and said, "Oh, I didn't hear you. Come on honey."

The police replied sternly, "She wants to get her stuff and leave. Because of the unpleasant situation, she can't stay here anymore."

Becky replied shocked, "Molly, her friend, is coming in the morning to get her stuff. She is supposed to pay me tomorrow."

The police said firmly, "She needs to get her stuff now. She can't stay here tonight."

Becky replied rudely, "She can't come in and get her stuff." She slammed the door in the policemen's face.

The policeman said frankly, "There is nothing more we can do. This is a civil suit with the courts if you want your stuff. I am sorry."

I said shocked, "Now I am homeless in the rain. Where am I going to go? I have no family here."

He said coldly, "There is nothing we can do."

The police didn't offer me a ride to a hotel or anything. I watched them return to their warm cozy police cars. They drove off and left me in the bleak rain like I was a drifter. I called Chantelle sobbing. I told her what had happened. She replied calmly, "Go to a hotel for the night."

In desperation, I replied to Chantelle, "I have no money until midnight when my direct deposit comes through my bank."

Chantelle replied kindly, "Where can you find shelter for the night?"

With tears falling down my cheeks, I said, "Maybe I can go to work and sleep on the benches in front of the hospital."

She said, relieved, "Yes, do that. Then in the morning we can get you a hotel."

I decided to use my overdraft from my bank to take a taxi to work. I remember walking into the main hospital and I laid down on the hard wooden benches in the hallway. My body was feeling chilly being outside in the rain all day. My temperature was rising and I was shivering. I was weak, delirious and had hyperthermia.

I walked slowly to the emergency room. I could barely make it to the front desk to check in. I was severely shaking. A kind nurse saw me trembling and she took me back to an exam room. She asked me to strip off my wet damp clothes and slip in a clean dry white checkered hospital gown laying on the white sheets on the hospital bed. I immediately felt warmth on my skin when the nurse wrapped three warm blankets around my body to increase my body temp.

I thought to myself, "I finally feel safe and loved. God has sent angels to rescue me and give me shelter for one night."

I was discharged from the emergency room 12 hours later. I called Chantelle that morning. I told her in a soft voice, "I have been in the emergency room all night with hypothermia."

She replied, relieved to hear my voice, "I'm so glad you're safe. I've been so worried about you."

Concerned, she questioned, "How much money do you have in the bank?"

I replied, happily, "The money just hit my bank today. My direct deposit came through for $450. I was going to use it to pay Becky."

Chantelle said disgustedly, "She kicked you out. Don't pay her. Go to a cheap hotel and pay for a week's stay. Call the bishop in your new ward to request his help."

I immediately called hotels in the area to make a reservation for a week. I found a cheap hotel close to where I worked and booked the reservation for the week. I hopped a ride with a taxi. When I arrived at the hotel, a nice man wearing black jeans and a white t- shirt told me there was a $100 deposit required with the reservation. I replied pleading, "I was not aware of this when I made the reservation on the phone. I only have $60 left in my account. If I can't stay here, I am homeless."

The hotel attendant was compassionate to my plea and accepted the $60 deposit. But now he had taken every last cent I had earned to purchase food. Later that afternoon, I remember smelling fresh clean towels laying on a soft white bedspread when I opened the green door to my hotel room. It was a simple room, but it was all mine. No more psycho landlord breathing down my neck every minute criticizing my every move. I had the freedom to turn on the lights, turn up the heater or turn on the television until after dark. I was surprised how decent the hotel was considering how cheap it was. Most hotels in San Diego were $120 a night and higher. I was lucky to get a deal for $50 a night for a week's stay.

I could hear my stomach rumbling; I was hungry. I hadn't eaten in almost two days. I called the Bishop of the ward in my area. But he didn't answer so I sent him a text, "I am new in your ward. I was just kicked out of my place by my landlord. I am staying in a hotel. I only have money to pay for a week's stay at a hotel. I am scarce on food. I have no transportation to go to work. I need to take the bus to work. Please help me."

The bishop immediately replied to my text with the number for the name of the person who helps with the welfare in the ward. I immediately called the number he gave me, and a nice man named Alan answered. I told him my predicament. He replied, "We can meet tomorrow at your hotel lobby to find out your needs."

Alan met me the next day in the lobby. He was very kind and helpful. He wore a nice blue suit and tie. He looked like he had just driven to the hotel from work. He handed me a bus pass for a month. He gave me a $100 Ralphs gift card to buy food. He said kindly, "The bishop can meet with me on Sunday to discuss how he can further help you."

107

I was overjoyed and I felt a sigh of relief that help had finally arrived. Meanwhile, on Sunday I met with the bishop. He wore thick rimmed black glasses and was highly intelligent. He was a young defense lawyer in San Diego, and he was one of the most caring people I had ever met. I was embarrassed wearing my scrubs to church. Literally, they were the clothes on my back when Becky kicked me out in the cold rain.

But the Bishop passed no judgment of my attire and told me with friendly eyes, "I can help you with your hotel stay and with food until you get paid again. Your situation is unique. Usually, I deal with people who can't hold a job. But you have a great job. You have had an unfortunate circumstance. I will not let you go homeless."

When he told me this, I cried out loud, "There is a God."

I stayed in a hotel for almost two months. Living in the hotel was perfect to take the bus to work. But I was having a difficult time finding the bus stop on my iPhone. Until I could figure it out, I took a taxi to work the next morning. I requested a ride and ran outside to look for my ride. It flashed on my phone: Your Driver has left.

My ride had five minutes left, giving me no time to catch my ride. I broke down in sobs. I cried out screaming, "Now how am I going to get to work? I'm going to be fired."

I walked aimlessly trying to find the bus stop. I tried to find the bus stop on my iPhone, but the further I walked my phone disconnected. I had been using the hotel's Wi-Fi because my phone had no data for some reason. I walked and walked having no idea where I was going. I was distraught and screamed to my dad, "I can't do this anymore. I can't catch a break. I want out of this life. Dad, please help me. If I can't get to work, that's it. I'm done. I'm going to jump off a bridge and leave this terrible life."

I suddenly saw a homeless guy and felt I should ask him where the bus stop was. He said, "Just up the street not too far down over there."

I listened to his directions and continued to walk and I saw the bus station. My heart leaped for joy. I hopped on the bus. Thirty minutes later the bus stopped ten minutes from my work and I walked the rest of the way. I was relieved it was 6:55 AM when I arrived at work. Thankfully, I was punctual for work. I cried out, "Dad, thank you. God, thank you. All you who helped me up there. You do care. You do love me!"

But almost derelict and living in a hotel took a toll on me. I knew the Bishop couldn't help me long term and I was scraping by trying to work to save money for another week's stay in the hotel.

Chantelle could sense my vulnerability and fragility. She called me every day to check up on me. I was so overwhelmed with everything that was happening in my life. Chantelle said calmly, "Take one day at a time."

I replied frantically and said, "What about tomorrow?"

She said sympathetically, "Don't think about tomorrow, just get through one day at a time. Are you paying your tithing?"

Tithing is 10% of our income in our church. We are requested to show gratitude to God for our blessings and to help the poor and the needy. Surprised by her statement, I replied, "I am poor and I am needy. I can't afford to give one cent away."

Chantelle was a successful multi-millionaire. She was very spiritual and she had a strong belief in God and in His plan. She had three beautiful children and a devoted loving husband who adored her. She was thin, smart and every year she could design a new line of modest bathing suits and modest dresses for her Diviine Modestee company like it was a walk in the park.

I asked her stunned, "How are you so blessed? Everything you touch turns to gold. Why?"

She replied happily, "I have always paid my tithing. I have always trusted God. I have had my share of trials. But I always put God first."

She said kindly, "Test it and pay your tithing consistently for three months. Have faith in God and his destiny for you. And you will see your life change drastically one eighty."

With my hands in the air, I replied, "Well, I have nothing. God has taken everything from me like Job in the Bible. What do I have to lose? I'm going to test it."

At that moment in my life, I turned my life over to God. But paying my tithing when I had diddly was not an easy task. It took a great deal of faith and God tested my faithfulness.

The next day at work, I felt a sore throat approaching me like an unwelcome guest. I was having a difficult time breathing. I decided to go to the emergency room to get checked out. The gracious nurse at the desk offered me a blue mask to cover my face from spreading my germs. I couldn't stop coughing. A few hours later a compassionate nurse took me back to an exam room. A doctor with dark blonde hair wearing glasses entered my room. He examined me and ordered a blood panel. He came back into the room a while later and said, "I'm pleased that you don't have pneumonia, but you do have a nasty case of bronchitis and need to rest."

I replied, concerned, "What about work? I need to work."

He replied kindly, "You need time to recover. Work what you can but you need rest to get better."

He was correct. I was very ill for three weeks and only had the stamina to work one day a week. My next paycheck I had only enough money to purchase food or pay my tithing. I had no financial means to pay for another week's stay at the hotel. I decided to test God and I paid my tithing.

The bishop called me the next day and told me happily, "I have a $100 Ralphs gift card to purchase food. I will pay for one more week at the hotel. But then you are on your own."

I couldn't believe it. Miracles and more miracles from paying my tithing. I decided to test it again and I paid my tithing every week for 30 days.

I instantly started to feel better. I was excited to go back to work, but the phone carrier turned off my phone service. I was $450 behind in my phone bill. I worked in the float pool and my employer would call me at 5:30 AM to inform me of my assignment that day. Without a phone, they couldn't contact me. They wouldn't allow me to work without a phone.

I was distraught. I thought to myself while sitting on my bed spread in my hotel room, "Now what? I need to work to pay for my hotel next week. The Bishop is no longer helping me."

I suddenly received a text from my tax place, "The funds from your federal and state income tax returns have been deposited into your account in the amount of $1000."

I screamed out in delight, "I am saved by God's grace of paying my tithing!"

111

I was blessed to pay for my hotel stay the following week. I had enough funds to pay my phone carrier to turn my phone back on. I had enough money to buy some new essential clothes. But slowly my money was dissipating again. I was trying desperately to find a place to live. But nothing worked out. I was feeling hopeless. The bishop arranged for me to meet with a therapist to help me get through some tough days. He could sense how distraught I was.

I declared to my therapist on our first session together rolling my eyes, "My life has been one whirlwind after another. People have encouraged me to write a book about my misadventure of a life. I decided to start writing two years ago. I was halfway finished when it was stolen from me. My landlord has all my belongings in her home. I call it the Norman Bates hotel of horror. She has everything I own including my manuscript and she won't return it."

She replied happily, "You should definitely write your story to the world. Maybe someday your experiences can help someone get through their trials. Just think about it."

I thought long and hard all night about what the therapist had shared with me. But the idea soon disappeared the following morning when I received a call at 5:30 in the morning from work requesting frantically, "You are needed on the instacare unit today to be a sitter for a suicidal patient."

When I arrived on the shift, the nurse with long sandy blonde hair and lovely green eyes sadly informed me, "The patient Phil almost died. His blood pressure and saturation dropped so low we almost couldn't revive him."

Later that day, Phil admitted to me why he had tried to commit suicide. He said teary eyed, "I have suffered from depression my whole life. I wanted the emotional pain to end."

I told him laughing, "Well let me tell you the story of my life and you will feel better about your life."

I relayed to him all I had been through in my existence on what felt like an emotional roller coaster of experiencing sunny days and stormy days. His chin hung low in awe of what I had just shared with him and replied, "Wow, that's berserk. Now I feel better about my life. You have been through so much. And you're here smiling. How?"

I told him laughing, "Oh believe me, I've had my dismal days. But something has kept me enduring. God has rescued me over and over. I don't know why."

He said benevolently, "Maybe all the pain you've suffered will help others to survive their own pain. You helped me today."

I left my shift that day in awe of what my patient had told me. Suddenly, I heard a text on my phone. Molly said: I have all your stuff. I feel responsible. I introduced you to Becky. She took you in as a favor to me. I feel I need to pay her what you owe her. Please pay me and leave Becky out of it.

I was upset that Molly had chosen to be involved in my affairs with Becky and replied to her text: You have no right to pick up my belongings. I didn't give you permission to do so. Becky kicked me out in the rain. I contracted hyperthermia. I had to go to the emergency room. I feel like you care about Becky more than you care about me. I will get back to you.

Later, I decided I was done with Molly. I just wanted my stuff back. I texted Molly back a few weeks later: I need to get my stuff. What do I need to pay you so I can get it from you?

I did not receive a reply from Molly. It soon escaped my mind when I received an unexpected call from my niece, Makenzie. She was serving her mission in San Diego for our church. She called me to tell me with a happy voice, "My mom asked me if I knew of anyone in San Diego who needed someone to house-sit for them. There is a family in my area with a senior mom who needs someone to take care of her at night for free rent. The mom's son's name is Tom and he is expecting your call."

Makenzie gave me Tom's number to call him. I danced for glee and thanked her for the number and called Tom immediately. Tom answered the phone. When he answered, I inquired, "My niece Makenzie gave me your number. Are you looking for someone to house sit for you?"

He eagerly replied, "Yes, we are looking for someone to house-sit for us for a month until our mom moves back home. She is residing in an assisted living place right now. But she's not content and she wants to move back home. We need someone to stay at night with her to make sure she's Ok and not alone."

I told Tom happily, "I am very interested in the position. I am living in a hotel. I need to find a place as soon as possible."

Tom replied empathetically, "Call my brother Jared. He is the big man in charge."

I called Jared immediately. He was very pleasant on the phone and said, "We have had a few other caretakers that didn't work out. We need three references from you to be considered for the position."

I gladly provided three references of three people to Jared. Jared replied courteously, "I will be in touch with you."

But I became worried about not hearing back from Jared in over a week. I remember one of the worst days of my life was how destitute I felt when the hotel informed me later that week that they had no vacancies for the weekend. Later the next morning, after checking out at the hotel, I was sitting on the hotel bench outside with a gym bag and a crammed suitcase packed with my minuscule belongings. I could feel the breezy ocean air brushing my cheeks. I cried out to God, "I can't be homeless. I can't do that trial. If that's your plan for me, then I'm sorry that I no longer want to prevail."

God is aware of how much we can handle. He had tested me to my last hopeful breath. He knew I was emotionally and physically done. I suddenly heard my phone ring-it was Chantelle. She said frantically, "I got your text? Are you really sitting outside houseless?"

I replied in tears, "Yes."

She said, "Okay, let me call you back. I will figure something out."

I never felt so much desperation and loneliness than I did that day outside the hotel. I suddenly received a text from Vannessa, a kind lady in my ward I had met. She was checking in on me to see how I was doing. I told her frantically in a text: I'm sitting outside with no place to go.

She sympathetically texted back: I will pick you up at the hotel. You can take shelter with me tonight until you can figure out a place to live.

I was relieved this sweet lady was showing me charity. But I had a feeling to call Jared to inquire about the position I had applied for a week ago. I desperately called Jared and he answered. He said apologetically, "I'm so sorry. I've been busy. My brothers are hard to get a hold of. But I checked your references. They love you. They couldn't say enough about you. We would like to hire you."

I told Jared in desperation, "I am homeless and I have no place to go."

He said, "Ok, we want to hire you. You can house sit for us for free rent for a month until Mom, Heather, moves back home. You can move into the house tonight. My brother, Tom, will meet you in an hour at mom's house in La Mesa."

I texted Vannesa and requested a ride to Heather's home in La Mesa. Vanessa thoughtfully picked me up from the hotel and drove me to Heather's home.

Later I was greeted at the door at a primitive home in a woody area by an ambivalent gentleman, Tom, who gave me a quick tour of the house. It was infested with various insects crawling in the bathroom in the shower and on the windowsills. There were nasty cobwebs hanging from the ceilings and it had a lingering strong stench. The house hadn't been lived in for six months since the flood when Heather was forced to leave. She took refuge at an Assisted living home until repairs had been completed. I studied the house after Tom left. I thought to myself smiling, I have a place to call home.

Chapter 11

God's Great Miracles

"If God is making you wait, be prepared to receive more than you asked for." Sarah Jakes Robert

Now that I was comfortable in my new place, I wanted all my belongings from Molly. I tried to get in contact with her, but she didn't reply to my texts or phone calls. Finally, I reached out to the bishop's wife, Amber, from my old ward at Chula Vista. I texted her: Molly has my stuff and I need it.

Amber's text replied: I will see what I can do.

Amber had finally gotten in touch with Molly. She sent a three-way text to me and Amber the next morning: Would love to talk to you ladies three-way tomorrow at 2:00 PM?

Both Amber and I replied to Molly's text: Yes, let's three-way tomorrow at 2 :00 PM to resolve the matter.

Tomorrow couldn't arrive soon enough. I had anticipated the call all day at work the following day. I scheduled my break time exactly at 2:00 pm. I remember anxiously sitting on the long wooden benches in the hospital lobby when I heard Molly's number ringing on my phone. When I took the call, I heard Molly and Amber's voices. I immediately said to Molly firmly, "I would like my stuff back please. I will pay you the money you gave to Becky."

Molly replied bitterly, "I don't have your belongings anymore. I gave it to the missionaries."

I gasped on the phone, "Are you kidding me? Why did you give my stuff away? What gave you the right?"

Molly replied angrily, "You told me you were mad and to not contact you."

I replied, "I tried to get in touch with you but you didn't reply. You could have contacted the Bishop to contact me to come and get my stuff. If I knew you were going to give my stuff away, don't you think I would've come to get it?"

She said haughtily, "Well, I gave your stuff away. You don't owe me any money."

I replied upset, "Dang right I don't owe you any money. You gave my stuff away."

Molly said coldly, "I kept your green filing system, your journals and albums. But I gave away everything else. I will drop those things off at Amber's house. Are you okay with that Amber?"

Amber replied nicely, "Yes, that is fine."

Molly replied quickly, "Okay then, settled."

Molly hung up rudely and abruptly ended the conversation. I was fuming inside and said to myself, "What right does she have to pick and choose what I keep and not keep?"

Molly had maliciously given my belongings away out of pure spite. She stole everything: keepsakes, Christmas presents, a DVD of my family reunion with my dad before he passed away and temple clothes. Also, my manuscript that I had been writing for two years about my life. She gave it away like it was yesterday's trash.

I thought to myself crying, "She was my friend. I thought she was an angel sent from heaven to rescue me. But she turned out to be my worst nightmare."

I was heartbroken. My whole world had been shattered by someone else's evil actions. I felt lost. I contemplated, "All that time I spent writing my book. It's all gone down the drain. How can I start over? Where would I start?"

I decided I would not pick up a pen to write again. I had a difficult time trusting people again after what Molly and Becky had done to me. But the Golden family slowly over time restored my faith in humanity. They were kind to me. They took me in with open arms. They treated me like one of their family members.

I house sat for the Golden family for six weeks. I enjoyed living alone but I didn't like the insects living there with me. I remember watching insects crawling behind the baseboards everywhere in the house. I felt itchy bug bites on my legs and arms. Heather's place was infested with bugs: spiders, big mosquitoes, ants and moths.

I decided to roll up my sleeves and I spring cleaned the entire house from top to bottom. I could smell fresh bleach as I wiped the dirty baseboards around the house. I felt lemon pine sol soaking into my white socks as I scrubbed the wooden floors of the house until they shined.

I opened the stained windows to release the toxic fumes. I discovered massive holes in the screens allowing those pesky critters to wiggle through. Upon my discovery, I called Jared to inform him of the unpleasant situation. He said kindly, "Page and I will come down from Los Angeles in a few days to put in new screens. I will call the exterminator to spray the outside of the house."

When I met Jared and his wife, Page, they were some of the kindest people I had ever known. Jared was a middle-aged gentleman. He was dressed in a farmer's gray hat that covered his almost bald head. He was dark tan and dressed like a lumberjack. Page was also a middle-aged woman with golden tan skin. She was wearing blue jeans and a black t- shirt. She had dark brown shoulder length hair and captivating blue eyes.

They both had driven from Los Angeles where they lived just to fix the screens. Jared got right to work when he and Page arrived. He replaced the damaged screens with new screens. Suddenly, a tall man with a large silver spray can dressed in a black uniform wearing a blue mask tightly on his face soon arrived. He sprayed a nasty, poisonous chemical gas outside the house and downstairs of the house. I also helped to catch the insects and set out ribbon traps inside the wooden doors of the house. I taped the baseboards around my bedroom to conceal cracks from any bugs entering. To my delight within a few days most of the insects had disappeared.

Jared called me a week later, "Mom will be coming home in a few weeks. We are paid up at her retirement home until the end of the month. You just need to be there with her overnight so she doesn't fall."

Meanwhile, a few days later I was working in the intensive care unit. I couldn't stop coughing. The contaminated air from one of my patients with pneumonia had infected my lungs. I immediately started hacking and hacking. By the end of my shift, I had a high fever and I could barely breathe. My throat stung and the symptoms showed I had pneumonia too.

I went directly to the emergency room after work. After waiting in the emergency room for a few hours, a nurse with a kind smile took me back to one of the exam rooms. A nice tall dark-haired man with friendly blue eyes saw me violently coughing and examined me. He ordered a full blood panel, intravenous fluids and intravenous meds for my throat pain.

Within thirty minutes the doctor entered my room and said with relief, "Luckily, you don't have pneumonia. But you do have severe bronchitis. I would recommend rest. No work for a week until you feel better."

I followed the doctor's orders and stayed home from work for a week. I tried to go back to work but I was still contagious and had no energy to work. Thankfully, I was housesitting for the Golden family for free rent. I was able to recover without the stress of paying rent.

But I was stuck in bed all day with my thoughts racing. I felt so alone and abandoned. I cried out to God, "How much longer do I have to be alone?

How much longer do I have to constantly be sick? I've been on my own since I was eighteen. I'm still single with no family to share my life with. What reason do I have to stay on this earth? I have no legacy to leave behind. Who am I here for? I don't want to be here anymore."

The next day I was finally feeling better enough to go back to work. It was a long day at work when I received a Facebook message from my darling niece, Makenzie. She said, "I got permission from my mission president to come visit you. I can't wait to see you. I miss you."

I was excited all day at work to see Makenzie. I don't know what it is about Chantelle's girls, Makenzie, Kalie and Kenna. But they always light up my life whenever I see them. They always make me feel special and loved. They would do anything for me, and I would do anything for them. I think of those three stunningly, kindhearted and playful redheaded nieces like my own flesh and blood.

I glanced at Makenzie pulling into my driveway at my house after working a long day at the hospital. When I saw my gorgeous niece walking to greet me, I ran to hug her. I could smell strawberry shampoo scent on her long glowing beautiful red hair blowing in the wind. She looked like an angel. I smiled and said happily, "I have this house-sitting job rent free because of you. I was homeless but you and your mom saved me."

She replied, hugging me tighter and smiled, "I know my mom is amazing. She is one of the most Christlike people I know."

I nodded and smiled in agreement. I invited Makenzie and her companion to the house. I looked at her black name tag, Sister Thomson, on her blue long dress that covered her knees. She looked so grown up. She was not like the little girl I remembered before her mission. Her companion Sister Smith was also wearing a long blue dress almost touching her ankles. Both missionaries were assistants to the mission president. I worked closely with other male assistants in the mission office in San Diego. I felt so blessed that Makenzie was serving her mission close to where I lived.

She and Sister Smith shared with me comical and heartfelt stories of their mission. We reminisced about Makenzie's family and how much she missed them. She lit up the room as I watched her playful girly laugh that could steal anyone's heart.

But when the dark night shadows called us we said our goodbyes. She gave me the biggest bear hug and happily grinned on her way out the door. I thought to myself with a smile, OK, I will stick around this crazy world. My niece showed me tonight she loves and cares for me. Makenzie Thomson you saved my life.

Later I remembered the phrase: When life gives you lemons, you make lemonade. This was applicable to how I felt when I met Heather next week. She was kind but very stubborn. I couldn't believe she was 98 years old. Her skin glowed, no wrinkles. She walked gracefully with her walker. Heather loved her beautiful garden, exquisite roses, daffodils and tulips. She adored sitting in her recliner and gazed out at her garden.

But she had been independent her whole life and she was having a difficult time adjusting to me taking care of her. She had dementia. Her short-term memory was slowly fading. She barely recognized who I was. Caring for Heather was like babysitting a small two-year-old child. She was into everything. She had tantrums a few times a day. She got up in the middle of the night, paranoid that someone was breaking into the house.

But I gave it to the old college try to make Heather happy. I remember smelling hot seafood at her favorite restaurants we ate at. I could feel the green grass on the bottom of my sandals walking to Heather's favorite parks. The scenic drive was breathtaking. I could smell the warm ocean air on our long drives to the beach.

Heather enjoyed the outings from her house. She always demonstrated good behavior. But as soon as she stepped in her front door, she was afraid of her surroundings. She would lash out her frustration, anger and fear on me. She was nice to me one minute saying, "I love you. You are wonderful" and the next minute telling me to, "Shut up" and shaking her finger at me angrily.

Jared and Page were always helpful to calm Heather down during her irate tantrums. They would call Heather at night to check in with her. Heather was not easy to manage but I was happy and content working for the Golden family. I slowly was able to buy a new wardrobe and replace some of the clothes Molly had stolen from me.

Meanwhile my certified nursing assistant license had expired on my birthday. I was having a difficult time renewing it. I offered to take care of Heather full-time. Jared happily agreed to my offer. He allowed me to use Heather's car to drive her to senior daycare during the day. I had become part of the family. Jared paid for Heather's and my food. He paid for all the cleaning supplies in the house and for our outings, dinners etc.

I was living the high life. Free rent, working forty hours a week making seven hundred a week. I had saved a thousand dollars in the bank in two months. Caring for Heather was the perfect job. It gave me the freedom to go running every day. and do my Pilates app at home. I was finally starting to get back into shape again. I was healthy. I had two months of pure bliss.

But Heather's memory was declining more and more. She only wanted her son, Jared, to take care of her. I was a stranger to her in her own home. One weekend, Jared came up to relieve me to give me a break from Heather. When Jared was entering his truck to leave to go back to Los Angeles, Heather raced out with her walker almost falling and screamed, "I want to go someplace else. I don't want to be here with her."

Jared closed the truck door and said with a sigh, "Ok I'm staying."

Jared had to stay for over a week to get his mom into a nice retirement home. Now I was out of a job again and without a place to live. I panicked inside, "Now what I'm I going to do?"

But later Jared relieved my stress and told me nicely, "You have been through enough. You have helped us so much taking care of mom. We don't need to add to your stress. You are out of a job because of us. You can stay here rent free until the end of the month."

I breathed a sigh of relief. I thought to myself, "Another angel sent from heaven to save me. God, you do love me."

But now I was unemployed until my Certified Nursing Assistant license was renewed. I was scheduled to take the skills and manual test in three weeks. I had saved a thousand dollars in my bank account. I thought to myself, I just need to make it until then.

I decided with all my free time to train for the San Diego marathon running four miles a day. But the wear and tear of my shoes were hurting my toes. It was giving me painful blisters. I stubbed my toenail the previous year playing a mean game of volleyball with my family at our family reunion. Over time, the nail created fungus and died.

One night, the pain was so severe I had to go to the urgent care to get my toenail treated. I anxiously sat on white paper on a leather black exam table swinging my legs back and forth looking at the physician assistant's awards that hung on a green wall. A nice lady wearing a white lab coat walked in the door. She examined my toe and nicely said, "Your toenail is infected. I need to cut off the end of your toenail to relieve pressure."

I can honestly say toe pain is the worst, but numbing the toe feels like torture. When the physician assistant stuck my big toe twice with a huge needle it felt like a large sharp drill pounding into my toe. My toe throbbed for four days after toenail surgery. I could barely walk on it. I lay in bed with ice and ibuprofen for the pain. Putting pressure on my foot killed me. I had to walk on the heel of my foot. But after soaking my feet in Epsom salt, bandaging it with Neosporin twice a day for three days, my toe started to heal.

But putting pressure on my toe when I tried to run, created painful blisters again. I couldn't jog outside for another week. I was feeling discouraged until later that week I was browsing through my Facebook post. I discovered a post of my friend Cari. She had posted that her brother had committed suicide hanging himself in her home. I was devastated by the frightful news. She had shared a Facebook message from one of the apostles of our church that read, "It's absolutely a lie that those who commit suicide go to hell."

I shared Cari's post on my Facebook post. A girl named Karina commented on my post, "Thank you so much for posting. My sister-in-law committed suicide two years ago from depression."

I felt I should send a private Facebook message to this girl. I felt I needed to share with her my suicide attempt and how my dad who had passed had rescued me from taking my own life. I told her, "I'm thinking of writing a book about this experience. But my friend stole the manuscript I was writing for two years so I gave up on the idea."

She immediately responded, "You have to share your story. People need hope. I am a published author. I will help you edit and get your book published."

I was baffled by her response and thought to myself, "Could this be true? Is this for real?" I have received this opportunity to write my book exactly three months after I had turned my life over to God. God has kept his promise and blessed my life beyond imagination just as Chantelle had said he would."

I jumped for glee and I messaged her back: OK you have inspired me to write my book.

It took me two years to write my first book. I was only halfway through when it was stolen from me. I finished this book in two weeks. I wrote every day. I stayed up until seven in the morning every night writing. The thoughts flowed into my mind to my pen and wouldn't stop. God gave me a window of opportunity to write my story to the world.

Chapter 12

Rescued In Heavens Eyes

"I believe in miracles because I am one. Because there's no doubt in my mind that I am only here today because of God's grace and mercy." Caroline Laughorn

Now, I am finished with my story. Now it's ready to be seen by the world. I have opened my life to the world. Why? If I can save one person from suicide by sharing my story, then everything I suffered through was worth it. If I can save a person from a lifelong addiction it was all worth it. If I can help someone feel Christ's love in their life when they feel God has abandoned them, then it was all worth it. If someone who is atheist or agnostic now believes in Christ and sees the miracles from God in his or her life, then it was worth it. If I can help one person believe that they are a Son or Daughter of God, it has been all worth it.

When I was suffering, I didn't see all the miracles around me. I didn't realize that there were many from the other side, like my dad, helping me. I didn't acknowledge the angels that God had sent from this life to help me. I didn't remember the quotes of my favorite apostles and prophets from my church and how they inspired me to survive when I wanted to throw in the towel. I experienced this quote from Kim Philips repeatedly as I battled through my trials. "I threw in the towel. God threw it back and said, "Wipe your face. You're almost done."

Dieter F. Uchtdorf once said, "Spiritual light rarely comes to those who merely sit in darkness waiting for someone to flip the switch."

Through my trials, I came to know that this is true. I spent most of my life thinking I was smarter than God, and that I could do everything on my own. I had a difficult time trusting God. Through the toil and the pain, I finally let go and cried out to God," I can't do this alone. I am not strong enough. I need Jesus Christ to carry me through."

After I had admitted I couldn't do it on my own, a miracle happened, and the weight was lifted. The trial was still there but the load was lighter. God would send me an angel like a brother, a sister, a bishop or friend to help me in my time of need.

But when I was going through the trial, I couldn't understand why I had to suffer. Why did God want me to survive? I cried out to God in tears, "What is my purpose? I'm just me? What good am I in the world? I'm not strong enough! Why do you want me here just to suffer?"

Eventually, I heard a voice pierce my mind, "Your mission is not finished. You were made to do great things."

I remember my cousin, Mickey, later sending me a beautiful song by David Archuleta. This song was first featured in Meet the Mormons and is titled "Glorious." It inspired me to write my story and share it with the world.

The lyrics are powerful:

There are times when you might feel aimless. You can't see the places you belong. But you will find that there is a purpose. It's been within you all along.

When you're near it. You can almost hear it. It's like a symphony. Just keep listening. And pretty soon you'll start to figure out your part.

Everyone plays a piece and there are melodies. Each one of us Oh Oh it's Glorious

You will know how to let it ring out if you discover who you are. Those around you will start to wake up to the sounds that are in their hearts.

It's so amazing what we're all creating. It's like a symphony, just keep listening. And pretty soon you'll start to figure out your parts.

Each one of us plays a piece and there are melodies . . . Oh Oh it's glorious

That you will feel that you will feel higher you will see it's like a symphony just keep listening and pretty soon you'll start to figure out your part.

Everyone plays a piece and there are melodies Oh Oh it's glorious

With God nothing is impossible. People told me throughout my life, "Wow you have been through so much. You are so strong."

I replied, "I am only strong with God. God is my anchor."

I truly need the Savior, Jesus Christ both in my hours of joyful sunshine and in my hours of stormy rain. I pray every day, "God lead my life today. Help me to see myself through your eyes as a child of God with a divine purpose."

I still face trials. I definitely still have high and low days. But my life has a purpose. There is an inspirational quote by Rachel Marie Martin that I now pattern my life after, "Sometimes you have to let go of the picture of what you thought life would be like and learn to find joy in the story you're living."

My life turned out to be nothing like I thought it would be. I lost everything in my life. I never thought I would lose the ability to bear my own children. Or that I would be ill for an entire year when I was always healthy as a young child. I learned what it was like to be homeless for a night and be hungry for days. I discovered what it's like to lose a father and my best friend. I experienced being sexually and emotionally abused. I endured being physically assaulted at my employment.

Chantelle told me amidst my suffering, "I can't believe what you have survived. You have lived ten lives in one life."

How did I survive? Only with God's great miracles. I wanted to check out and give up. But God rescued me through sending my dad from the other side again and again. God saved me by sending an angel like my brother, sister, Bishop or friend. Why did he save me? I don't know, but he did. And maybe he saved me so I could share my message with the world. Our stories have not yet been written. God is the author of our lives. He can make more of a life than we can if we turn our lives over to him.

C.S. Lewis, a renowned Christian author and novelist has said, "Imagine yourself as a living house. God comes in to rebuild that house. At first, perhaps, you can understand what He is doing. He is getting the drains right and stopping the leaks in the roof and so on; you knew those jobs needed doing so you are not surprised. But presently he starts knocking the house about in a way that hurts abominably and does not seem to make any sense. What on earth is he up to? The explanation is He is building quite a different house from the one you thought of- throwing out a wing here, putting on an extra floor there, running up towers, making courtyards. You thought you were being made into a decent little cottage: but he is building a palace. He intends to come and live in it himself."

We are glorious in the eyes of God. We were made for greatness. God will give us a window of opportunity to be great and shine. But we have to seize that window of opportunity he gives us. He gave me a small window of opportunity to write my story. I had to seize that opportunity, to write day and night and give my whole heart and soul to write my story. It wasn't easy. I faced roadblocks along the way. I had to relive every trauma I experienced to be inspired through the pain. But I knew that maybe, just maybe my story would help someone through their dark days. What joys would you be missing out on if you ended your life today?

Let's find out.

Chapter 13

There is Peace in Christ

"He knows my name. He knows my every thought. He sees each tear that falls and hears me when I cry his name." -Tommy Walker

January 2020

I was sitting patiently on the exam table as I looked at the medical diagrams, my legs shaking from the drafty paper robe I was wearing. The door swung open, and in walked a handsome Asian man, who examined me. After a moment, he said, "I can feel it. You have a tumor."

My mind raced back to the past few months. I had endured mammograms, ultrasounds, and constant Emergency Room visits complaining to the ER of severe chest pain. had been so intense, it hurt to breathe. While each test came back normal, I knew in my heart something was seriously wrong with me.

I remembered being in bed one night and the pain was so severe in my left breast that I thought I would pass out. I made an appointment to see my primary care doctor that afternoon. My doctor was an old, gray-haired gentleman with a kind smile. He was concerned about the breast and chest pain I was experiencing. He referred me to a general surgeon despite other tests suggesting I was fine. I was grateful he was concerned about my health and well-being. I scheduled the appointment to see the general surgeon the following week.

I was happy I was seeing the surgeon but terrified it could be breast cancer. I felt such great anxiety that I couldn't sleep or eat anything. I thought to myself, "Am I dying? What if it is cancer? Am I ready to die? Who will take care of me? I can't take care of myself."

My racing mind was interrupted by my doctor's kind voice. "Marci, did you hear me? You do have a tumor. I can do lumpectomy surgery in two weeks and remove the tumor, especially if it is causing you this much pain."

I was relieved to learn there was a tumor and that it wasn't something I had fabricated in my mind. Dr. Yen had finally found the source of my issues. He was one of the best breast surgeons in San Diego. I was confident in him performing the surgery.

I walked outside of his office after I finalized the paperwork for the surgery. I pushed open the steel doors. I felt the warm breeze brush my soft cheeks. I could smell the ocean air and missed being at the warm sunny beach. I hadn't been to the beach in months, due to my unstable health. I felt like I was a prisoner in my own body. Unable to do the things I loved, like running in the warm sun for miles. I remembered how I felt at that moment. Sweat dripped down my body as I felt my breath inhale and exhale. I felt like a competitive runner, trekking up steep hills for miles. Keeping the pace strong I push my tired body. I hit a peak, my legs cramp and my heart races. I forced my body to continue, until I had a second wind. The adrenaline rushes through me. I pushed past my fatigue to victory and won the race. I loved every moment.

Suddenly, I heard my iPhone ring. It jolted me back to reality. When I answered it, I heard my sister Chantelle's voice. She asked, concerned, "What did the surgeon say?"

I happily replied, "My surgeon felt the tumor, and he is going to do the surgery to remove it!"

She was happy I was getting the surgery as well, but she became emotional on the phone and started crying. "What if you have breast cancer? What will you do?"

I answered with certainty. "I've already thought about it. If I do have breast cancer, I'm going to deny treatment for it. I've endured multiple surgeries since I was 29. It has caused me more and more painful health issues in my thirties and forties. I feel like I've been on an endless, dizzy

merry-go-round, with one health issue after another, spinning around faster and faster, never stopping. I just want to jump off the ride and land free in a beautiful, grassy meadow in heaven."

I heard whimpering on the other end of the phone. Chantelle said, "I don't want to lose you as my sister. I love you. I can't believe this is happening!"

I pondered in my mind. If I do die, I would miss Chantelle. Chantelle and the T girls (as I called them) - Kenna, Makenzie and Makalie -were my life and love. I couldn't imagine my life without them.

I had endured this terrible ordeal for months. I found out how many people truly cared about me and loved me. My "Rescued In Heavens Eyes" Facebook page now had 750 followers. For some reason, people admired me and loved my posts I shared on a daily basis, in an attempt to lift them up and inspire them. When I became ill with my breast tumor, people on Facebook sent me daily personal messages, expressing their love and concern for me.

Though I had the support of many caring people, I did not have my Mom in my life. We had grown apart over the past few

135

months. It felt like we couldn't bury past regrets and hurt feelings. I tried to shrug it off, telling myself that I didn't need her in my life. That I only needed my close friends and family. But I knew deep inside I was lying to myself.

The day of surgery arrived. It was like a dark abyss. I was alone and terrified of what awaited me in the surgery room. I felt cold inside and shivered at the thought of my thirteenth time going under the knife. I felt like I had lost my womanhood when I had my hysterectomy in my late thirties (due to chronic endometriosis). Now I was going to lose the beauty of my breasts also?

The surgeon had told me at our last visit in his office that he would need to make a large incision in my breast to remove the tumor. I had thought to myself in sheer horror, "How can I recover from this? Who would ever want me with all of these nasty scars on my body?"

I sat in the hospital bed; tears streamed down my face. My body trembled all over, that once again I was treated like a pincushion-prodded and poked, just to survive. A kind, dark-haired lady with a stunning smile entered my room. She asked me, in a soft, soothing tone, "Would you like your friend Jared to be here with you?"

I looked up at her with tears in my eyes and replied with gratitude, "Yes!"

A smile came over me and my eyes gleamed with delight when the gray- haired gentleman entered my room. He gently held my hand and said to me, "It's all right, kid. I'm here. We will get through this."

Jared was like a big brother to me. He said to me sweetly, "You are like the sister I never had."

I was like family to the Golden Family. I had won their hearts and they had won mine. They were like my angels sent from heaven. They had rescued me by taking me in and treating me like family. I had been a live-in CNA for a few months when Heather, Jared's mom, needed 24 hour care for her dementia. After Heather's passing six months later Jared and I became like brother and sister. He had taken me under his wing and had been my rock facing my new health challenges since December.

But now I was about to face the Operation Room alone. It horrified me to my bones. The OR nurse walked me to the Operating Room and as soon as I saw the vision of terror of machines hooked to other machines and scalpels in the middle of the room I spun out of control and said, "I can't do this."

I tried to dash out the door to make a clean getaway, but the nurse placed her arm around my shoulder and said to me with a soothing tone, "Close your eyes. I know surgery is scary. Just take deep breaths."

With my eyes closed I trusted her kind tone of voice to lay me on the surgery table. Immediately I felt a mask over my face. I inhaled the gas. I was brought into a peaceful feeling where I wanted to be forever. But soon my tranquil feeling was interrupted when I awoke to the most excruciating pain in my life. I heard a kind voice, "Do you need more pain medicine."

I cried tears of suffering and said, "Yes please."

But nothing could remove the intense pain I felt from every bone and muscle in my body. It felt like a thousand knives, stabbing me, bruising me and bleeding every pore of my body. Finally, after the nurse gave me three doses of strong IV pain medicine, there was some relief so I could go home.

But home was not inviting to me, when later that night my left breast grew twice its size. It felt like a huge balloon expanding. The pressure was pushing on my chest wall. I was fighting to breathe. Jared had kindly offered to take care of me for a few days at home. I screamed in pain and almost stopped breathing. Jared saw me struggling and rushed me to the ER.

Later at the ER the waiting room was full of other sick people too. We waited for four long hours. Jared finally complained of my agony to the OR nurse. The nurse escorted me to an exam room in the ER. Jared did not leave my side. He was hungry and tired, but he unselfishly stayed with me all night.

The on-call surgeon who resembled a dashing, handsome man in a fairy tale, entered the room and examined me. He said to me, concerned, "You have a hematoma - blood clot in the bruise and there may be internal bleeding, You will need surgery again in the morning."

The surgeon immediately admitted me to the hospital that night. Jared was relieved I was being admitted to the hospital. He felt confident he could leave me in good hands with the medical staff. The next morning, I felt groggy from the pain medication the floor doctors had administered to me through my IV for my unbearable pain.

My surgeon came to visit me early that morning and examined my left breast. He said to me kindly, "I would rather avoid another surgery because I'm afraid it could cause a blood clot. I'm going to keep you in the hospital for pain management until you can comfortably take oral pain medicine at home."

My surgeon had a reputation of one of the highest skilled and compassionate surgeons in San Diego. I trusted him and his medical decision to allow me to heal, without another surgery. In a few days he discharged me from the hospital when my pain was under control with oral pain management at home.

February 2020

After I returned home that night I sat in the recliner chair and the pain returned. I felt intense chest pain and it was moving to my left lung. I could barely dial my phone to call 911. I was gasping for air. When the paramedics arrived 10 minutes later I was unable to walk. I cried out in agony. The paramedics helped me onto a narrow yellow stretcher outside my house. They rushed me to the local ER. I was immediately taken to a room in the ER and the ER doc ordered an immediate CAT scan.

I don't remember more details, only that I was in severe pain. I felt like I could faint. I just remember hearing a kind lady's voice that said, "You have a pulmonary embolism - left lung blood clot."

She immediately admitted me to the hospital. She started me on a IV heparin drip and gave me IV pain medication. Within a few days of being in the hospital, the heparin drip was healing both my hematoma and blood clot. I was relieved.

But the day I was discharged to go home I experienced chest pain and abdominal pain. I was nauseated and vomiting. I reported my symptoms to the nurse, but she was anxious to discharge me. She shrugged it off like it was the stomach flu.

After I was discharged from the hospital a dark, lean, older man, my Bishop from my church, was kind enough to pick me up at the hospital. I drove home from the hospital, with him and his sweet wife when I yelled, "Stop the car. I'm going to throw up."

I felt the car stop instantly. I rushed out of the car and violently vomited. The Bishop was concerned I was sick but reassured me,

"It's probably because you haven't eaten or drank anything all day."

He dropped me off at my house a few minutes later. He drove off in the black, starry night. I walked into the house and within ten minutes I vomited excessively every 15 min. I had terrible diarrhea. I was dehydrated, weak and I almost blacked out. I called 911. When the paramedics arrived I vomited more in the ambulance when they rushed me into the ER.

At the ER the doctor was kind, but he said to me "You have been to the ER so often that they wrote in your chart that you have drug seeking behavior."

I was livid and told him, " I've never done drugs in my life."

He was a compassionate doctor and said to me, nicely, "I will order a CAT scan. Give you a shot of nausea meds and do blood work to see if there is anything wrong. But I can't give you pain medicine right now. I'm sorry,"

I lay in bed in insufferable pain until he came back into my room 30 min later. He said angrily, "I could yell at those doctors who treated you at the hospital. You have appendicitis. You need emergency surgery. I don't care what the records say about you. I'm giving you some pain medicine."

I was overjoyed that he finally was going to relieve my body of the blood curdling pain I felt. A kind nurse dressed in blue scrubs, immediately came into my room 10 min later. She administered IV pain meds in my veins. I instantly felt a rush of euphoria and my pain subsided. I groggily drifted off to sleep.

A few hours later my sleep was interrupted by a soft voice," Hi Marci I'm Doctor Zu. Your CAT scan showed your appendix is about to burst. We need to do emergency surgery. We need to take you off the blood thinners you're taking for your pulmonary embolism. If we don't, you could bleed out."

I thought to myself, "Are you kidding me about another surgery? When will this suffering end? Haven't I been through enough?"

But I had only experienced the tip of the iceberg. I was about to feel what real torture felt like. After my 14th abdominal surgery I was in the hospital to recover for one day. I was sent home with oral pain medication. Unfortunately, my body wasn't healing correctly. Experiencing another surgery so close to my lumpectomy caused a whirlwind of pain and suffering that I never knew a person could endure. The surgeon had put me back on the blood thinners to try to heal the blood clot, but now the hematoma wasn't healing. The pressure of the blood clot in my left breast felt unbearable to handle. I was screaming in pain.

I laid in bed trying to sleep. The pain was intense. The oral pain medication I had taken didn't touch the pain. I grabbed my iPhone. I frantically called 911. When the paramedics arrived 10 min later I was crying. I was doubled over in pain. The paramedics helped me onto a yellow gurney. They tightly strapped me on the gurney covering me with a gray thin blanket.

When I arrived at the ER the charge nurse instructed the paramedics to take me to a small room in the ER. The doctor immediately entered the room and examined me. He was concerned I was suffering from both surgeries so close together. The ER doctor immediately called my surgeon. They decided to admit me to the hospital. They submitted orders for the IR team to drain the hematoma.

I was overjoyed. I was finally going to be receiving relief for my blood curdling pain. I stayed in the hospital for a few days for

141

pain management. The day of surgery. I had conflicting thoughts of another painful surgery, but the hematoma was causing me more pain than I could endure. I was ready to cut into my own breast myself, just to relieve the pressure that was inflicted on my body.

To my amazement, the nightmare had only begun. A tall, dark, haired lady walked into my room with a cruel look and said, "I'm the cancer specialist in this hospital. I've decided you don't need surgery. Another surgery would do more harm than good. It could cause another blood clot. You only had a small tumor removed. People live with hematoma for months to years. You need to live with the pain."

I looked at her with steam coming out of my ears and said, "Well I'm not going to live with the pain. It's my body. I'm overriding your decision"

She left in a huff and said, "We will see. I'm going to talk to the other surgeons about it."

A few minutes later a man wearing blue surgeon's scrubs walked in and said, "Your lung blood clot has disappeared, but the blood clot scarred your lung. Your breathing won't be normal for a few months until the scar is healed. Performing the surgery could cause another blood clot or an infection. It's too risky to do the surgery right now. I'm sorry."

As he walked out of my room, I felt empty inside. "Was there nobody to save me from this pain?" I contemplated to myself.

My surgeon discharged me the following day and invited me to come to his office. He said kindly, "I will try to offer you relief in my office and drain the hematoma with a syringe."

I accepted his kind offer. I left the hospital in terrible pain. A few days later I visited my surgeon's office. He drained the hematoma. Immediately, I felt instant relief for about a week. Then the pressure of the hematoma returned on the incision site. It caused excruciating pain.

I returned to my surgeon's office for a few weeks. Each time he drained the dreaded hematoma that afflicted my body, black blood clumps clogged the syringe forcing him to stop draining. The procedure gave me minimal pain relief.

Finally, my surgeon was more evasive in his efforts. He drained the hematoma on the incision site. He numbed the incision site with lignocaine. I felt the huge needle pierced into the incision site on my left breast. It felt unbearably painful. I prayed for the sweet release of death. I pictured the Savior and the Garden of Gethsemane and I thought to myself, "This is my Garden of Gethsemane. This is more pain than I can bear. How did Jesus suffer so greatly for the sins of the world?"

My love and appreciation for the Savior intensified a hundred-fold. Finally, the pressure on my left breast released. The surgeon had shrunk the hematoma. I cried out, "Thank you God."

After a few more visits to my surgeon's office for the same procedure, the hematoma drained to half its size. I finally felt relief after 6 weeks of indescribable pain.

Meanwhile following my appendectomy, I did not have an appetite. Food was not appealing to me. Its flavor had lost its taste to me. The first week post-surgery I couldn't keep solids down. The second week I couldn't take in stomach liquids. The third week I couldn't keep an ice cube down without vomiting. I was severely dehydrated by the third week.

To make matters worse I had endured this suffering alone. I had no one with me to hold my hand or wipe my tears. I felt like God had abandoned me. I cried out for God and my dad's presence to be with me, but I felt a hollow empty void. I wondered if this was a test of my faith. I pictured in my mind how the Savior must have felt when he cried out to God, "Oh God, why hast thou forsaken me?"

But he felt only an empty void. Jesus carried on the burden of the Garden of Gethsemane alone. I was alone also. I felt God had forsaken me too. I shared some of the feelings of sadness and despair Jesus had felt. I felt closer to Jesus than I ever had in my life. I cried out to Jesus in pain, "You have felt what I feel. You suffered it all. Please give me the strength to endure this. I can't do it alone."

After my heartfelt prayer, I felt comforted. Jesus had given me strength to go on. Meanwhile, Chantelle had been in close contact with my family. She had reached out to them through a family text. She asked my family, especially my mom: "Please reach out to Marci during this trying time in her life. She has suffered through it alone."

I was appreciative of the kind text she had sent to my family. But I felt I needed to do my part too. I made amends with every family member I had hurt or lost touch with through this trying time in my life. My family's hearts were softened by my heart-felt love for each of them through texts and phone calls.

Many family members like my mom, Carlie, Brian and Levi sent me care packages, money and cute letters from my nieces and nephews. I felt loved and tears filled my eyes of the charity my family showered on me.

I honestly felt like I was dying. I wanted to leave on good terms with my family, especially my mom. I was ready to go. I was off my rope of being trapped in a sick, painful body, just to survive. My mom called me soon after my text to her: I'm ready to die. I'm not receiving any more treatments to live. I love you. I'm sorry I haven't been a better daughter to you. You have done so much for me. I appreciate you.

My mom and I began planning my funeral on the phone. At first it was difficult for my mom to hear me give up on life, but I had been severely dehydrated for five days. I could feel my body shutting down. I was barely voiding. My stool was tarry, dark. I had a few tremors a day. I couldn't stand without almost falling over. Delirium was settling in. It felt like an out of body experience. My body floated to the other side. I felt loved ones, including my dad in the room with me. It was a peaceful, euphoric feeling. It felt better than any high I had experienced, and I wanted to go to heaven.

My mom wouldn't allow me to die alone. She wanted to fly me out to Chantelle's so that I could die with the family holding my hand. I agreed and decided to talk to my doctor about finding a hospice nurse to take care of me. I had decided that I was not going back to the ER to get treated anymore. I refused to go through the torture of them trying to get an IV only missing because I was severely dehydrated. I was over the ER treating me like I was a druggie when I

I was just trying to save my life. I decided God was either going to heal me or take me because I was not going to receive any more treatments to survive.

But the next morning I felt a sudden change of heart. I decided to give it one more try to allow God to heal me before I gave up on living. I sipped a cup of water. I ate a small cup of yogurt. I vomited excessively for 10 min straight. My throat was raw from the nasty stomach acid. I started to lose my voice. God definitely was not healing me.

I made the definite decision to let my body naturally shut down from dehydration. That's when lightning struck and shook my plans of impending death. Suddenly the country and the world was infected with a nasty coronavirus from China that was spreading through human contact. It stayed alive through air borne. It was attacking the respiratory system. Many people who had it reported, "It felt worse than the flu."

Many people were being hospitalized and were dying all over the world by this deadly virus. Suddenly the whole country was on lock down. Businesses were closing. Doctors' offices were only having phone consultations with their patients. Beaches and parks were closing down in San Diego and all over the world to prevent this virus from spreading any further. People were instructed by law to wear masks to cover their face, at the grocery store and any public place. It felt like a scene from a horror movie. I had never seen anything like it.

Meanwhile my friends, Mission President, my family and Facebook friends were praying I would be healed. My brother Brian and my mom called and texted me on a daily basis to send their love and concern. I will never forget the conversation I had with Brian the day before it all turned around. I told Brian on the phone in a flood of tears, "I'm ready to die. I can't endure this pain and suffering anymore"

Brian replied confidently, "It won't happen, you have too many people praying for you."

The next day my primary care doctor called me for my phone appointment. He encouraged me to go to the ER and be treated. He was very concerned that I was severely dehydrated and had black, tarry stool that may have caused a GI bleed. But wild horses couldn't drag me to call 911 and go to the ER again. I thought to myself, "I would rather die than go through the torture of being stabbed and pricked to get an IV, when they can't get one. I don't want to be healed. I have made the firm decision that I want to die."

146

I remember laying in bed one night. I felt dizzy and delirious. I was too weak to get out of bed or lift my head up. I suddenly received a text on my iPhone from my editor Katrina. She sent me a nice text expressing her love for me and didn't understand why I was suffering so much: I don't get it. I've watched you and it breaks my heart to see you like this. It's like you're just suffering to suffer.

Her words hit me to my very core. I replied: I am losing my trust in God. I don't know why he just wants me to suffer like this? It's cruel and just heartless. Just to survive, I've endured unbearable pain. People think I'm strong. I'm not strong. This one did me in. I just want to die.

She replied: "I don't understand it either but here is a quote I hang up on my wall by Henry B. Eyring." If you are on the right path it will always be uphill. Sometimes you have to go through the worst to get the best."

Eyring had always been one of my favorite apostles in my church. I requested the talk from Katrina that he gave to Brigham Young University students in 2005 titled "Raise the Bar."

Immediately I read Eyring's talk and when I read it I decided to put it to the test. He said in the talk, "We need the Spirit in our lives. We should pray for it every day to guide our lives. We will have great trials in life, but with the Spirit of God, he will be there to help us and inspire us in our dark days."

I fell on my knees. I prayed earnestly for the Spirit. I prayed a very humble prayer, "God I can't do this alone. I need your Spirit to be with me. My doctor wants me to go to the ER but I can't do this alone. I need my dad here with me to get through it."

I climbed off my knees and I immediately heard my dad's voice, "I'm here. I will not leave your side."

I felt the warm comfort of my dad in the room with me. He gave me the strength to call 911. I called 911 and when the paramedics picked me up they were all wearing masks covering their faces, because of the coronavirus pandemic. They refused to go inside my house. They instructed me to walk outside wearing a mask, when I could barely stand. They strapped me onto the stretcher table

I felt alone and hopeless. But suddenly I felt someone sitting next to me. I felt my dad holding my hand and I saw him in my mind. He said to me, "I'm right here. I will not leave your side."

On the way to the hospital I felt nauseated and dizzy. I could barely feel my body. My heart rate was racing over a hundred. It felt like my heart was beating out of my chest. I knew I could go unconscious if we didn't arrive at the ER soon.

When we finally arrived 10 min later, the hospital had a strange atmosphere. The medical staff were all wearing masks and instructed me to keep my mask on because of the coronavirus pandemic. A lady dressed in a yellow mask, yellow protective gown and blue plastic gloves met us at the ER entrance. She instructed the paramedics to take me down the hall to a secure room.

I was having a difficult time holding my head up. When we arrived at my room I was too feeble to walk. The paramedics helped me onto a steel soft bed. They exited the room. I changed into the blue gown laying on the bed. I looked around the dark empty room. But I felt calm. I felt my dad with me. It gave me a peace and comfort I hadn't felt in months.

A dark haired, tanned skinned man entered my room. I was nauseated and in stomach pain. But the doctor was cruel and attacked me verbally. He said, "You have been to the ER multiple times. You have received so many oral drugs in the past months it's unreal. You are on our records for drug seeking. Why are you lying to us that you are sick? I'm not going to give you pain medicine"

148

I looked at this brutal man who showed no feeling and said, "That's it. I'm done. I'm trying to save my life and you are accusing me of being a druggie. I've never done drugs in my life. I've had two serious surgeries in the past two months that caused a blood clot and hematoma. I'm going home and dying. I'm done."

The doctor walked out of my room in a huff. I sat on my bed ready to go home and allow death's door to come take me to the other side. When suddenly he entered my room again. He had a change of heart. He said nicely, "Are you sure you don't want any treatment like fluids and nausea medication."

I sat on my bed and part of me was already dead inside. I thought to myself, "Is there any hope of humanity left in these ER doctors?"

But I felt I should stay and allow the doctor to treat me. He refused to give me any pain meds and I said, "Fine, I don't care. I need a shot of nausea medication and some IV fluids."

He told me, "I can do that. I will send in one of my best nurses to do an ultrasound IV, get blood work and give you a shot of nausea meds."

A few minutes later a kind nurse entered the room to do an ultrasound IV. I was surprisingly calm. I felt my dad gently holding my hand when she stuck me with a large needle. She tried three times to get an IV and both times my veins blew. I didn't move each time she pierced me to thread the needle in my vein. I felt my dad by my side. I was confident he wouldn't leave me.

The nurse reported to the doctor that she was unsuccessful in starting an IV on me. The doctor told the nurse to give me a liter of water to try to hydrate me with oral fluids. The nurse came into my room 15 min later and gave me water to drink. I held the cylinder of water in my trembling hands. I tasted the cold ice water in my mouth and I swallowed it. My thirst was quenched, but within 5 minutes I felt nauseated and vomited. The doctor suddenly walked into the room. He said disgusted with himself. "Wow you are sick. I was hoping you would keep that down. We have beat you up pretty bad. I'm going to give you some IM pain medicine, another shot of nausea meds and a GI cocktail to numb your throat. Your throat must be raw from excessive vomiting. If we can get an IV on you, we will admit you to the hospital."

I cried out in the deepest gratitude and said, "Thank you."

A few minutes later the nurse came back to my room. She gave me a shot of pain medicine, nausea medication and a drink of the GI cocktail. I finally felt some relief. I closed my eyes and

drifted into a peaceful sleep. The nurse came in 10 minutes later and tried to get an IV. But, once again, she was unsuccessful. The doctor came in shortly after and told me, "I can't admit you without an IV and this is the worst time to be in the hospital with the coronavirus anyway. I called into your pharmacy a plethora of nausea medication. Go buy Mylanta to coat your throat and stomach. It's a lot like the GI cocktail we gave you."

I was disappointed that I wasn't being admitted. I couldn't keep anything down. I was nauseous and in pain. The IM shot of nausea meds and pain meds that the nurse administered improved my symptoms, and I agreed to be discharged.

The nurse wheeled me out of my room to go outside to wait for a taxi service to pick me up. Outside there was a group of tables and chairs of medical staff checking in patients, but they weren't allowed inside the hospital until someone escorted them in and they were wearing a mask. The coronavirus pandemic was affecting everyone, especially those who worked in health care.

I waited patiently in the dark, cold night for my taxi ride to pick me up at the hospital. A yellow cab pulled up to the curb 20 min later.

On the ride home in the cab I could smell vanilla from the freshener that hung on the car mirror. I could hear 80's music playing on the radio. The city looked like a ghost town.

The governor of California had instructed us to stay inside only to go out for necessities like medical supplies and groceries. The beaches and parks were all closed. It was the most eerie feeling.

My ride dropped me off at my house 10 min later. I shivered and walked inside the cold frosty house. I hastily turned on the fireplace switch in the dining room and immediately felt warmth. I walked into the kitchen and I cried out to God, "Okay God. You need to heal me if you want me to stay alive. I can't keep going on this roller coaster of endless medical problems. I'm alone. I have no one to hold my hand and comfort me. Everyone else is happy and married. Why can't I be? You have taken everything from me, including the one gift I've always wanted, to birth my own children. I have served you well. I went on a mission, but all my nieces and companions are now married who served missions like me. How is that fair? If you want me to live, for whatever crazy reason I can't comprehend, then we need to make a deal. This lonely, painful experience has healed me from the pain and abuse I endured with Troy, my ex-boyfriend. I want to be married and adopt children. I can't experience another Christmas or surgery alone. It's time for me to be healed and take a break from these endless painful medical issues that make it impossible for me to want to survive. I have endured this trial and now I'm asking for the blessings of my faithfulness. If things don't change and I continue down this lonely horrifying path, I'm not going to receive any more treatment and let my body die. I'm losing the will to live."

Chapter 14

God Kept Me Broken To Keep
Me At Jesus Feet

"Sometimes God Breaks You Just So He Can Fix You" -
Loren Thomas

I was at my lowest, but I held on to hope of better days. I thought to myself, "'I've hit rock bottom, but I've climbed through the muck alone and am terrified to endure another day. It can't get worse than this."

But, I was about to experience more pain and agony than I could possibly imagine. Later that night I awoke to severe, sharp chest pain. It hurt to breathe. I still wasn't able to keep anything down. I had terrible stomach pain. My throat was raw from vomiting. I climbed out of bed and sucked on a few ice cubes to try to numb my sore throat. I called my doctor that same day to report my symptoms and he suspected that I may have a tear in my esophagus. We agreed to talk the following Monday to see how I felt over the weekend and if my symptoms became worse or not?

I slept all day feeling more miserable. I felt weak and shivered with chills. I was burning up with a high fever. I was dehydrated and each breath I took was more shallow. Suddenly I received a text from my Bishop of my church: We can help you with rent for April but your family needs to help you with food and your Verizon bill going forward.

Then I got another text from Verizon: Your promise to pay agreement is today to pay your past due amount of $350 please pay this to avoid service interruption on your phone.

I fell onto my bed in a puddle of tears after I received both of these texts. I had reached out yesterday to my Bishop and asked for help for my rent, food and Verizon bill. I was grateful he was going to pay my rent to Jared, my landlord. "But how was I going to pay my Verizon bill and for food? I have been out of work for three months now. I was supposed to be recovering from my lumpectomy surgery for two weeks. But the complications post-surgery when it caused a hematoma, pulmonary embolism and appendicitis extended my recovery longer. Why was this happening to me?" I contemplated to myself.

I felt helpless to go on. I was trying to get back on my feet. I kept getting kicked down over and over again. I thought to myself, "How can I keep doing this? I can't go back to work until I get my income tax return. I had filed my taxes online, in hopes to pay my taxi rides for transportation, when my doctor released me back to work. But my severe health problems caused my doctor to be concerned about me returning to work."

I fell on my knees and cried out to the Savior a heartfelt prayer, "I can't do this anymore. I don't want to suffer and be in pain anymore. If you want me to live, then I need a miracle. I can't do this alone anymore. I need to know that you love me. If you want me to stay then I need to know why?" I need strength to endure because I am emotionally and physically drained. I have lost the will to live."

Later that night I felt only more suffering. I was up all night unable to sleep. The hematoma in my left breast was moving into the incision site causing painful pressure again. I was fighting to breathe. I finally voided my urine, but it smelled of old fish. It reeked. The severe dehydration was affecting my kidneys now. I was literally off my rope and pleading to God to die.

At 5:30 am I drifted off to sleep while laying in the recliner chair in the TV room. I heard a text message on my phone from my Mission President, Marsden Blanch: Lynette and I would like to help with your Verizon Bill. Do you have a Venmo account?

When I read the text I was sobbing in tears. This amazing man had rescued me just like my dad had done, more times than I could count on one finger

When I was 24 years old I served a LDS Mission on Temple Square Salt Lake City for 12 months. The remainder of my mission I served in San Bernardino for the last 4 months, but I was sent home two months early because I became sick with h pylori virus. Marsden Blanch had been like my second dad on my mission and his wife Lynette Blanch like my second mom. They were one of the most compassionate, caring people I had ever met. We bonded instantly when we met and President Blanch expressed to me in our weekly interviews, "You are amazing Sister Zollinger. I've seen you serve so diligently. You have such a sweet, strong spirit"

This beautiful man always saw me through God's eyes, just like my dad. His jet-black hair, lean figure and kind smile reminded me of my dad. When my dad passed away, he kept in close contact with me. His love and compassion for me felt like a soft blanket wrapped around me. He comforted me in my time of need, especially after the complications I had experienced of my current surgeries.

Every day he offered me words of encouragement to keep me going when I wanted to throw in the towel. The true miracle happened that morning when I received his kind text offering to help me with my finances.

I replied to his text: This has been the worst week of my life. I'm severely dehydrated and my throat is raw from vomiting. Now there is a cramp in my legs that moved to my chest. I'm having severe chest pain. I have never experienced months of more pain and suffering than these past few months. I'm always weak and sick. I prayed to God "I can't do this anymore. Please heal me or take me. I've lost the will to live. I need a miracle to fight because I am physically and emotionally exhausted. I've been up all night ill with chest pain and a raw sore throat. My hematoma is collecting in the incision site causing more pain again. I've been crying in pain all night." I received your text. You and your sweet wife are my miracle. Thank you I love you both more than you could ever know.

He replied: We love you. You are a dear friend.

I sat in the recliner chair and felt an overwhelming love from God. I cried out to God, "That was a miracle. Thank you. You do love me."

I drifted off to sleep and awoke a few hours later to a text on my phone from the pharmacy that my medication for acid reflux and stomach acid was ready for pick up. I called for a taxi service.

10 min later I walked outside into the warm sunshine and felt a light breeze kiss my cheeks. I opened the door to climb into the back of a lovely black suburban station wagon waiting for me near my house. I sat in the passenger's seat. I stared at the foreign man that drove me to the pharmacy and reality slapped me in the face once again. I sadly said to myself, "Even he has a car.

My car broke down a few months ago just before my lumpectomy surgery. Now I have no transportation. I'm so pathetic. How am I going to live without a car again? I can't do this?"

155

The sun was warm and inviting, but my heart was cold and bitter. When I walked into the pharmacy after the taxi driver dropped me off what I encountered was not what I had expected. The store clerk was wearing gloves and a mask. The pharmacist technician was dressed the same. Us shoppers were not permitted to stand ten feet from each other because of the coronavirus.

I felt like I was in a jail cell and my freedom was being taken away from me. I stood in a long line. I felt anger inside because this nasty deadly virus had taken over the world's lives.

I wanted to leave to enjoy the beautiful sunshine. After I picked up my medication from the pharmacy I walked outside. The warm sun usually brought a smile to my face. But, I had checked out emotionally. I didn't want to be alive anymore.

I walked slowly to the mall from the pharmacy that was less than a block away. I felt faint and my breathing was compromised. I shook my hands at God and yelled, "Why do you want me here? I don't want to be here anymore. Now I have respiratory issues from a scarred left lung. You are making it impossible for me to want to exist. If you are going to keep taking everything from me then let me die. Please."

I dragged my feet and walked around the mall. I noticed my favorite yogurt place and thought to myself, "I don't care if I vomit it up. I need something delicious to taste to make me happy."

I walked closer to open a steel door of what I pictured to be like paradise but the sign on the door haunted my vision, "Closed because of the coronavirus for your health and safety. We will notify you when we resume business." I felt that my life was over. How could I ever be happy again?" I sadly thought to myself as I scanned the mall. More disappointments of each door closed by the same dreaded sign, "Closed." The only stores that showed any human life in them were some local grocery stores.

I rode home on a taxi ride. A feeling of despair washed over me. I walked alone into a house where there was no laughter of kids playing in the yard. There was no husband to come home to share my day of joys or sorrow. I never felt more alone. I was feeling weak and sick from sleepless nights. I drank a cup of the liquid of medication I had bought at the store. I wanted to be numb and sleep. Sleep was the only place I felt painless. I felt sleepy immediately after drinking it.

I walked into my bedroom and I fell into the covers of my bed into a deep sleep. I woke up a few times during the night. I couldn't feel my body. But I welcomed the feeling. I wanted to be free of my sick, painful body. I wanted to be with my friends and loved ones who had passed. Before my lumpectomy surgery I had a strong feeling that I needed to get my life in the proper order and heard my Dad's voice, "Are you ready to come home?"

Meanwhile in and out of sleep all night I was confused that I was still here. I prayed a heartfelt prayer, "Why I'm I still here? What work am I supposed to do so I can die? I'm ready to go."

I awoke 12 hours later and glanced at my cell phone. I read a few text messages. My sister Carlie texted me and her message stood out to me: I've been reading a lot about being broken as a human. I'm learning that there is strength in being broken. There is also an intense amount of humility in being broken and there is also an incredible amount of beauty in each of our brokenness.

I read this today:

To be alive is to be broken; to be broken is to stand in need of grace. Being broken keeps us at Jesus' feet.

This made me think this: Satan wants us to cure our brokenness, to obsess about not being or becoming broken. This very thing then distracts us from Jesus' feet and pulls us away from him.

This is why I've realized brokenness brings strength which ultimately comes from Christ. Brokenness brings humility which continually drives us to stay at his feet and not leave. Brokenness brings beauty which comes from Jesus' love and seeing ourselves through his eyes. I wish I would have known these simple yet powerful truths as a teenager and even young adult. I always strived to appear put together. To appear close to perfect. To not let my weaknesses, insecurities, faults and imperfections show. I associated those things with appearing weak, appearing broken. And now I see I was so wrong. There is strength and so much beauty that comes from being broken. The fact I am human and will always be broken keeps me at the Savior's feet and that is exactly where I need to be....everyday"

This text spoke to my heart and it was like a light bulb came on. "Was God keeping me broken to keep me at Jesus' feet?" I thought to myself.

Chapter 15

Heaven Is Cheering Me On

"My home is Heaven. I'm just traveling through this world."
-Billy Graham

March 2020

I remember feeling deadly ill one morning and too dizzy to walk out of bed. Two months had passed. I couldn't keep solids or liquids down. My throat was raw from chronic vomiting. I had severe diarrhea. I was nauseated. I had a high fever and had tremors constantly. I awoke covered in sweat. I walked to the bathroom. I almost collapsed from weakness. I undressed and looked in the mirror at my frail almost lifeless body. I had lost 20 lbs and my skin was sunken in. I shook when I opened the shower door and turned on the shower knob. Immediately, I felt and tasted warm water dripping down my body. It felt good to taste something. I was extremely thirsty for water, but my body shook more and I felt faint. I could barely find the strength to walk on the cold aluminum floor in the bathroom to grab a towel, to wrap around my trembling body. I was too weak to stand any longer and collapsed to the floor shaking uncontrollably. My entire body felt like a rumbling earthquake. I wept uncontrollably. I was exhausted physically and mentally. I prayed to God, "Please release me from this painful body. I want to die."

Suddenly, I felt a warm touch sitting close by. It was my dad. I could see him in my mind. I felt him stroke my wet cold head. He whispered in my ear, "We will be together soon. Hang in there kiddo. Your suffering will be over soon."

The visions of my dad continued that night as my body got weaker and weaker. The veil was lifted. I saw other loved ones from the other side too. There were times I could feel my body and other times I couldn't feel my body. My body had lost the desire to be present in this life.

The GI doctor called me for our phone appointment the next morning. I reported to her my unfortunate situation and she replied concerned, "I am concerned that you are severely dehydrated, with chronic diarrhea, fevers and chest pain. If you don't get fluids in you soon your organs like your heart, lungs and kidneys will start to shut down. Go to the ER if it gets worse. I'm scheduling you for an emergency endoscopy and culture test next week. I think you may have bacteria in your colon and intestines from the antibiotics they gave you post surgeries because your symptoms started after your appendectomy. I'm calling in some medication to help your condition. My physician assistant will be calling you to set up the endoscopy appointment."

I thanked the doctor, "Thank you for your time and concern for me. I will go to the ER if I get worse."

I hung up the phone and gazed out the window. The sun was beaming through the translucent white drapes. I felt the warm breeze brush my face when I opened the glass door. I wanted to stay in that peaceful moment forever. I contemplated my life and if I wanted to live or die.

I received a disturbing call from a lady from Medi-Cal," Your Health insurance has lapsed because you earned too much money before your surgeries."

I replied in tears, "My situation has changed dramatically. I had two serious surgeries; a lumpectomy to remove a tumor and an appendectomy because my appendix almost burst. I had life threatening complications from both surgeries; a left lung blood clot and a hematoma. Both of them are healing now, but I've been ill with

160

a GI issue. I haven't been able to keep anything down since my appendectomy."

The nice lady on the phone said, "It takes 10 days to be reinstated, but I will put in an emergency for this to be reinstated. Sorry for all you have been through. Are you getting better?"

I replied, "No, worse."

She replied, "I'm so sorry. I will keep you in my prayers." and then the phone went silent.

I sat in the recliner chair in the living room. My body began to shake again. My eyesight was blurry. I felt my body slipping out of the chair. I almost collapsed when my heart raced faster. I heard a voice from my Dad, "You will be home soon my dear."

Later that night I had a vision from heaven. I saw the Savior. He had set a place for me at his table in heaven. He took my hand to follow him and said softly, "Well done thou good and faithful servant. Your afflictions have been but a small moment and God will exalt you on high. I have prepared a place for you in my mansion."

I woke up with a big smile on my face. I thought to myself, "Maybe I have suffered and I'm not married with my own children because I am here on this earth to help others through their pain and suffering. Twenty long years of loneliness and suffering are now going to end. I can finally find my bliss. Maybe, my husband is on the other side and I can finally be happy and meet him. I don't want to be lonely and in pain anymore. Soon I will be in heaven with my dad, Ryan- my cousin, Kirstin, Aaron, Tayva, my dear friends and my Grandpas and Grandmas who had also passed. I will be with my best friend, my Savior."

My heart was beaming with joy that I was going to heaven. But I knew my passing would not be easy for my family and friends. Every time I tried to discuss the possibility of me dying with my family or friends they couldn't accept it. I thought to myself, "Maybe in time they will see how happy I am near to death. The veil lifting, experiencing wonders from the other side undefined to us mere mortals. They will accept my passing in time. I'm ready to go."

The closer I felt to death the more the veil was lifted from my eyes. I was experiencing tremors now regularly. During the tremor my whole body shook and my heart raced. I felt my spirit floating up to heaven. I saw heaven in all its glory. I saw a bright light. Angels were drawing near to me. The light got brighter and a heavenly being appeared. I saw a vision of Jesus and beautiful white angels were surrounding him. I saw an angelic small child with long dark blonde hair smiling. She was holding out her hand to me. I felt that was my little girl. I have never felt so much love and peace in my life. I heard a soft voice from Jesus, "We are waiting for you to come home."

I felt the entire room full of spirits from the other side. I felt people I had done temple work for in my church. I felt my friends and loved ones who had passed. I felt patients I had cared for as a CNA when they passed in their home and in the hospital. I felt they were all waiting for me. My spirit was longing to be there. My spirit was ready to go home and leave my sick, painful body. I smiled at the thought of going to heaven. I was distancing myself from the world. I wasn't interested in watching TV or movies as much now. All I wanted to do is listen to spiritual uplifting music of the Savior. The more sick I became the more I wanted to go to heaven.

Meanwhile my family was in denial of how deathly ill I really was and sent me texts of their cute kids singing cute songs to me: Feel better aunt mouse - (my nickname).

I tried to reach out to my sister Chantelle and mom to tell them I wasn't getting better. I knew how much my family loved me and didn't want to say goodbye. I told them, "I am dying. My doctor told me that in three days my health will decline rapidly without fluids. My heart, kidneys, brain and liver will start to shut down."

162

But I felt from my Dad I needed to give my family a chance to say goodbye to me before I leave this world and join those who are waiting for me on the other side. I didn't want to die alone. I wanted to die with my family holding my hand. I prayed that my family and friends would accept my decision to die and let me go.

Unbeknownst to me my family and friends were praying I would be healed. They weren't ready to say goodbye.

That night I awoke to excruciating pain in my stomach. I was severely dehydrated and started to hallucinate. I tried to hydrate myself with Gatorade ice chips but I vomited it back up. My breathing was becoming more shallow. I was in a severe amount of pain. I prayed to God, "Please I need my Dad right now. I need to go to the ER. I'm in too much pain and nauseated from vomiting. Please I need the ER doc to be nice to me and help me."

I had a strong feeling I should bring my heating pad with my other belongings I packed in my black bag. I called 911 and the paramedics arrived at my home 10 min later, but they were not kind to me and said cruelly, "OH it's you again."

I replied, fighting to breathe, "My symptoms are worse. I can barely breathe and my chest hurts. I've been vomiting with severe diarrhea."

The paramedics helped me onto the stretcher into the red ambulance parked near my house on the street. In the ambulance one of the paramedics said rudely, "Have you thought of calling a taxi service rather than calling us? You don't get in quicker with the ambulance"

I looked at this cruel man who had no empathy for my suffering. I was fighting to breathe. My heart rate was over 100. I felt dizzy and weak like I could go unconscious at any time. I fought to take my next breath. I watched my saturation level decline on the machine I was hooked to in the ambulance.

163

Luckily one of the female paramedics showed me more compassion when she wheeled me to the ER from the ambulance and told the nurse, "She is a potential COVID-19 virus."

The charge nurse wheeled me to an isolation section of the ER. I saw nurses and doctors in PPE gowns and masks. The kind nurse helped me into bed. A green gown laid on the white sheets on the bed. When the nurse exited the room I scanned around the cold isolated room. I felt so alone. I suddenly felt a warm hand touch my shoulder and I felt my dad. I heard him whisper in my ear, "I am right here."

My dad's presence calmed my scared, troubled heart. A handsome doctor with kind, blue eyes entered my room 15 minutes later. He was genuinely concerned about me and my symptoms that resembled the COVID-19 virus. He ordered three panel tests for pneumonia, COVID-19 virus and bronchitis. He also ordered blood work, IV nausea meds and IV fluids.

A few minutes later a beautiful, compassionate nurse entered the room. She was the same nurse who had taken care of me the last time I had visited the ER. I felt calm knowing she genuinely cared about me. I told her happily, "I brought my heating pad this time to help my veins pop out. They used heating packs to get IV for my surgeries. They seem to have better luck when they wrap my arms in heat."

She replied joyfully, "Good idea."

She stuck me with a large needle to start the IV. I cried out to my dad who I still felt in the room with me, "Please dad send angels from heaven to get this IV in my scarred, tiny veins."

I felt the pain of the needle piercing my skin and the nurse weaved it in a vein. I felt the room filled with angels from the other side. I heard a sweet voice, "I got it. I finally got it."

164

I looked at the IV fastened to my vein and smiled and said, "Thank you God. Thank you Dad and the angels. You saved me. I love you."

I felt cold fluids streaming through my veins. I felt drowsy and less nauseated from the IV nausea meds the nurse gave me. I had a big grin on my face when I drifted off to a peaceful sleep. I awoke half an hour later to a soft voice, "Marci, your labs are normal. The chest x-ray is normal. I don't know what is going on with you. But this is the danger zone. You don't want to be here. I am sending you home with some nausea meds. If you get worse, come back to the ER."

I laid in bed and contemplated to myself, "How am I ever going to get better if they don't admit me to the hospital?"

The nurse entered my room a few minutes later with my discharge papers. She walked me out of the hospital to the waiting area for my taxi ride to arrive. I sat in the cold, dark, black night. After 30 minutes a yellow cab pulled up to the sidewalk.

On the drive home from the hospital in the cab I felt a wash of helplessness to survive. I walked into my lonely home and climbed into my cold bed. I drifted off crying myself to sleep.

I woke up the next morning in a cold sweat. My body was burning up with a high fever. I crawled out of bed to eat and drink something. I was thirsty and so hungry. But my body would not keep it down. I vomited it back up. I ran to the bathroom a few minutes later and everything came out in stool liquid. It wouldn't stop coming. It was like a hot lava just pouring out of me in buckets. I was severely dehydrated and covered in salty, wet sweat. I stumbled into the shower and turned the silver knob. I could feel warm water cascaded down my cold sweaty body. My body trembled. I fought to hold my body up. I prayed, "Please let me die. I don't want to do this anymore."

I spent the next five days in a state of delirium. I felt near death. I was too weak to get out of bed and slept 13 to 18 hours a day. My breathing was shallow and there were times I stopped breathing, but my body took one more breath to keep me alive. My whole body trembled every few hours. I felt my dad more often. I was waiting for death's door to open and invite me in.

But the suffering continued. I remember waking up one morning and cursed God that I was still alive. My hematoma was pushing on the incision site on my left breast and causing me unbearable pain. I laid in bed and I didn't care if I lived or died. I was tired of being sick, alone and feeling depressed.

I climbed my weak body out of bed and I dressed in my workout clothes. My body had transformed in 30 days. I lost most of my muscle tone. I was leaner than I had been in years. I measured my waist and I had lost 4 inches. My stomach was flat. I smiled at the picture I viewed in the mirror. I had finally lost all of the weight I had gained from my multiple surgeries over the years.

I happily walked out the door. I could smell the fresh air. Suddenly I felt elated listening to Spotify on my iPhone of all my favorite music. I felt alive and I ran faster on the wet cement. It was damp outside from the rain all week, but my heart welcomed the damp, warm weather. I was in my happy place. I hadn't ran in months since I had been so ill. I jogged for half a mile and didn't want to stop. But my weak lungs weren't strong enough to go any further. I walked back to my house sweating from head to foot. I turned on the shower in the bathroom. I felt the warm water drip down my body. I felt like the old me again. I spent the rest of the day overjoyed to be out of bed.

Dreams are like miracles from heaven. The next morning felt like a beautiful dream. My fever was gone and my chest was clear to breathe. I drank sips of Gatorade and miraculously kept it down. I thought to myself happily, "Maybe God has finally healed me."

I was anxious and walked to the bathroom. I decided to doll myself up for the first time in six months. My long, golden-brown hair cascaded down the middle of my back. My lean, flat tummy slipped into my black- spandex workout pants and black tank top. I felt beautiful and youthful for the first time in years.

I called for a taxi to pick me up at my house. The sun was beaming and the birds were chirping. I felt joy. I was pain-free and healthy. The taxi driver picked me up five minutes later at my house. I was beaming ear to ear viewing the beautiful weather when he dropped me off at the Eye Center at the mall in La Mesa where I lived. I had scheduled an eye appointment a few days ago.

I remember sitting on the cement porch outside beaming with joy. I felt the sun rays glaze my face. My mind envisioned a life of happiness and gladness. A life of marriage to a dark, handsome, kind man. Two adopted twin, Korean babies I embraced lovingly in my arms. A life of pain-free, healthy, wonderful times at the beach feeling the strong gust of wind, pulling me into the salty ocean. The waves crash over my head as I dive into the water to catch my first wave. My heart was bursting with a feeling of enchantment of this wonderful vision.

But my beautiful imagination was interrupted by a kind voice, "Marci, are you ready for your eye exam."

I walked slowly through the reality of feeling lonely once again. But, I was relieved to be getting new contacts. I had lived with the discomfort of a ripped contact for over a month now. My eyesight was poor and it was difficult to see with one eye. I inserted new contacts into both of my eyes. I could see clearly again. For the rest of the day I was on cloud nine. I posted pictures on Facebook. I sent pictures to my family of my new healthy and lovely life. They responded with happy hearts and were overjoyed that I was healthy.

But like all things that come to an end in my life, this one did, too. I awoke the next morning and I felt very ill. I fought to breathe, I could only sip on Gatorade ice chips that I couldn't keep down for

167

long. I was malnourished, dehydrated. I was in severe pain. I finally called a taxi to take me to the ER. But before I did I prayed, "Please, I need my dad with me. I can't do this alone.

The taxi service picked me up at my house 15 minutes later and dropped me off at the ER in Grossmont, close to where I lived. I felt a wisp of sadness that filled my entire body with despair. My eyes watered with tears as I thought to myself, "My life has been a series of ER visits once a week for severe dehydration for two months. I feel like this will definitely be my life and it scares me to my very core."

When I arrived at the ER they were able to admit me quickly because of my poor condition. The nurse took me back to the exam room. She kindly instructed me to slip into a gown on the white sheets on the silver steel bed. I lowered my head and tears flowed down my cheeks to my lower, quivering lip. I sat on the white sheets of the bed. I felt like I would be in pain and alone forever. I suddenly felt a loving presence beside me. I felt my dad. But his presence felt different. I felt he was weeping for me and he said softly, "It pains me to see you in this much pain."

A calmness came over me. I felt confident whatever I had to endure I could pull through with my dad cheering me on. A tall dark-haired man with a golden smile entered the room. He treated me with compassion and understanding. He ordered blood work and an X- ray because of my discomfort of pain and nausea. He entered my room 30 min later with the test results and said, "Your blood work showed dehydration. The X- ray showed that your lungs are filled with fluid. You have pneumonia. I'm ordering an IV for fluids, nausea meds and pain meds IM."

He gave me a prescription for oral antibiotics and said, "We can't admit you. You need an endoscopy to find out why you're vomiting and have diarrhea. We don't do that in the hospital now that we have patients with the coronavirus. It's too risky. You need to see your GI doc ASAP. I will prescribe you pain meds and antibiotics for your pneumonia."

168

Once again, I was sent home with oral medicine that when I tried to swallow, it got caught in my throat and I vomited it up. The pain medicine was tiny and stayed down to give me some relief. But each passing day my health declined more and more. A few more days passed. My fever was over 100° degrees. I was fragile. I could barely get out of bed. My heart was beating quickly. I felt weaker and weaker. My body felt like it was slipping more and more, but I felt free of pain and only felt joy the closer I felt heaven.

The more I felt heaven the more I long to be there. But I continued to pray that God would heal me or take me to that beautiful place free of suffering and pain. I tried to eat and drink one last time. I vomited for 15 minutes straight. I quickly bolted to the toilet to dump diarrhea. I sat on the toilet and vomited more with diarrhea pouring out of me. I was done. I knew that God was not going to heal me. It was time for me to go and be free from my sick inflicted body.

Miracles happen when we least expect it. That night Chantelle called me to inform me that the family had been talking and they didn't want me to be in pain anymore. She said softly, "We have accepted that you want to die and don't want to suffer anymore. Mom wants me to talk to your doctor to verify that you were dying without treatments. Mom or someone will drive down to pick you up to say goodbye to the family who will be here to hold your hand so you don't have to die alone."

I thought to myself, "This is a miracle. Maybe that is why I haven't passed yet. I need to say goodbye to my family.

I agreed and said to Chantelle happily, "Ok I will call my doctor tomorrow and call you."

Chapter 16

The Incurable Diagnosis

"I Finally Threw In The Towel But God Through It Back and Said, 'Wipe Your Face Girl We Are Almost Done" -Anne Kennedy

May 2020

The day was like any other, but I wanted to be free from this body of clay causing pain and suffering. I called my surgeon. I needed him to drain my hematoma one last time. It was building up in the incision site again and causing me great pain. I set up an appointment to see him Tuesday at 11:30 am.

I was crying after I got off the phone with the front office secretary. "Tomorrow I will be going into my surgeon's office for the last time. This kind man had been there for me when I had no one. He had taken care of me for four months now. He held my hand when he admitted me to the hospital. I was screaming in horrific pain from the complications of the surgery when I could barely breathe. He sat with me in his office almost in tears of the pain I was enduring from a surgery that was supposed to be 2 weeks recovery to now 3 months recovery. He definitely had been an angel sent to me while I experienced the misery of it all." I contemplated to myself in tears.

My mind raced back to all the pain and suffering I had endured the past three months. I shivered as I recalled the torture of the ER nurse unable to get a vein. Her sticking me over and over with giant sharp needles trying to thread a small IV into my weak scarred vein. I had endured horror, curdling pain from the hematoma that presented itself post lumpectomy surgery. The hematoma was as big as a grapefruit pushing pressure on my chest making it difficult to breathe. More suffering continued when I went to the ER and almost stopped breathing when they discovered I had a left lung blood clot. Then, the ordeal of being on blood thinners to try to heal the blood clot prevented the hematoma from healing. To add salt to the wound I was in the ER again the day I was released from the hospital vomiting violently every 15 min. The ER doc called the emergency surgeon to do appendectomy for an almost ruptured appendicitis.

I had endured 12 weeks of unbearable pain, vomiting and diarrhea because my body isn't digesting food or liquids. Anything I swallowed I vomited back up choking because it got stuck in my throat. I was aspirating and had pneumonia.

I thought to myself, "I'm done. My body is emotionally and physically done. I can no longer take the pain and suffering just to survive. I had already overdosed four times and tried to take my life. But that isn't the way I want to go. Maybe God has finally heard my cries and answered my prayers. Maybe God knows I can't do another day in this pain, sick body anymore. Maybe God knows I can't do another Christmas or Birthday alone. Maybe God realizes the physical ache I feel watching my siblings and their own families now having children of their own with a painful heart knowing I never will be given that blessing in this life. Maybe God does love me and wants me to be happy?"

As I contemplated my life in heaven I had a huge smile on my face. I pictured seeing my dad walk towards me with a big smile on his face and embracing me in his loving arms. I pictured meeting the Savior. Would I fall at his feet? Or stand in awe of his perfect love and light?

My home is heaven. I'm just traveling through this world. I was ready to be called home to heaven. But the agony of my physical body haunted me and I felt the pain of my earthly existence continue.

171

I remember waking up one night in a pool of sweat. I barely had stamina to get out of bed. I stumbled to the restroom and slowly undressed to wash my weak sweaty body in the shower. I almost fainted in the shower. I could barely stand. I was dehydrated for 5 days. I had tried to force myself to eat or drink to stay hydrated but within 5 min I was vomiting.

My surgeon, doctors, family and friends pleaded with me to go to the ER again to get IV fluids but I had checked out. I thought to myself, "I'm not going to go to the ER to be treated like some druggie, get IV fluids and sent home to go back to vomiting again. The dehydration starts all over again. I'm still miserable and not healed. I don't care if I live or die anymore."

But my Primary Care doctor was not ready to give up on me. He was concerned about the time frame I had been sick and vomiting for 3 months since my appendectomy. He was afraid that my

declining health could turn life threatening quickly. He ordered an emergency endoscopy and told me that the GI (gastrointestinal) doctor should be calling in a few days to set up the appointment. I waited patiently. The weekend came and went. I didn't receive a call from the GI office.

I prayed to God and said, "Why am I still here? I've lost the fight to live and endure this pain any longer. If you want me here you need to give me a good reason why? I need a miracle to give me the fight to stay."

The sun was beaming. I could hear the birds singing in perfect harmony. I woke up the next morning. I was depressed that once again, I laid in bed sick from dehydration. I decided that I definitely didn't care if I lived or died. I was going to be happy. I decided to go for a run.

I drank a few sips of Gatorade before my trek up the steep hills of San Diego where I lived. I immediately spit out a huge chunk of stomach acid. I couldn't keep it down. But I didn't care. I was outside. I could feel the asphalt of the cement on the soles of my tennis shoes. I could smell the warm air and feel a light breeze kissing my cheeks. I started to jog down a windy narrow road. I ran faster and faster each stride I took I felt alive again. My body began to sweat. I could feel the sweaty, salt dripping down my back. This was my happy place.

But I had to stop a few times on my long trek. My lungs were working twice as hard because I was dehydrated. A few times I felt like I could have a heart attack, but my fatigued body wouldn't give up yet. I continued to hike back to my house. I felt like I would pass out from heat exhaustion. I said out loud in desperation, "Dad please I need help to get home."

My legs felt like jello and I couldn't move another foot. I felt something carry me. I felt my dad and loved ones from the other side carrying me home. It felt like I was floating. I heard my dad say, "We can do this, but you need to take one step at a time and we will help you."

I stepped one foot and another foot. I felt light as a feather. I finally made it a short distance to my house. I ran into the house almost collapsing by the fridge. I clumsily opened the fridge door, grabbed a cold Gatorade and drank sips, trying to quench my thirst. But, after a few sips of Gatorade, I felt sick to my stomach. I immediately vomited back up what I had drank.

The room was spinning, and I barely made it into my air-conditioned room. I passed out on my bed unable to move or want to move. I slept for hours. I was weak and severely dehydrated. I called my doctor to let him know how I was feeling and that I was still unable to keep fluids down. My doctor was very concerned and said" I am worried about your health. I'm going to have my nurse call the trauma hospital in La Jolla to let them know you are coming in to be seen. I know you have had issues with other hospitals admitting you and treating your condition seriously, but I'm confident that this hospital will take good care of you and give you the IV fluids you need desperately to survive."

I agreed with my doctor that I needed to be seen at the ER for medical evaluation. I called a taxi service to pick me up. When I arrived at the ER I was showered with love and concern that I was weak from severe dehydration from chronic vomiting. The Nurse took my vitals and my BP was low and my heart rate was over 100. Another Nurse immediately took me back to a room in the ER. The nurse instructed me to wear a green, plaid gown laying on a white sheet on the hospital bed. I slipped into the drafty gown and pulled the warm blankets up over my trembling body.

I was weak and unable to keep my head up. I laid back on the hard mattress. A nice lady in a PPE yellow gown and blue latex gloves entered my room. She said in a kind voice, "Your symptoms of shortness of breath, chest pain, and abdominal pain are concerning. We need to test you for the coronavirus."

The test was invasive. It felt like the swab the nurse used for the test was going far up inside my nose that it hit my skull. I was relieved when it was finally over. The rest of the night felt like a blur. My body was shaking. I felt nauseated. When the ultrasound nurse came in to start my IV I didn't feel present in my body. I barely felt the huge needle piercing my scarred veins, for the nurse to advance the catheter. But when the nurse started the fluids in my IV I suddenly felt the cold stream in my veins. My body drank it up, feeling starved of fluids.

I was still very weak and sick. The doctor came in about a half hour later and told me that I had a kidney injury. I was not surprised by this bad news. My left kidneys felt like someone was repeatedly stabbing me in my upper back under my ribs. I hadn't peed all day. I couldn't void any urine for eight hours in the ER, even with IV fluids. The doc was very concerned that my creatine levels were high and said 6 words I had been longing to hear for months, "We are going to admit you to the hospital."

I was happy someone had taken my condition seriously, and felt it was life or death if I wasn't admitted to the hospital. I was transferred to a busy section in the hospital the next morning. The medical staff were kind to me and treated me with great care. The Nurse tried to draw blood from my hand. She was so close to my knuckle, she hit the bone. I pulled my hand away and cried out, "I can't do this, it's too painful."

The Nurse was empathetic and felt bad I was in so much pain. When the medical floor doctor made her rounds that same morning I begged her to order a PICC Line for me so I wasn't stuck in the most painful places to give blood in the morning for routine blood draws to monitor my progress. She was kind to my plea.

A nice PICC line nurse arrived a few hours later. She put in a PICC line, but she hadn't numbed my arm enough when she tried to thread in the line. The pressure was strong. I almost jumped out of my skin, when I felt the huge catheter going into my upper left arm. She immediately gave me more lidocaine to numb the area. She finished threading the long catheter in my vein.

The whole procedure caused a large bruise that made it difficult to lift my arm. She called the nurse, who took care of me that day, to bring me an ice pack to bring down the swelling. My arm was aching and swollen at the PICC line site for the rest of the day.

The next three days I was in the hospital were like I was in a trance. My kidneys were trying to recover. The nurse put a cannula in my nose to help me breathe. I was so weak. My body wanted to sleep. My veins were consistently pumped with an IV fluid bolus drip. I had a slight fever. The doctor wanted me to try to keep liquids down. But when I tried a few sips of vegetable broth and Gatorade I vomited it back up.

The next morning the GI team was called in to treat me. They did a series of tests to figure out why I was chronically vomiting. The first test they did was an endoscopy. They sedated me while they put a camera tube down my throat to look at my esophagus and intestines. The test revealed that I had gastritis inflammation of my stomach. The second test was a gastric emptying study. I was given an egg sandwich to eat, water to drink that had a radioactive liquid in it to track how long it took my digestive system to digest liquids and food.

The results were positive for gastroparesis - a motility disorder that had paralyzed my GI tract. I was not digesting food or liquids correctly. The test results concluded that the food and liquid was staying in my esophagus for 30 min after I consumed anything. It caused acid reflux then projectile vomiting. Whatever was left moved into my stomach. It camped out there for four hours, causing more acid and indigestion.

The GI team was relieved with a diagnosis. They instantly put me on medication to try to increase my motility. Unfortunately, it made me crazy. I literally felt out of my skin, like I wanted to jump out the window. I was so relieved when the medication wore off. The GI team abruptly discharged me the next day even though I was still vomiting. They told me to follow up with their motility doctor and that he would be the one to help me.

I looked out the window. I felt sad and discouraged about the disease I had been diagnosed with, which had added to my other medical problems. I looked at my discharge paperwork the nurse had given me when she discharged me a few hours later. I was horrified by every word I read. "Gastroparesis is a non-curable disease requiring anti- psychotic medication and possible surgeries to survive."

176

Life as I knew it, would be on disability because I couldn't work with chronic vomiting. My blood sugars would be imbalanced and I could be diabetic. I would be in and out of the hospital, with feeding tubes from malnutrition, severe dehydration leading to kidney failure and other organ failure.

I dropped the white paper on my untidy bed. I stared in a foggy haze, out the window. I literally wished I could open the window and leap to my impending death. I dreaded living this nightmare life anymore. I knew God was not going to heal me and that I could die.

I was severely depressed by the new diagnosis that haunted my life. I didn't want to live anymore. I had so many close calls of death. But I was still here enduring this sick body of pain and suffering. I felt like this diagnosis was a death sentence. I suddenly received a text from my landlord, Jared, to check up on me on how I was doing? He, Chantelle and Brian were so good about texting me their love and concern. It meant so much to me because my mom couldn't come with me because of the COVID - 19 virus pandemic. I had reached out to her a week earlier with phone calls and multiple texts pleading with her, "Mom I need you right now. Please call me or text me. I definitely can not do this alone anymore."

Chapter 17

Service with A Smile

"We are here to serve the Savior and all else become secondary." -Doug Zollinger

June 2020

I remember when my dad was alive, he was an example of Christlike love. He loved to help others. He was always a helping hand to anyone who needed him. He would say to me "Service with a smile. We are here to serve the Savior and all else becomes secondary."

Chantelle and Brian were so much like my dad in that aspect. They were always selfishly willing to be there for me all hours of the day or night. I remember when Brian called me before I had been admitted to the hospital. I was not in a pleasant mood. I was delirious from severe dehydration. I was tired of vomiting. I told Brian, "I'm done. I'm going to let my body shut down naturally - my kidneys etc. I'm not going back to the ER for any future medical treatment. I'm done being sick. I've been sick for 20 years in and out of the hospital with one diagnosis after another. Why does God just want me to suffer?"

Brian replied, "I can't imagine what pain you must be enduring just to survive. So many are helping you financially and emotionally. What are you doing to give back?"

Brian's words hit me like a ton of bricks. I remembered the day after I was discharged from the hospital. I decided that I was tired of feeling depressed. I was going to pay it forward. I wanted Brian to know how much he meant to me, of his sacrificing and devoted love. I called his wife Susan. I asked her to pick up Brian's favorite meal from his favorite restaurant. I sent her money from my bank through Venmo. She received the funds immediately. Susan had been kind enough to video him on her iPhone when she gave him my present. She sent me the video.

On the video Brian was happy that someone had taken the time to think of him. He was surprised to discover it was me. I will never forget the happy expression on his face, when he read the card I had attached with a yummy meal of steak, mashed potatoes, salad and cornbread.

He sent me a text thanking me for thinking of him. It felt good to see Brian happy by my small gesture. I decided I wanted to give the same gift to Chantelle. I called my beautiful niece Kenna. I asked her to pick up Chantelle's favorite meal at her favorite restaurant. Kenna was more than happy to help me surprise my sister with a gift from her little sister. Kenna also recorded the experience. Chantelle was surprised like Brian that the surprise was from me.

I felt joyful inside that I had shown both my two kind siblings of how much I appreciated and loved them. I decided I wanted to serve more so when I received Jared's text the following day: We have that big fruit orchard outside. It would be nice if we gave back to those in your ward who may need it right now. Many may be out of work because of the COVID - 19 virus?

After I read Jared's text a light bulb came on. I texted the Relief Society President who is in charge of the welfare system for the ladies in my ward: Jared and I would like to contribute yummy fresh fruit from our orchard to needy families in the ward.

179

She immediately replied: Yes, that would be nice of you.

I immediately went outside, picked boxes and bags of fruit in the hot sun. I didn't care how dehydrated I felt. I was happy to be helping others and feeding hungry families who needed it.

But, after a few hours, I started feeling like I was going to faint. I collected the boxes and bags filled with fresh, tasty fruit. I stacked them on the wooden bench outside to be collected by the Relief Society President of my church.

I stumbled into the house. I felt faint. I ran to the fridge, almost collapsing. I was shaking. I grabbed a bottle of Gatorade from the cold fridge. I gulped most of it down. After a few seconds I vomited it back up. I couldn't keep it down to hydrate myself.

I felt dizzy. The room was spinning and spinning. I clumsily walked into my room. I fell onto my soft bed. I was too weak to move. I slept and awoke a few hours later to a voice message on my iPhone. It was the nurse at the trauma hospital. She was inquiring how I was doing since I had been discharged a week ago.

I called back the nurse at the trauma hospital. A kind voice answered. The Nurse asked me, "How are you?"

I replied sadly, "Not good. I'm worse. They discharged me from the hospital vomiting and diarrhea. I'm home now dehydrated again and feeling more sick. I had kidney failure in the hospital because of severe dehydration."

She replied, "That is not good. I'm scared for you. I'm ready to call 911."

I said, "No, that is okay. I will call a taxi service to take me to the ER. I've been debating whether to come or not. It's expensive. I can't afford it right now. I've been out of work for four months now. I've been so sick."

She replied, "Let me check something and get back to you."

A few minutes later she called me back and said joyfully, "I checked with your health insurance and you have free medical transportation to the hospital, doctor visits etc. Now you don't need to pay for a taxi service."

I was overjoyed by the news and promised her, "Okay I will come in."

I called the medical transportation and arranged for them to pick me up at 5 am. They needed at least a 12 hour notice to pick me up.

5 am couldn't come soon enough. I felt dizzy and lightheaded like I could pass out at any moment.

As soon as I arrived at the ER at the trauma hospital I was greeted with kindness and love. A nice nurse lady took my vitals and saturation levels. My BP and heart rate was high. She immediately had another nurse take me back to a room in the ER. I felt sick, nauseated and thirsty.

A kind, good looking, sun kissed, blonde hair, male nurse came in to get an IV and blood with the ultrasound, but he was unsuccessful because I was severely dehydrated. He had to stick me six times in the most painful places on my body. He wanted to try my feet, neck, knuckle and thumb. I told him, "No way. I would rather die."

He couldn't get an IV in my scarred veins. He exited my room to talk to the doctor about it. When he left I sat on the hard, uncomfortable bed and cried. I felt alone and hopeless. I threw up my hands and said, "I'm done Heavenly Father. I can't do this anymore."

I heard a soft comforting voice, "I know."

Ten minutes later the nurse entered the room again and said kindly, "We are going to get it this time. I'm going to try a longer catheter. It may sting, but I think I can get it."

I laid in bed, ready to be stuck again, by a large needle. I cried out to my dad, "Please dad bring all the angels from heaven to get this IV in my arm."

I felt a huge pinch. I could feel the nurse advancing the catheter. He said, "Happily, I got it. It's in."

The nurse hooked up my IV to a bolus of IV fluids. I instantly felt fluids running through my thirsty veins and sighed saying, "Thank You God, Dad and the angels who rescued me. I can feel my veins drinking up the fluids."

The nurse gave me IV nausea meds that instantly gave me relief. I immediately fell into a deep sleep. My body was exhausted mentally and physically. But soon my dream of full sleep was interrupted by a voice, "Your labs look fine. We gave you 3 L of IV fluids. You can go home now your kidneys are okay."

I replied, "I'm chronically vomiting and I keep getting severely dehydrated. Can't you admit me."

He replied sternly, "No if you're dehydrated again come back to the ER. If your kidneys are failing, we can cross that bridge when we come to it."

I sat in bed fuming inside and thought to myself, "So basically you don't want to avoid a potential kidney failure. You just want to treat it when it's present. It may be too late. I could die."

I collected my belongings and left the room. Now that I was hydrated I had an appetite again. I bolted to the cafeteria. I purchased an egg sandwich, chicken soup and a bottle of water. I sat outside with other medical staff under the umbrellas at the steel grey tables. I drank half a bottle of water. I ate a sandwich and some soup.

Within 5 minutes I felt nauseated and had to stop eating and drinking. I raced to the bathroom. I vomited for 10 min straight. I called medical transportation to come pick me up.

I rode home in a fancy limo car. I looked at the beautiful scenery of green palm trees and beaches close by. When the driver pulled into my driveway I thanked him for the ride, I walked into the house feeling alone and scared of my future. I was tired and hadn't slept well all night. I climbed into the warm covers of my bed and fell into a long peaceful sleep.

The next four days I only ate a spoonful of applesauce to take with my medications. I couldn't take one more day of vomiting, nausea, chest pain and stomach pain from drinking any fluids. The fifth day I was severely dehydrated again. I lost the strength to get out of bed. One night I almost stopped breathing. I no longer felt connected to my body. Each day felt like I was in a prison cell. I longed to be free in heaven with my dad and loved ones who had passed on.

Chapter 18

Losing The Will To Live

"Waiting For Death's Door To Invite Me In" -Marci Zollinger

The dawn breaks, the night falls and someday my soul will be free from its torturous shell. I woke up the next day in excruciating kidney pain. I pushed my weak body out of bed. I walked to the restroom. I couldn't not void. I hadn't peed in 12 hours. My kidneys were in distress again. I had decided if I did go into kidney failure or liver failure I would go to hospice. I was now at a crossroads in my life. Did I want to continue living like this or to give up? I decided that I wanted to be free and break through the painful shell that housed my sweet soul.

I was ready to say goodbye to my journey of life and go be with my loved ones in a better place. I sent out a group text to my close friends: My health is declining more every day. My kidneys are in constant stress from severe, chronic dehydration. I have decided if I do go into kidney failure I will go to hospice.

When I sent out the group texts, immediately I had close friends responding like my Mission President and my close friends who live in Utah. I heard my phone ring. It was Lori, a dear friend who had been like a sister to me. She had always been there for me through the past twenty years of medical problems after medical problems. She was one of the most compassionate people I knew. She was crying when we talked about my potential end of life coming near. She said tearfully, "I can't lose another sister."

I replied sadly, "I don't want to lose you either. You are like my sister."

We talked for two hours about my experiences of Heaven. She shared with me her experiences she had with her sister and granddaughter who had passed. It was lovely and brought peace to my heart, that I could say goodbye to my sweet, dear friend. She said to me crying, "I want to come to California to say goodbye. Please let me know when you are in hospice, so I can come see you."

We continued to cry on the phone, until we said goodbye. That day, I felt a radiant ray of light all around me. I was severely dehydrated. I started to feel my body lifting. I knew that my body was slowly wanting to go. But I wasn't ready to go yet. I wanted to say goodbye to my family and close friends. I staggered to the kitchen to eat a spoonful of applesauce. I heard my dad's voice, "Are you ready for me to come and get you?"

I almost collapsed. I was feeling lifeless and replied, "Yes dad you can come get me, but not yet. I need to say goodbye to loved ones."

It was miraculous, as soon as I said this I could feel my body again. I thought to myself, "What a loving God that he not only wants me to feel peace about passing on, and for my loved ones to feel peace about it too. He is keeping me around so they can say goodbye. He doesn't want me to die alone."

The next morning the sun was shining. It was too inviting to lay in bed weak and depressed. I crawled out of bed and dressed into my work out clothes. I sipped some Gatorade. I stepped outside and could feel the hot sun on my cheeks. I could feel the cement under my tennis shoes while I ran down the hill. I ran and ran. I didn't want to stop running. I felt alive.

185

But I started to feel weak and had to stop. I vomited up the Gatorade. I felt like I was going to faint. I fell onto the grass and my head was spinning. I knew if I didn't get help, I would die.

The Grossmont hospital was close by. I stumbled into the ER too weak to stand anymore. A nurse saw me struggling and immediately took my vitals.

She raced me back to a room in the ER. My heart rate was 130. I could barely hold my head up. A lady in scrubs came into my room to start an IV with the ultrasound machine. I had been to the ER so frequently now with chronic vomiting causing severe dehydration that the hospital knew my medical history. They knew I was a hard stick.

I laid in bed crying out to my dad, "Please bring angels from heaven to get this IV. I can't handle the pain of them sticking me over and over again."

I felt my dad holding my hand and heard him say, "We are all right here with you."

I felt my dad, my cousin Ryan, my Grandpa Zollinger, Grandma Zollinger and other close loved ones who had passed in the room with me. I started to cry, feeling their presence close by. I was calm. I closed my eyes. I felt these beautiful angels from heaven, helping me to endure the pain of the ultrasound nurse sticking me with a large needle to thread into my vein.

It was a miracle when I heard her say, "I got it. It's in."

I said with a smile on my face, "I could kiss you. You deserve a raise. No one has been able to get it on the first try."

She smiled and replied, "I'm so glad. Thank you."

I looked up and I could still feel the room filled with angels from the other side. I had tears in my eyes and said, "Thank you sweet angels."

Another nurse entered the room wearing green scrubs. He told me, "I'm going to be your nurse today. I have some IV fluids and nausea meds here for you."

I instantly felt the IV fluids and nausea meds flowing through my veins. My veins drank it up. I asked the nurse nicely, "Can I get some ice chips. I'm dying of thirst."

A few minutes later the nurse brought me a cup of ice chips. I immediately grabbed the cup. I sucked and swallowed the ice chips. I felt the coldness go down my raw, dry throat. There was a relief of thirst, until 5 min later I vomited. The doctor came into my room 30 min later and said calmly, "Your white blood cells are high. You have an infection. I'm not sure where the infection is? It could be a stomach infection from gastroparesis. There isn't more I can do without evidence."

He immediately discharged me. I called medical transportation to pick me up. They were not available for an hour. I waited in the cold, black night. When transportation finally arrived I was trembling and freezing. A nice, kind dark haired scruffy man dropped me off at home 10 min later.

I walked into my dark house, turned on the lights and the fireplace for warmth. I was hungry and thirsty now that I had IV fluids to hydrate me. I called the food service to order a steak burrito. When the food service arrived 30 min later, I ate the burrito with a few Gatorade ice chips. Within 5 minutes I felt nauseated. I vomited for 10 min and the stomach acid burned my throat.

My stomach felt like a semi-truck had run over it. I had excruciating stomach pain. I felt nauseated like I had a terrible stomach flu. I crawled into bed and I prayed to God, "I want to die. I've lost the will to live."

It was then, I truly knew I made the decision to die. I was inflicted with this debilitating disease. I had no quality of life. I was discouraged from ever healing. I felt like it was my choice to stay or go. I had chosen to go. I was sick all night long and too weak to move. I decided, no more treatments, no more surgeries, or no more IV fluids. I wanted to die. I knew it would only be a matter of time before my body shut down for good.

The next week was my birthday. It was the worst birthday, but miracles did happen. I was dehydrated and couldn't go to the beach to celebrate. My mom reached out to me and sent me $120 for my birthday. I used the money she sent me to buy me a yummy birthday dinner. It

tasted so good going in, but I felt nauseated within 5 min and vomited it up.

I realized this would be my life if I chose to stay. I felt I had made the right decision to die. A week later I had a phone appointment with my Primary Care doctor. We had a serious discussion about my declining health. I told him that my ER visits felt like torture because my veins are so scarred to find an IV.

My doctor told me sadly, "The next step is a feeding tube."

I replied, "No way. No feeding tubes. "I'm not going to receive any more treatments. I want to go to hospice."

188

He replied, "Give me a week to research to see if there are any treatments we have missed to treat the disease. Then we can discuss going to hospice in my office when I evaluate you."

I agreed with the terms and called Chantelle to tell her the news. Chantelle couldn't believe it had come to this and that I was really dying.

She sent out a beautiful text to my family: Family pls read up on what happened to this lady. This is exactly what happened to Mouse when she had her appendix surgery. The surgeon accidentally took her life. She severed the vagus nerve. This nerve runs from the brain to your face, to the thorax to the abdomen. And when it was severed it left her GI tract paralyzed that she can't keep food or liquids down she vomits them back up.

She has to keep going to the ER every 4-6 days to rehydrate and now they can't find a vein because of being so scarred. She was told today by the DR she will need to go on a feeding tube - she has prayed and will not be doing this. There is no cure! This is not the quality of life she wants. She will be going to the ER one last time & talking to her Dr next week to make arrangements to go on hospice. I am going to add her back into the family group text - please show major kindness. This is real. This is happening. She is dying, so any feelings you have for Marci that are unkindly pls keep them out of this and please know she needs your FULL love & support right now! This angers me that a surgeon has done this to our sister! This is a time if ever to come together as a family, unite together for each other & our beloved Mouse! Family I am in tears to soon lose our beloved Mouse.

Many of my siblings like Lymster began to reach out to me after they had received Chantelle's text. Lymster called me and we talked for an hour. He said concerned, "Is it okay if I am on the conference call with your doctor. I would like to record it to send to the family."

189

I replied, "Yes that would be fine."

He said, "I'm so sorry you're going through this sissy. I've been talking to my girlfriend who is an ER doctor and telling her about what you have been going through. She knows some doctors in Canada that specialize in motility disorders. I'm in the process of collecting information from her to try to help you."

I replied, "That is kind of you bro thank you. I will talk to you later. I'm feeling really sick and need to rest."

I hung up the phone and ran to the bathroom to vomit. I had a small bowel movement. What I had eaten a few hours ago I vomited back up. The laxative pill I had swallowed was now working. I could not have regular bowel movements without laxatives because of chronic dehydration. I broke down and cried. I was at my breaking point. I prayed that my doctor would put me on hospice.

That night was insufferable. I couldn't keep hydrated. I was excessively thirsty. I sipped on Gatorade, but I couldn't keep it down. I had watery diarrhea from the laxatives. My stomach and kidneys hurt from chronic dehydration. I tried to take over the counter pain medicine, but on an empty stomach it felt like stabbing pain. I was suffering in intense pain and feeling nausea for hours. I finally grabbed my heating pad to relieve my pain. I fell asleep exhausted from vomiting and diarrhea.

The sun's rays were beaming through the white blinds in my small room the next morning. I called my doctor to make an emergency appointment that day. I was determined to go to hospice and end this horrific nightmare. He agreed to see me and I called medical transportation to pick me up in a few hours.

When I arrived at my doctor's office they buzzed me in. They instructed me to wait in the waiting room. It had been a few months since I had seen my doctor in person. The COVID pandemic was still going on. Most clinical doctors were only seeing patients via phone appointments to avoid spreading the virus to other patients. I had already been tested three times for the virus in my visits to the ER. Luckily I tested negative for the virus.

A nurse approached me 10 minutes after my arrival at the doctor's office. She asked me to stand on the scale and she took my weight. I gasped when I saw my weight. I had lost 30 lbs since my last visit. This horrible disease was making me not only deathly dehydrated but malnourished as well. The nurse took my vitals. My BP was low and my heart rate was over a hundred. Not a good combination. The nurse told me nicely, "The doctor will be in soon."

I sat on the black chair in the doctor's office. My mind imagined what it would be like to be in heaven. I imagined a life pain free and only feeling joy. I couldn't stop smiling. But then my dreamy thoughts were interrupted by a calm voice, "Marci, did you hear me? You don't qualify for hospice."

My bleak, painful reality had returned. Dr. Randall had just uttered the most dreaded words of my life. I sat in his office and it was like I was in a trance. I called Lymster to join him in the conversation with my doctor. Lymster recorded the call. He was planning to send the recording to Chantelle and my mom to update them on the prognosis, but I didn't say a word during the call.

It didn't matter what was said. All I could think about was, "that I'm going to suffer longer. I'm

not going to heaven yet. I have to stay in this insufferable body for days, maybe weeks until my organs start to shut down from this painful incurable disease."

All I can remember from the conversation is Lymster asking Dr. Randall, "How did she get gastroparesis?"

191

Dr. Randall replied, "Both GI docs that have treated her are certain it was the vagus nerve that was severed during her multiple abdominal surgeries."

Lymster replied, "So it wasn't from the appendectomy only?"

Dr. Randal replied, "No, an appendectomy wouldn't do that. It was from multiple abdominal surgeries. But I am hopeful. I'm putting her on an antibiotic that I think could help with the vomiting."

Lymster said warmly, "Well, we are happy she isn't going to be in hospice. Thank you doctor for your time. Love you sis. I will send this recording to the family to let them know what was decided today. We will talk to you soon."

Dr. Randall hung up the phone and said to me happily, "I'm sending over this antibiotic to the pharmacy. I'm hopeful this should work. It's a liquid form so you can keep it down easier."

I replied, "What if it doesn't work?"

He replied hopefully, "I'm hopeful it will, but if not, I'm going to refer you to a motility specialist."

I walked out of his office and pushed open the steel doors to feel the warm sunshine on my face, but I was not hopeful. I had lost the will to live. Part of me wanted to dart out in front of a car to just end it all. I did not understand why God wanted me to continue to suffer just to survive. I cried out in sheer horror, "What do you want from me? Why do you want me here? Why don't you love me? I've been so faithful to you and this is how you treat me? If this is what it takes to get to heaven then it's not worth it. If you really love me then I need a miracle because I'm losing faith in you."

Chapter 19

God's Tender Mercies

*"There is nothing in this universe you need more desperately
than Christ." - R.C. Sproul*

July 2020

I am not going to lie. I was angry at God for days for keeping
me in my painful body. I had made the decision that if he wasn't
going to heal me, then I was going to let my body shut down
naturally. I could only survive on IV fluids.

I was determined to leave this diabolical, nightmare life. I
wanted to go to a place of peace and serenity. My faith was tested
greatly. I felt weaker and weaker from dehydration for six days. I
only allowed myself the bare minimum to drink. I couldn't bear
the pain of drinking a few sips of Gatorade causing nausea and
then vomiting.

I remember sitting in bed depressed to move or want to move.
I could feel my kidneys starting to shut down. I was barely peeing.
I could feel fluid building in my spine, in my ribs and upper back
close to my kidneys. I had made the firm choice not to go to the
ER for IV fluids. I couldn't bear the thought of being tortured by
one more IV in my poor, scared veins.

Meanwhile, Jared texted me and told me he was coming up to
the house to clean more stuff out of the house. He wanted to get
the house up for sale in a few months. I had stayed in close contact

with him about my decision to go to hospice. I texted him the terrible news: I didn't qualify for Hospice

Jared responded to my text: That is good news

Jared was my family. He had always been there for me. Especially, when my health had declined. He was concerned for my health. He and his sweet wife showered me with love.

Jared arrived the next day. He went about his business clearing out the house for a few days. He ran errands for me to buy Gatorade, apple sauce - the only food and liquids I was consuming. I was only taking a tablespoon of applesauce with my medication because the pills were getting caught in my throat when I tried to swallow them with liquids.

I remember feeling deadly ill the day Jared left to go back to Los Angeles, California. I felt delirium and intense pain from severe dehydration. I was so thirsty I was dying for a drink of water. But I couldn't keep a simple sip of water down to hydrate me.

I laid in the recliner chair in the living room. I felt the room spinning like a merry go round. I felt like at any moment I could faint. I looked up through what felt like a foggy haze and saw Jared next to me. He said kindly, "I don't want you to die. It concerns me that you want to die. When I met you were so vibrant and full of life. Now you are sick and losing the will to live. I know we all are supposed to die, that is part of living. But I can't watch you die yet. Please keep living. It isn't costing me much to have you stay here, maybe try going back to work for a day to see if you can. If you can't then I'm sure they will let you go and you can collect unemployment. If you work one day a week you can live until maybe the motility doctor can help you. You can keep staying here. You will always have a home until I sell the house."

195

I looked at this wonderful, kind man who loved me. I smiled and replied, "Okay I will keep going for you. I will go to the ER tonight and get IV fluids. I love you and you are my family."

He smiled and walked out the door to his big red truck. I watched him drive away to go back to Los Angeles. I said to myself, "God you do love me. Jared is my miracle from heaven."

God's tender mercies didn't stop there. I called medical transportation to take me to the ER at the trauma hospital I worked at. Since they had knowledge of my diagnosis of gastroparesis they were efficient in giving me plenty of IV fluids on my ER visits.

When the driver picked me up I stumbled out of his car and almost collapsed walking. Each step I took felt like I was climbing a huge mountain. I could barely feel my body anymore.

When I arrived at the ER the nurse immediately took my vitals. My BP was dangerously low and my pulse was 120. She walked me back to a room in the ER and told me to dress into a green gown laying on a small bed. I could barely lift my arms to undress.

I fell into the bed. My legs felt numb. I had no more strength to stand. A nurse dressed in blue scrubs entered the room with an ultrasound machine to start an IV. The medical staff knew me well at the ER and that I required an ultrasound IV. I looked at the huge needle about to pierce my tiny vein and I prayed to God, "Please let him get the IV on the first try. I can't handle the torture of being stuck again and again."

The nurse was earnestly trying to find a vein on my arm with the ultrasound machine, when a bald kind man entered the room. He said, "I was reading your chart. You have gastroparesis. I'm so sorry. Let's get you hydrated and get some blood work. I want

196

to make sure your kidneys are okay. I'm giving you some IV fluids, IV nausea meds and something for pain."

I felt a painful piercing in my left arm and I felt a sharp needle going in. The nurse said happily, "I got it in."

I looked at the IV placed firmly in my arm. I praised God for another miracle. I watched the IV fluids streaming through my veins. I felt dizzy and nauseated. I felt the cold fluids bringing my lifeless body back to life.

The rest of the night the medical staff treated me with compassion and understanding of my suffering. The doctor was concerned I wasn't peeing. My blood work showed my kidneys almost in failure again. He kept me in the ER to watch me to make sure my kidneys were normal again.

I was discharged from the ER the next morning. I felt groggy from the IV medications. When I called medical transportation to pick me up I almost fell asleep in the car. When the driver drove me home from the ER I don't remember more details.

I just remember when I came home I crawled into my bed and I had the most peaceful sleep I had in weeks. I felt God's arms tightly around me. I was pain free for those blissful hours of sleep.

I awoke later that night. I was hungry and thirsty. I felt like maybe I could eat something. I unrealistically hoped I could keep it down.

I was craving Chinese food. I anxiously ordered delicious Chinese food from my favorite restaurant. When the food was delivered I could smell it and almost taste it. I hadn't eaten real food in over a week. I was famished. I took a few bites. I tasted pure, heavenly joy.

But a few more bites and I felt nauseated. I couldn't finish my plate. I immediately vomited up most of what I had eaten.

The nightmare continued. This disease affected my quality of life indefinitely. I felt that it could take my life, but I just didn't know when. I knew without a shadow of a doubt that God loved me and wanted me in heaven soon.

I prayed to God, "Please give me strength to endure what I need to endure until I can finally be in heaven with thee and my dad."

I wish I could say that the next few weeks were blissful, but they weren't. They were some of the most difficult days of my life. My boss from the trauma hospital called me to tell me that I would need to come back to work by the following week or I would lose my job. I thought in a sheer panic, "How am I going to work when I'm vomiting and nauseated all the time."

I decided to try different foods to see if I could keep any of them down to get through a 12 hour day of work. I was unsuccessful in keeping fat down. But fish and cooked vegetables did feel better on my stomach. I only vomited a little. I drank tiny sips of water after my meals. They seemed to stay down better than when I drank with my meals. I doubled up on my nausea meds. I took them before I ate or drank liquids. It helped control the excessive vomiting and nausea.

I felt like I was making some progress, but I was severely depressed living with this painful, incurable disease. My primary doctor referred me to a psychiatrist. I had a phone consultation with the psychiatrist a few days later. But he did not bring me comfort.

He prescribed me two anti-depression meds that made me feel suicidal and crazy. I stopped taking them when I felt like I was hearing voices and hallucinating. I felt hopeless. I felt like I was just existing.

I woke up depressed to get out of bed. I was unhappy I was still alive and in pain. I had no reason to keep living. I prayed, "Please let me die."

I remember for days I felt like I wanted to run in front of a train or car. I wanted to swallow a bottle of pills. I wanted to die. I was upset at God that he was keeping me alive, sick and in excruciating pain. I prayed, "If you don't take me then I'm taking myself. You have given me more than I can handle. I'm done."

God knows how much we can handle. He knew that I was off my rope. He knew I was ready to end it if he didn't give me something to keep me going.

I received a text from Lymster the next morning: How are you feeling today?

I replied: Same no improvement

I instantly saw a FaceTime request from Lymster. I immediately answered it. I saw the most beautiful sight to behold. My wonderful brother was smiling and brought me instant joy that he cared about me to call me. We talked for hours. We talked about our childhoods and about our dad. We shared our hopes and dreams. I felt like me again before this sickness plagued my body. I laughed for the first time in weeks. I never wanted this feeling to end.

After we said our goodbyes I decided I needed to keep on living. I could never hurt my family, especially Lymster and end my life. I decided that I was going to keep living my life and have faith in God's plan for me. It was a scary thought to lose control and allow God to take the reins. I had never been able to completely trust him. But now I knew I couldn't survive without him.

I felt ripples of sadness the next day trying to endure Father's Day. I dreaded this day, since I had lost my dad seven years ago to a brain disease. I wanted to stay in bed and not think about my dad. It was too painful.

When I finally awoke in the late afternoon, I noticed multiple texts on my phone from family members paying tribute to my dad for Father's Day. It was beautiful and touching. I decided to share in the group family text the song my dad dedicated to us kids before he died by Cristy Lang `I'm with you tonight." I shared my love and memories of my dad with my family.

My mom called me within a few minutes of my sharing and we talked for an hour. I hadn't heard from her in days so it was a nice surprise. We had a pleasant conversation about my dad and the spirit world. It was one of the best conversations we have had in months. I felt like we were connecting as mother and daughter. It warmed my heart and I wished it could always be like this.

When I hung up the phone with my mom I listened to the song "I'm with you Tonight" by Cristy Lang.

I missed my dad deeply and needed to hear the comforting words from the song.

I'm With You Tonight

You won't feel my breath whispering in your ear

But I'm that little voice telling you I'm right here

You may not feel my arms wrapped around you tight But take comfort in knowing that I'm with you tonight Consider me your best friend always cheering you on Consider me the shoulder that

200

you can always cry on Don't look back on the past when the future is bright Take comfort in knowing that I'm with you tonight Hope your path is easy

Hope your skies are blue

You may never need me

but just in case you do

I will be the warmth inside one corner of your heart even though we may be miles and world apart

Your eyes may not a fix me in their sight

But take comfort in knowing that I'm with you tonight Take comfort in knowing that I'm with you tonight

Tonight

As I listened to this beautiful song I heard my dad whisper, "I'm right here."

I broke down in a puddle of tears. I knew my dad was watching over me from heaven. I smiled at heaven above. I felt that God had showered me with his heavenly love. I felt my room filled with God's light and peace. I have never felt so happy.

I remembered how my dad always felt joy even when he was sick. He never cursed God and wanted to die. He always embraced life and when I would ask him, "Dad how are you?"

He would reply, "A hundred percent with a thumbs up."

The month before he passed away it was his seventy third birthday at Chantelle's home in Utah. The disease had taken his speech and he had been unable to speak for a year. But he was still smiling. When I asked him, "Dad, how are you?"

He held up his weak thumb as if to say, "Hundred percent."

201

He always found joy in everything. He was a good example to me of being happy in his trials. I realized that maybe that was the missing piece of the puzzle before I died. To find joy in being sick. I knew in my heart of hearts I could die from this incurable disease. Maybe I needed to give joy to the world of light and love. Maybe I needed the world to know before I die that God loves us and wants us to be happy.

Chapter 20
My Trip To Heaven
"Jesus is the Light of the world" John 8:12

Prayers are like the highway to heaven. My prayers were now about God's will for me. I would pray, "What is missing? What do I need to do before I die? I'm ready to go, but I'm still here. I feel like I'm going to die soon. What do I need to do before I die."

The answers came slowly to my heartfelt prayer, but they did come. The rest of the week was one of the worst weeks of my life. I was unable to consume solid foods because it got stuck in my esophagus. I choked on the food vomiting. I could only drink fluids that came right back up too.

I was losing more hope every day that I would be healed from this crippling disease. I spent the next few days in bed. I was losing strength to lift myself out of bed. I had a high fever and chills. I couldn't stay hydrated. My stomach pain felt like a cramping dull ache. My kidneys felt like stabbing pain under my ribs and around the small of my back into my spine. I could feel the fluid build up in my spine. The pain was so unbearable that I took baths to try to relieve the pressure in my stomach and kidneys.

I slept for hours. I felt too feeble to move. I awoke late into the night. I clumsily walked into the kitchen to make me a smoothie of frozen peaches, skim milk and MiraLAX to give me a bowel movement. I took my medication with the smoothie and within 10 minutes I was vomiting. I cried out to God, "I can't do this anymore. I can't live day after day vomiting. How am I going to work? I'm too weak to get out of bed. I can't get married or take care of kids when I'm this sick. I have no quality of life. Please let me die."

I was looking lifeless and felt dizzy like I could faint. I heard a voice from my Dad, "It will be over soon. I promise."

I felt a rush of unconditional love and God spoke to me, "You have suffered long, but your suffering will end soon. Well done thou good and faithful servant."

I knew at that moment that I could die. I could be in heaven soon. I felt my body floating. I felt a rush of peaceful euphoria. I felt only an abundance of love.

I reflected on old memories that had brought me to this point in my life. I remembered when my dad became ill. He sat me down in the kitchen at my parents' condo and said, "If I have to die I'm going to haunt you and make you come back to church."

He did just that. He rescued me from an abusive relationship with Troy, my ex-boyfriend. He rescued me from almost taking my life twice. He had always been there for me from beyond the veil.

I thought to myself, "Was he meant to guide me to go to the other side? Was that the plan? Was I supposed to endure sickness and pain just to survive? Was this my last and final test? My dad endured great pain and suffering when he got sick. Now he is helping me get through my cross too. My sickness had brought our family closer. My mom and I have buried the hurt feelings of the past. We are becoming like mother and daughter."

I felt an overwhelming feeling that my sickness would keep our family bonded. I felt my dad nearby. My family and friends were still praying for a miracle, but I felt I would not be healed from this nightmare disease. I felt it would take me home to heaven very soon.

I had heard of people knowing that they are going to die close to when they do. I felt I was going to die closer than my family and friends anticipated. But I decided to live to the fullest while I was still here.

I was determined to keep running outside in the beautiful sunshine and go to the beach to soak up the sun's rays. I pressed on hoping for a miracle to be healed, but I continued to suffer day after day alone and hopeless. My life now was weekly visits to the ER at the trauma hospital, where I worked, to get IV fluids to rehydrate, from severe vomiting and diarrhea.

Then a bolt of lightning struck and the unexpected happened. The LDS missionaries from my church called me to see if there was anything they could do for me. They offered to give me a blessing when I shared with them my declining health. I accepted and they came by the next day to give me a blessing of comfort. "God loves you more than you can comprehend. He has a plan for you that you may not be able to understand. You will do the surgery. The doctors will be directed to know what to do during surgery and you will be healed."

After the blessing I was taken back by the blessing because I hadn't mentioned to the Elders that I was thinking of having surgery. I recalled in my mind the days I had spent in the trauma hospital when I was diagnosed with gastroparesis. The floor doctor mentioned a surgery that can be done called a neurotransmitter that is implanted into the lower abdomen to give shocks to the vagus nerve that has been severed. It relieves vomiting and nausea. I remembered after the doctor told me about it I researched its success online and a lady posted, "I had the surgery done and haven't vomited since."

My thoughts were interrupted by a voice, "Did you hear us, is there anything else you need.?"

I responded, "I text and called the Bishop a few weeks ago and left messages, but no reply. A few days ago I had to trek in the hot sun to go to the store for groceries. I couldn't keep hydrated. I vomited along the way, dehydrating me even more. I had to carry bags of groceries home, almost passing out. I need someone to pick me up from the store to take me home. My car broke down and I have no transportation."

The missionaries replied kindly, "We will reach out to the Bishop to help you."

I gave the missionaries a bag of fresh fruit from our beautiful orchard outside. I thanked them for coming to give me a blessing. All day, though, I received no call from the Bishop. To make matters worse, medical transportation services had stopped taking me to the ER because of the COVID - virus pandemic. Now I had no transportation to the ER to get my weekly IV fluids to keep me alive.

The next few days were insufferable. I was severely dehydrated and had terrible kidney pain. I decided I was tired of being in bed depressed. I was going to take my last breath in the beautiful sun. I made a beach day for myself on the patio. I laid on a long chair on my beach towel, my sunshades on, my suntan lotion glistening my tanned skin in the gorgeous sun. I ate what I wanted because I knew I would vomit anyway. I had a good day basking in the sun, drinking tiny sips of water to try to stay hydrated. This was my happy place. No one was going to take this moment from me.

The next morning, I was jolted back to my incorrigible reality. I was suffering from unbearable kidney pain. I had stopped voiding for 12 hours now. I felt my kidneys were in distress. My only option was to trek up 2 miles to the ER to get IV fluids. It was scorching hot outside. I was extremely dehydrated. I made it halfway to the ER by foot when I felt my whole body going numb. I felt my right cheek hit the hard cement with a giant thud. I had fainted. I heard a voice say, "Are you okay, do you want me to call 911."

I nodded yes. I don't remember more details except I heard voices around me trying to wake me up, but I could not respond. I was unconscious. I was in septic shock from the nasty fall, heat stroke and being deadly dehydrated. My liver was shutting down.

I remember the paramedics swarming around me rushing me to the ER. I kept going in and out of consciousness. The nurses, doctors and techs introduced themselves, but I could not respond back. I heard voices saying, "We are losing her. She is having a seizure. Her temp is 103 now."

I felt the voices keeping me in my body for a short time. But then I felt my body slipping more and more. My whole body went completely numb. I couldn't speak. I suddenly felt no pain. I didn't hear the voices around me anymore. I was out of my body and I saw the afterlife on the other side. I went to heaven.

I remember seeing a beautiful mirage of colors and clarity unlike anything in this world. It was like I was watching a 3D movie. The mirage opened to a mystical world of a beautiful yellow butterfly flying over my head. The image looked bright, glorious of dark green trees, tall brown mountains, green grass of valleys with glass blue water streaming down. I saw beautiful, angelic children dressed in white who were singing and dancing.

Then, I saw a bright light coming towards me brighter than the naked eye could see and it welcomed me to come to him. The light got closer and closer. I felt light as a feather. I was flying and what I experienced on my journey in heaven was God. I was pulled to this beautiful, radiant light. It was the Savior, Jesus Christ. There were no words spoken, only minds speaking to each other. I heard a soft voice that sounded like thunder, "Do you want to go?"

I immediately replied, "Yes I want to go."

I heard a soft voice reply, "You need to finish your second book."

I had never felt so much perfect love and acceptance in my life than from this striking light that spoke to me. I felt at home in his presence. I recognized him and felt how much he loved me. I felt my dad and other loved ones who had passed on. I felt they were all happy to see me. I didn't want to leave this perfect world of joy and peace. I had never felt happier in my entire existence on earth.

Then the beautiful light disappeared and I heard a voice, "Okay, Marci are you ready. She isn't responding"

I had seen patients being bagged before at the trauma hospital where I had worked, and it petrified me. I knew what was coming next. I finally responded and said, "No I have my rights. Don't bag me."

The doctor replied, "We got her back. It's okay."

I heard the Nurse respond bewildered, "How does she know that word?"

Slowly my body was coming back to reality. But I was not happy I was coming back. I wanted to stay in the beautiful, glorious and pain free mystical world, but now I knew my mission and why I was still here. I was to give this gift to the world by writing my second book "Just Passing Through On My Way to Heaven."

One of the nurses came into my room a half an hour later and said, "Wow, it's like you are a new woman. It's a miracle. We almost lost you."

Recovering from a deadly fall that almost took my life was not easy. I still couldn't believe I was alive. The doctors and nurses were overjoyed that I had been saved. They treated me with love and compassion. The doctor was concerned about my mental status and he admitted me to the hospital. I realized, when I felt my face with my soft hands, that I had a large bruise on my right eye from my nasty fall.

The doctor immediately ordered an MRI that showed a concussion and herniated disk on my L3 - spine. I was in excruciating pain. I felt like a huge semi-truck had crushed me. I was unable to get out of bed. I applied ice on my neck and back to relieve the screaming pain.

The doctor was concerned about my concussion. He wanted to keep an eye on me for a few days. He was kind enough to give me strong IV meds for my pain. When the doctor felt it was safe for me to go home I was discharged from the hospital.

The hospital called a taxi service to pick me up to take me home. I was still so out of it from the concussion and herniated disk in my back. I don't remember the taxi ride home. Everything felt like a blur. When the taxi service dropped me off at home I climbed into my soft bed covers and fell asleep.

I slept for a few days. I wasn't eating or drinking fluids. I was too weak to stand most days. I lay in bed until the pain was so severe in my kidneys and in my abdomen, I called for a taxi ride to take me to the ER.

When I finally arrived at the ER and the nurse took my vitals. I had tachycardia with a 140 pulse. Within a few minutes another nurse came racing out to take me to a room in the ER. She said, "Slip into this gown, I will be back to start an IV. Your blood pressure is really high."

I was shaking profusely. I couldn't stand it. I was too weak to undress myself into the plaid green gown laying on the tidy bed. Suddenly, the nurse came back in and helped me with my gown. I crawled into the cold covers on the bed, shivering.

The nurse thoughtfully brought in two warm blankets and wrapped them around me for warmth. I immediately felt the warm heat going into my cold clammy skin.

The nurse set up her IV ultrasound machine. She proceeded the dreaded process of starting an IV. I was so severely dehydrated that she was still unsuccessful after sticking me five times.

She left the room and told me, "Let me find someone who can try to get a vein,"

For the next hour the room was filled with doctors, nurses, ultrasound techs who tried to get an IV on me. But once again, to no avail. The doctor who treated me said, "I'm very concerned about your heart rate, it's too high. I could wait for the IV team in the morning to get an IV on you, but you could get worse and die if we don't get fluids in you. Your CT scan also showed that you have colitis - bacteria in your bowels. We need to get IV antibiotics in you. I'm going to do a central line in your thigh and admit you to the hospital"

The doctor was concerned and compassionate, while gently putting in the central line in my thigh. He talked me through it. He gave me lidocaine to numb my whole leg before inserting a long catheter in a large vein in my upper thigh. I could feel pressure in my leg when he stitched it up so that the catheter wouldn't come out.

I told him, "Thank you for being so gentle and kind."

He replied, "You did great. Very brave, now we can get some more blood, get some IV fluids, pain meds, nausea meds in you."

I smiled happily that the torture of being stuck over and over again was over. I could barely feel my body. I was weak and almost in cardiac arrest. The doctor ordered an IV fluids bolus to push IV fluids in me STAT. I was in the ER all night, until they could find a bed for me upstairs to admit me. I couldn't sleep. I felt nauseated.

In the early morning, the doctor wanted me to try some food and liquids to see if I could keep it down. My heart rate was coming down now that he was giving me round the clock IV fluids. The doctor gave me food and oral fluids. He was hopeful it would stay down and he could send me home, but I vomited as soon as I had a few bites of food and a few sips of liquid.

An hour later the nurse from upstairs on the third floor of the hospital came into my room with a wheelchair and kindly said, "We are going to admit you. I'm here to bring you upstairs."

She proceeded to collect my belongings and wheeled me upstairs. We were greeted by two nurses when she wheeled me into my new tidy room. I sat on the bed while the nurses proceeded to hook me up to a tele monitor to check my heart rate twenty-four seven.

The medical staff treated me with the utmost of respect and kindness. The nurse immediately gave me IV pain medication and nausea meds. She went over my list of medications I take at home, to be sure I was getting the proper dose of medications while in the hospital. She hooked me up to more IV fluids and said, "Your potassium is low. Take these potassium tablets. And we are giving you a bolus of IV fluids to rehydrate you."

The nurse left the room to attend to other patients. I looked around the room and a feeling of warmth came over me. The hospital had become like my second home. I was being admitted almost weekly for severe dehydration and malnutrition. I felt so alone with no one to sit with me and talk to me. I had caring doctors and nurses who took good care of me, but I needed my family support.

My brother Lymster was my new go to guy. He texted me almost every day to see how I was doing. My mom texted me a few times, too. I felt my dad close by, and that was all I needed to endure one more day with this debilitating disease. I had accepted that this was my life. It didn't matter how much my loved ones and friends wanted me to get a feeding tube to endure more days I couldn't do it. I had lost the will to live. I knew one day my body would shut down and release me from this pain and suffering.

My friend who is a nurse told me a few days ago in a text: Marci this is absolutely heartbreaking. I've only known you for a short time. In that time you've gone from energetic and vibrant to one

of the sickest people I've known. I'm so very sorry this has happened to you! And all from an appendectomy?"

She was right. This incurable disease had stolen everything from me. I was too weak to work at the trauma hospital anymore. I was too dehydrated to run miles like I used to without passing out and getting a concussion - like what had happened to me a few days ago. I had to go to the hospital every week and stay a few days to get rehydrated. I had no quality of life and I was severely depressed.

212

But God still wanted me here for a reason, because the suffering didn't end. I felt like a shackled prisoner in my own body. "How much longer could I endure this alone and so sick that it hurts to breathe? When would God finally call me home as he had promised to do in so many visions I had when I went to heaven? When would I be truly happy again?" I thought to myself.

Meanwhile I stayed in the hospital for four days for IV fluids and antibiotics for my colitis. I was feeling so ill and weak that I didn't get out of bed other than to go to the restroom. The doctors put me on a full diet to see if I could tolerate it with nausea meds, but I vomited everything I consumed.

I was sick, nauseated and in unbearable pain. The doctor on my floor decided to put me on a liquid diet, in hopes I could keep that down with strong nausea meds, but my esophagus was filled with stomach acid from vomiting and it burned. The doctor gave me some pain medicine and anti-acid pills. I stopped eating or drinking anything shortly after. I only ate jello to take with my medication. I was exhausted of being in pain and nauseated every time I tried to eat or drink anything

The doctor came into my room the next day bearing bad news, "There isn't much else we can do for you. You won't accept a feeding J-tube."

My mind was racing with terrible thoughts of what the future held if I accepted this J-tube of doom. I envisioned weeks and weeks tethered to this IV pole in the hospital, alone and hopeless for better days. My happy days in the warm sun at the beach and running outside feeling the soft breeze kiss my cheeks, would be over. The thought of this kind of life terrified me to my very core.

I heard a voice interrupted by my nightmare of thoughts, "Did you hear me Marci? There is nothing more we can do for you without a J feeding tube. You won't eat anything and your potassium levels are low."

I replied, "I would rather die than live with a feeding tube."

I watched the doctor leave my room to start the papers to discharge me. I felt sad to leave and be alone once again to start the process of feeling too sick to get out of bed; to endure chronic dehydration from chronic vomiting, but the alternative horrified me worse. I thought to myself, "I'm not going to live through this disease. This disease will take my life.

Chapter 21

God's 5 Miracles

"Only God Can Make A Way Where There Seems To Be No Way" Don Moen

August 2020

God is a god of miracles. I prayed for a miracle a day for five days if God still wanted me here to publish my second book. I had already started writing it before my near-death experience. My Mission President had encouraged me to write it, but I didn't know how to end my book at the time.

After my near-death experience, when I went to heaven and met the Savior, I was told I could go when I wrote my second book, "Just Passing Through On My Way To Heaven."

I finished my book while in the hospital. My trip to heaven added beautifully to the ending of my book. I finished what the Savior had asked me to do. My book was ready to be published on Amazon soon. I now wanted to go be with my dad and the loving, beautiful light I felt in heaven. But I felt conflicted to go just yet. I recalled all the fond memories I had experienced here on earth and all the wonderful people I had met along the way.

I felt tears trickling down my chin of sad thoughts that I would not see my loved ones if I died. I was longing for the joyous reunion with my dad and loved ones who had passed. I cried and cried. I couldn't endure my life of sickness any longer. I made the firm decision to stop all treatments, no longer go to the ER for IV fluids or get a feeding tube just to survive. I was ready to die and say goodbye to loved ones.

But I felt a need to make mistakes right before I died. I needed to make amends to family members I may have hurt or hurt me along my path of life. I knew that I had to forgive them before I could feel at peace to go. I knelt on my knees and prayed to forgive everyone who had hurt me or judged me.

I wanted to be more like my Savior. He forgave even those who judged him, spit on him and crucified him. I knew I would never reach his pure Christlike love in this life, but I had never felt closer to Christ than these past eight months of my terms of endearment bearing my own cross.

I also posted on FB a post saying goodbye to my beloved Facebook family: My amazing dad has been my rock through the worst 8 months of hell of being so sick I can barely get out of bed now. My dad has been there to hold my hand through it all alone and scared to endure another day of pain and suffering, but my health is declining more every day. I almost died when I fainted and went unconscious. I went to heaven. I saw heaven in all its glory, and it was amazing. I was told I needed to finish my second book and then I could go.

My last visit to the hospital the doctor told me that I'm malnourished, and my potassium levels are low. He told me without a feeding tube I will die. I've stopped eating and drinking. The pain is just too severe to vomit one more day. I've been strong through this, but there are some things a person can do and some they can't live with. I can't live the rest of my life with a feeding tube and enduring it alone. I feel peace about it. I've been to heaven and now I'm ready to go be with my dad. I just finished my book "Just Passing Through On My Way to Heaven"

After I sent the post my mind raced back to the blessing from the missionaries I had received a week before my near-death experience, when I went to heaven. At the time the blessing gave me zero comfort when it told me I would heal from surgery. I wanted to die. I didn't believe I would be healed, but now I couldn't stop thinking about it.

I was feeling conflicted if I did want to die. I was crying thinking of so many loved ones I would leave in this journey of life. At the same time, I felt those from the other side calling me home. I felt it was now my decision to go or stay. I prayed for another miracle if God wanted me to stay awhile longer.

I suddenly received a FB message, Miracle 1, from a sweet man on FB: Marci, I am so sorry for all that you are suffering. I purchased your first book. It's wonderful! If you are looking for a cover image for your second book I'm happy to provide one at no charge. If so, message me and I'll send you my contact info.

When I received his message I cried and responded to his message: I'm so happy you liked my book. Yes, I would love a cover for my second book. I'm too sick to get out much more with my health declining. My editor is my angel from heaven and was my inspiration for my second book. She is doing all she can to get it published before I pass on. I would love to see it published on Amazon before I go. Thank you for your kindness. It means the world to me. You are my miracle from heaven. This wonderful man and I spent a few days designing a beautiful cover for my second book.

Meanwhile, I also sent heartfelt texts to family members saying my last goodbyes to them. I thanked them for opening their homes to me in the past while I was sick during my multiple surgeries. My sister-in-law Tally responded to my text the same day - Miracle 2: Thanks for the text. I'm sorry you are so sick. I don't want you to be alone. Will you come up to Spokane and stay with us?

I almost fell off of my bed when I received the text. My brother Levi called me and said, "We want you to come stay with us in Spokane and then go to Utah for Mackenzie's wedding. But if you have to go to the ER every week that won't work. We could fly you out to Utah for the wedding and pick you up at the airport."

I was beaming with joy. I said, "Yes! But I can only stay a few days because I'm so sick. I can go to the ER the day before to get fluids. I may be okay to fly to make the trip."

He said, "Okay let's book the flight. Call me tomorrow."

I hung up the phone. God had just provided me with another miracle. I thought to myself, "Only God can create a Way Where There Seems To Be No Way." For the first time in months I fell asleep without crying myself to sleep.

The next morning I woke up feeling optimistic, but once again vomiting sips of water. The pain and nausea continued. I desperately wanted to go to the store to buy jello. When I was in the hospital I kept tiny bites of jello down taking my medication for nausea and cramping pain. But I was out of funds now, not working for so long. I was also in need of essential items like contact solutions and other grooming supplies. I felt so hopeless that I prayed for another Miracle.

I felt after I prayed that I should create a GoFundMe page on FB for people to donate funds to me to be able to survive, especially if I did have the surgery. It's an invasive surgery and I would be unable to work or lift over 15 lbs for 8 weeks. I felt I should send the link to close friends via text message and on FB.

This was my GoFundMe post:

"I have lost the will to live. I am so ready to die. But, in my recent near-death experience when I went to heaven I saw a bright light and met the Savior. He asked me if I wanted to go and I said, "Yes." He told me I needed to write my second book. "Just Passing Through On My Way To Heaven." I just finished writing my first book "Rescued In Heavens Eyes", published on Amazon. I feel like I need to be here a while longer to publish my second book. I prayed for a miracle if God wanted me to stay to publish it.

My wonderful sister-in-law Tally contacted me and told me she didn't want me to be alone anymore. She and my amazing brother Levi could possibly fly me to Utah for 3 days to see my beautiful niece get married Aug 20. I can stay with family and be able to see close friends, relatives, who are so dear to me. They texted me and called me crying that I just wanted to die. After I got Levis' call, he offered to help me. I am giving it one more fight to know I tried everything to beat this incurable disease.

God told me in a blessing that the surgery will cure me. I need another miracle. I have endured 14 abdominal surgeries including my last surgery, an appendectomy that severed my vagus nerve paralyzing my G.I. tract. It caused a motility disorder called gastroparesis, that caused excessive vomiting and nausea. I'm unable to keep anything down. I have suffered with this motility disorder for eight long months. I have been unable to work and even care for myself at this point living alone. I make constant weekly visits to the ER for severe dehydration and malnutrition. My weekly visits are now turning into hospital stays for kidney injuries, low potassium for severe dehydration.

On my last hospital stay a week ago the doctor told me that I would need a feeding tube or that I could possibly die without one, because of malnutrition. There are some things a person can do, and God knows I can't live like this.

219

I prayed and prayed. I felt as said in my blessing that if I received surgery then I would be healed.

When I was in the hospital the doctor told me about a surgery that could be done to help my terrible painful symptoms of nausea and vomiting. It's called gastric electrical stimulation. It is a device that is surgically implanted into the abdomen to deliver electrical pulses to the nerve and muscles of the lower part of the stomach. This stimulation may reduce chronic nausea and vomiting. I looked online at the success of the surgery. A lady posted that she had the surgery done and she has not vomited since.

The surgery is excessive. I will not be able to work or even lift anything over 15 pounds for eight weeks. I talked to my doctor about the surgery. We are in the process of trying to get my 15th surgery done as soon as possible. I have had so many wonderful people help me through this excruciating painful disease, but I need more help. I am unable to work because I am too sick now and getting worse. To make matters worse my car broke down. I have no transportation to go to the ER. I would need to call 911 every week and that's just not feasible.

I tried to walk to the ER to get fluids but I ended up fainting. I went unconscious. I almost died with a terrible concussion and heat stroke followed by septic shock. I am so dehydrated when I go to the ER that I have almost gone into cardiac arrest a few times. The doctor told me if I don't get IV fluids I will die.

I have no other option than to go to the ER to get IV fluids - because I'm severely dehydrated from chronic vomiting. At the ER the nurses use an ultrasound to get an IV. The whole process is so painful and sometimes unbearable - because they have to dig for a larger vein that won't blow.

I'm continuing this torturous process to live to publish my sequel book and stay a little longer for loved ones. I need financial assistance for funds for Lyft rides to the ER. I haven't been able to work in 8 months when I had a lumpectomy for a mass removed. It caused one complication after another including hematoma, pulmonary embolism, and appendicitis. I had two surgeries within three weeks that my surgeon told me had put too much trauma on my body, causing my health to decline more.

I am also two months behind in my cell phone bill that they have been generous to work with me but they cannot do it much longer without a payment. I need money to live and not working now. I need your help and prayers please. Thank you from the bottom of my heart."

I spent all day creating the GoFundMe page. I missed my opportunity to go to the store for jello and Gatorade. Luckily, I had been blessed with a Cal fresh EBT card for food stamps for $300. A true blessing from heaven.

But the 3rd miracle happened at 11pm. I received a message from my Venmo Account that my dear sweet friend Lori had just donated $100 to my Venmo account. When I received the text I cried and immediately sent her a reply text: I know it's late so I didn't call you. But I'm weeping that you donated again, you have no idea what you just did. I've been crying because I don't have money to buy a contact solution anymore, so I had to sleep in my contacts last night. I prayed and prayed. I felt I should send close friends to my GoFundMe page. God gave me the miracle I asked for- you. I can't wait to give you the biggest hug when I see you in Utah in two weeks. You are one of the most Christlike people I know. God bless you my dear friend.

I went to bed that night optimistic to press on to live a little longer. But the next few days everything fell apart. My brother Levi called to tell me, "We can't fly you out to Utah for Makenzie's wedding anymore, We don't think you can make the busy trip being so sick. I'm sorry."

I was sad at first when I received the news, but after we hung up the phone I went to the restroom to pee. It was a dark brown color. I hadn't eaten or drank anything in four days. I was dangerously dehydrated. I tried to eat and drink again. I just vomited and vomited with diarrhea. I felt so hopeless. I can't win. I wanted so desperately to go to Makcnzic's wedding. My beautiful niece was getting married. I wanted to see her and rejoin my loved ones again. It didn't matter what I wanted, though. My body was not healing and I'm ready to die." I thought to myself.

I remember waking up the next morning feeling gloomy and depressed to still be living. I had checked out emotionally. I was ready to die of dehydration and malnutrition. I stayed in bed until the late afternoon. I was physically drained from vomiting last night. My insides ached. I was hopeless to go on. I was severely dehydrated. I laid in bed in a trance to fight one more day. I prayed for a miracle to keep going if God wanted me to keep surviving this life-threatening disease.

God blessed me with a 4th miracle, and he gave me a big one. I received a FB message from a lady from FB: Hey sweet friend. Please post a pic of your cell phone bill here and I'll pay it for you.

I was in shock by this FB message that I replied: Are you kidding me this is way and above beyond?

I received her loving reply: No, I'm not kidding. You need your phone. Please send me a pic and I'll pay for it.

I replied: I'm speechless of your charity and kindness. Thank you for being my angel from heaven.

222

She replied: God bless you and keep you in His care! I'm so glad this small gesture gives you hope. Sometimes that's all we need. I was just listening to God. He told me to pay your phone bill for you. He's so good every day.

I cried and cried. God had given me hope to endure another day. The following day Miracle 5 happened. I was dehydrated and feeling very sick. I needed to go to the hospital to get IV fluids, but I had no funds to take a taxi service to be seen. I laid in bed most of the day, weak from dehydration. I felt hopeless to rehydrate myself. I woke up at 5 pm to a message on my phone that two people on FB, my two dear friends, had just donated $20 each through the GoFundMe page. Their kind gesture gave me enough money to go to the ER. I thanked God for the 5 miracles he had given me that week and rescued me through his earthly angels. I prayed with tears of gratitude. It gave me hope to fight another day.

Chapter 22

My Second Trip to Heaven

"God's Plan for Me" Marci Zollinger

July 2021

I woke up in a sheer panic. So much time had passed. and I was definitely not healing. I reflected back through my life to the past year. I had endured more pain and suffering than I could imagine one person could endure. The painful, incurable disease that plagued my body had taken control of my life. I felt like I was a prisoner in my own body. I was still unable to keep liquids or solids down. I was now in the hospital every 4 days literally fighting for my life severely dehydrated and malnourished from chronic vomiting causing my kidneys to shut down.

To fuel this fire I was discouraged that my Primary Doctor wouldn't release me to go back to work. But he couldn't because now I was basically living in the hospital. My boss from my work was disheartened to let me go from the trauma hospital I had been employed at for a year before I became deathly ill. She told me on the phone "It breaks my heart. You did nothing wrong, but it's been a year now. We can't keep you on staff anymore without a physician's release."

I had just lost my dream job and any chance of finishing school to be a Registered Nurse. I was so depressed feeling my life was slipping away. I was living in San Diego, CA. One of the most beautiful places in the United States. But I was too sick to enjoy going to the beach. Going out for a nice dinner without vomiting.

To make matters worse I was battling this painful incurable disease alone.

My family tried their best to help me however they could. But I needed help with grocery shopping and picking up my medication at the local pharmacy. I needed a shoulder to cry on. I prayed to God, "Please send me an angel to help me."

God answered my prayers. A week later my friend Lisa came to visit me. We met on Facebook and became good friends. Thanksgiving Day arrived a few weeks later. I was so disheartened I was spending this joyous holiday alone again. Lisa could sense my melancholy through texts we had shared that week. She surprised me and brought over some friends from her singles ward from our church to cheer me up. I wanted to be a good host so I cooked yummy frozen pizzas for them. I could smell the sandy ocean on their clothes from being at the beach all day. They were famished. and scarfed down the pizza.

I was so overjoyed I wasn't alone on Thanksgiving. I relished in meeting all four of these wonderful people. They brought a ray of sunshine in my dark world that night. We laughed and talked for most of the night. It felt so nice to be around people again.

We instantly connected. I became close friends with one of the guys, Travis. He was a tall, good looking guy with sandy hair. He was so easy to talk to. He was one of the kindest men I had met in a while. He would come visit me twice a week. He brought me my medication from the Pharmacy. He picked me up from the local store so I could buy my groceries.

I adored Travis. He adored me. We enjoyed hanging out with each other. He treated me with kindness and respect. I felt like the real me with him. I was coming alive again as the carefree, self-assured, feisty, spiritual, kind-hearted woman I had hid for so many years in my six year abusive relationship with Troy. It felt

225

so good to shed my broken shell. To shine through with light and beauty.

But Travis was not the only angel Heavenly Father had brought into my life. Jared, my landlord and I had formed an unbreakable bond. He would come to the house to clear more stuff in the basement. He was getting ready to put the house up for sale soon. I was in awe of the charity his family continued to show me. He allowed me to stay in the house for free as a house sitter until he sold the house. I knew without a doubt Jared and his family were true angels sent into my life. They were meant to help me endure this hellish lengthy illness. Jared always reassured me, "You will always have a home here. We don't want you to die, we are praying for a miracle."

Jared and his altruistic family were not alone in their tireless prayers for me. My family and close friends, including Facebook Friends, were praying that I would heal. But each passing day I wasn't healing. I felt so hopeless. One night I poured my soul and prayed to God, "Please heal me or take me. I can't live like this anymore."

But the next morning I took a sip of water with a cup of soup. I immediately vomited it back up. God was definitely not healing me. My family and close friends were concerned about my declining health. They encouraged me to get a blessing. I asked Travis to give me the blessing. He accepted. He came over a few hours later. He gave me the most beautiful blessing of comfort. In the blessing Heavenly Father told me I would pass on, "Heavenly Father loves you. He is pleased with you and your faith in him. Your pain and suffering will end. You will be healed in the Lord's way. As time progresses those beyond the veil and your family here will help you transition to go to the other side. There is a lot of work to be done on the other side. You will be a beacon of light for others through your example. You will bring others closer to Christ. Have patience that you will go on the Lord's time and in the Lord's way."

226

When I received that beautiful blessing from my loving Heavenly Father I knew that I was going to die. I didn't know how or when I would pass on, but I knew in my heart it would happen soon. I had a close call the following month. I remember the day vividly when my heart almost stopped. My chest was hurting. I could barely breathe. I was severely dehydrated. My heart was racing. I called 911.The paramedics arrived at my house 10 min later. I felt dizzy like I would faint. I could barely feel my body. I could feel myself going unconscious.

The paramedics helped my weak body onto the yellow stretcher. I took a few steps and my legs buckled under. The paramedics caught me before I hit the ground. I was too weak to stand. I heard a loud siren sound and a voice on the speaker in the ambulance, "We are bringing in a potential heart attack patient."

It was like I was not in my body. I felt myself lifting. I had no awareness of my surroundings. I just felt myself lifting higher and higher. When the ambulance arrived at the local hospital the medical team helped me into a green gown laying on the steel bed in the ER. My amazing high was gone when one of the nurses was sticking me over and over again to get an IV, but to no avail. I was screaming in pain after the fifteen stick and said, "No more. I would rather die."

The nurse exited my room. A tall, dark-haired doctor came into my room 5 min later. He looked very concerned. He said to me, "We need to do a chest port. We can't get an IV. You need IV fluids STAT or you could die. The IR team is coming in a few minutes to take you to the IR to place the chest port."

Five minutes later I saw a kind man in blue scrubs open the glass door to my room. He wheeled me to the IR room in the hospital. An older gentleman in blue scrubs and a blue surgical cap covering his head smiled at me. He said with a soothing tone,

"We are going to place a chest port. You should feel pressure but not pain. We will give you something to relax you so you don't feel pain."

Suddenly I felt an euphoric feeling. I felt pressure like the doctor said, but I didn't feel any discomfort. The last thing I can recall is being back in my hospital bed with a huge bandage on my chest and neck. I pulled the bandage down. I gasped when I saw the incision on my neck that the doctor had made to insert the catheter into my clavicle in my right chest. I was in insurmountable pain. I shakily pressed the red button on the call light next to me to request pain medicine from the nurse. A few minutes later a beautiful lady dressed in blue scrubs administered pain medicine through my chest port. I immediately felt pain relief. I drifted off to sleep.

I awoke to Jared's text: I'm worried about you, Haven't heard from you since you texted me you called 911

I told Jared what had happened to me via text: I am severely dehydrated. I almost died because they couldn't get an IV. They put in a chest port to get IV fluids in me. I'm now living with a chest port for survival.

He replied to my text: I'm going to write a letter to your family and inform them of your poor health. Maybe they can come out and help you, especially your mom. I've prayed for a miracle. But it's been 16 months. You're still not healed. I'm facing the painful fact that you could possibly die.

A few days later I was discharged from the hospital in the early afternoon. Jared picked me up from the hospital. He wanted to make sure I was okay. He was very concerned that my family was not here to help me. Jared said to me when I climbed into his shiny red truck, "I sent the letter to your mom via e- mail."

I said, "Thank you. So thoughtful of you."

Later that day when I was taking a nap at home I received a call from my mom. She said frantically, "I read Jared's e- mail. Can I talk to Jared?"

I handed Jared my phone and he turned on the speaker so I could listen. He said to my mom, "I have seen your daughter at her best and her worst for 16 months now. Before this happened she was working full time. Training for the San Diego Marathon. Spending her days at the sandy beach. She was vibrant and full of life. Then out of nowhere poof this happened. Now I've seen her look worse than death. This is real and it's bad."

My mom replied, "Thank you for letting me know. This is just so sad. You are the greatest Christian taking in my daughter like you have."

Jared replied, "Well she is helpful for us as well. She brings up the value of the house. She has been a wonderful house sitter for my family until we can sell the home. She is very clean. We enjoy having her in the home."

My mom said, "Well I want to meet you. I am trying to figure out a way to fly out to see you and be with Marci."

Jared replied, "I know that Marci would love that."

When Jared hung up the phone with my mom he said to me happily, "Well now we have opened a door for your mom to come see you."

The next morning Jared packed up his things.to go back to LA. He walked to his shiny red truck in the gravel driveway. He pulled the silver handle to his truck and climbed in the black leather driver seat. He gave me a warm hug and said, "Hang in there kiddo. See you in a few weeks."

I watched his tires skid on the driveway driving down the gravel hill. I saw a beautiful yellow butterfly fly by and landed on a red rose in the front garden. I looked at the huge acre lot all around me of fresh fruit growing on the trees. I wanted to pick the fruit and eat it. But fruit was the enemy for my digestive system. When I ate it in the past I would get nauseated. The acid would burn my throat when I vomited it up in chunks almost choking.

I recalled the day I was sitting in my bed at the hospital feeling so sick from dehydration and malnutrition from chronic vomiting. I had a cannula in my nose to help me breathe. My kidneys were failing again. I cried out to my dad for comfort. I heard a soft voice whisper, "We are all right here."

I felt the entire room filled with angels from the other side. I felt my cousin Ryan, my Grandpa Z, Grandma Z and other loved ones who had passed on. I started to cry. I felt a warmth in my heart that heaven was cheering me on. It gave me strength to continue to endure what it was I needed to conquer to graduate to the next life.

Although I had these comforting angels in my life, I didn't understand why God continued to allow me to suffer. I was physically and mentally exhausted from fighting one more day. I felt like I was just existing. Family members would send me pictures and videos of them vacationing with their families. It gunned me. It felt like my heart was breaking into a thousand pieces. I said to myself with tears streaming down my face, "I am alone and will be for the rest of my life."

I remember one night I felt so alone. I was so sick in bed. I was nauseated from vomiting all night. I felt hopeless to go on. I cried out to Heavenly Father in heartfelt prayer with sobbing tears, "Why did you take the gift of having my own children away from me? Why am I on this earth to never be blessed with a family to love and nurture in this life? I need some answers for me to continue to endure this lengthy and painful trial."

Later that same night I had a burning high fever. My right kidney felt like thousands of knives stabbing me. I could feel my kidneys failing again. My heart rate was 140. I felt like I was having a heart attack. I was in excruciating pain. I grabbed my right chest with my weak trembling hand. I tried to move my body to reach for my iPhone to call for help. I couldn't feel my body. I could feel my soul (spirit) slowly lifting from my body. I felt light as a feather flying like the speed of light to a white curtain of a veil that opened into heaven.

Suddenly, I was pain free flying above. With every glimpse of heaven I felt a rush of joy I had not experienced in my 50 years on earth. I saw the golden pearly gates. I saw a windy road paved of gold with huge mansions. Inside one of the mansions was a beautiful, blonde hair, angelic child. She was smiling at me. Her smile spoke to my heart and to my soul. I felt the Savior, Jesus Christ close by. He conveyed to my mind that this mansion was being prepared for me. He told me that the beautiful, angel child that looked 4 years in age was mine to have. I saw ordinary people working on the gold streets planting flowers in God's kingdom. The clarity and colors of the flowers were exquisite beyond anything in this world. I saw two large marble brown steps leading to God's huge throne of brass. Jesus' brass throne was on the right side of Heavenly Father's throne.

A glorious bright light appeared. A beautiful Heavenly being walked towards me. It was Jesus. Every fiber of my being shedded tears of joy being in his presence. He had on a white robe covering his head with a striking light around him that drew my soul to his. I saw him through spiritual eyes.

231

In heaven I was who I was in the pre- existence when I knew him. I walked with him. I talked with him. My spirit longed to be there with Jesus. I didn't want to leave. I was home in heaven. Jesus was magnificent in every way. I couldn't believe I was seeing the beautiful being I loved so dearly. I could feel his unconditional love wash over me like a perfect rainstorm - pouring into my heart and soul.

Then everything went black. I saw the devil and his demons in hell. He is pure evil. He looked scarier than anything I had seen in movies. He had no body and no soul. I felt fear in his demonic presence. If people saw what I saw they would never follow him. Then hell and the devil vanished. Jesus' glowing white light appeared again. I was comforted by his presence. Jesus shared with me that Satan wasn't allowed to be around his light. He told me, "There are those angels in heaven who carry this light. Others are drawn to their light. The light brings others joy and peace."

I felt an overwhelming love from the Savior that he knew what I was going through. He had sweated blood and tears for me in the garden of Gethsemane. I felt no judgment. But I felt he only wanted to hold me in his arms through my mountain of trials. I felt that no one could ever love me more than Jesus. I asked Jesus," I'm I going now? Am I crossing over permanently and that's why I've seen glorious heaven?"

When I spoke to Jesus he did not speak to me with his lips but through our minds. He said kindly, "No it's not time yet. You need to go back and share this with others. Then you will go."

Suddenly just like magic poof the veil and Jesus disappeared. My fever was gone. My kidney pain and chest pain were evanescent. I had been healed. I was mesmerized by what I had just seen in heaven.

I realized that my Heavenly Father had answered my prayer. My second trip to heaven brought more clarity and peace than I had felt in years. I knew why I had never been given the gift of bringing a beautiful baby into this world; to have a wonderful family of my own. When I saw the angelic child in my beautiful mansion I knew from Jesus that whatever I had not received in this life I had earned in the next life. Joy filled my heart and soul of the amazing blessings that God had in store for me beyond the veil.

God revealed to me in a blessing I received two years ago before I became ill, "You have important work to do."

I didn't know what that meant until now. I realized I wouldn't have written this book if I hadn't been single and lost my ability to have children. Or I wouldn't have had my first NDE (near death experience) followed by months later experiencing an awestruck, second NDE. A moment of feeling more joy and love beyond anything that I had felt in my whole life.

God revealed to me in heaven the map of his plan for me. Now I was not afraid to die. I wanted to move on to the next chapter of my life in heaven. Jesus wants my story to be told. I know now without a shadow of a doubt my Heavenly Father is preparing me to die.

September 2021

Three months have gone by. My family is 700 miles away. No one in my family had come to pay me a visit in the 19 months since I had been sick with gastroparesis. I could feel myself becoming deadly ill. When I tried to express the severity of my illness to my family they replied, "You have been playing the death card for 19 months now and you're still here. We just don't believe it will happen."

233

I, like my family, was growing tired of hearing my own voice, "I'm going to die." I began to doubt it myself. I remember the day so clearly when I cried out to God in pouring tears, "I'm done. I can't live alone anymore and be so sick too. I feel myself doubting my faith in you. I feel you just want me to suffer. I believe as my family believes. I don't believe I'm going to die from this illness. I'm taking my own life this week if you don't take me. I don't want to go this way, but you have given me too much to bear. I'm done."

God had tested my faith to the limit. I had been alone, losing myself, to a debilitating, incurable illness for 21 months now. But now my reward of keeping faithful was about to be evident.

The week following, I was only keeping small bites of jello down. I had been vomiting everything else I tried to eat or drink. I was slowly becoming weaker and weaker. I was exhausted from my weekly routine visits to the ER for dehydration and malnutrition. I wanted to see if I needed my weekly hospital stays.

It had been 8 days since I had stepped foot in the hospital. I remember feeling like the room was spinning like a merry go round. I wanted to get off this ride, but I couldn't because I could barely see straight. I felt like I was drunk as I arose off the recliner chair in the living room.

The room was spinning more and more. I clumsily took a few steps to turn off the dining room light to go to bed. I wanted to curl up in the covers of my warm bed and go to dreamland.

The room was pitch black. I was laying on the cold aluminum floor in the living room on the left side of my body. I couldn't move. I was numb from the waist down. I could not see a phone to call for help. I panicked. I realized that I had fallen and blacked out.

When I fell it was light inside the house. Now it was dark. I tried to move onto my elbows towards my bedroom to call 911 But, I couldn't see the hallway. I was too weak to try to muddle my way in the dark. I fell unconscious for another few hours. When I came to it was light outside. I felt a seizure of pain rush through my body. I knew if I didn't try to make it to my room for help, I could die. Part of me wanted to just lay there and pass on. But the other part of me felt like, "It's not time yet. But soon." I prayed with all the courage I could muster. "Please give me the strength to call 911."

I pushed my body up onto my right elbows. I reached to unlock the glass wooden door outside to the living room. I pulled myself down onto the aluminum floor pushing on my elbows. I was sliding my body towards my bedroom. It felt like this long journey would never end. I felt so tired. I was profusely sweating down my back. I finally reached my bedroom. I scrambled for my phone on my nightstand to call 911. I heard a voice, "911 what is your emergency?"

I replied, "I fell and blacked out. I'm on the floor. I can't walk, I can only move my arms. I'm numb from the waist down. I unlocked the outside door in the living room for you to come help me in my bedroom."

I heard a concerned voice say, "Help is on the way."

I lay on the cold wooden floor in my bedroom helpless to move. I heard voices 10 min later. "Hello, where are you?"

I yelled, "In here. In my bedroom down the hall."

Suddenly a yellow stretcher came barreling in my room and two dark haired gentlemen dressed in a dark blue shirt labeled "Paramedics" arrived and lifted me up onto the stretcher.

I had no feeling in my legs. It scared me to no end. The red ambulance lights were moving quickly to race me to the local hospital. When we arrived at the hospital I was carried onto a steel bed by the two paramedics. A kind nurse in dark blue scrubs entered the room. She helped me into a green gown. She immediately took my vital signs. She accessed my chest port drawing labs. She covered me with two cozy warm blankets.

Twenty minutes later an older doctor entered the room and said, "Miss Zollinger, I'm the attending physician. Your labs show that your white blood cell count is 40,000. A normal WBC is 100. Your liver is shutting down. It's attacking your muscle cells on your left leg. It's filling your leg with fluid. We are going to do a MRI on your left leg to see what is going on. From the report the paramedics gave us you were unconscious for 7 hours. Your labs show you are dangerously dehydrated. I'm admitting you to the hospital. I'm giving you round the clock IV fluids. I'm also giving you strong pain medicine."

God works in mysterious ways. That day I had a huge wakeup call that my life was about to change in a fundamental way. My body was slowly dying. I could feel my liver shutting down. The MRI showed that I had severed a peripheral nerve in my left leg. I hurt the L disc in my back and hurt my left hip. The feeling in my right leg came back. But my left leg from my toes to my knees were completely numb. My leg was full of fluid. I could not wiggle my toes or move my calf. I could not walk on my left side.

I contacted my family, Jared, and my close friends on Facebook. I shared with them the terrible news. My brother Lymster called me in a sheer panic after he received my text, "Mouse (my nickname) you can't die. You need to come to my kids' wedding and their kids' wedding. You just can't die."

It was then I realized that the prophecy was being fulfilled like my Primary Care Doctor had predicted two weeks ago, "The chronic vomiting of 21 months is going to cause your organs to shrink. Especially, your liver, kidneys are going to start shutting down. It will cause a domino effect when you least expect it."

236

Like a fortune teller he had foretold the months following. My doctor was very concerned that my high WBC was not decreasing like he had hoped. The next few days he was in a sheer panic that I may not recover. He increased the IV fluids to 500 ml an hour to treat the fluids in my left leg.

The next day my WBC finally decreased. My doctor was relieved. But it took a week to fully recover. When my labs were stable again my doctor wanted to send me to a rehab/ nursing facility. The fluid had decreased in my left leg. But my toes to my knee were still numb. I was still unable to walk on my left leg.

I called my family and Jared to share the bad news of my recent condition. They all agreed to my doctor's recommendation to send me to a rehab facility. I had hit my lowest. I couldn't believe that I was living in a rehab/ nursing home. I had to share a room with a lady who was snoring. She kept me awake all night. I begged the staff to be moved to another room. They promised they would move me in a few days. It never happened. I wanted to get out of my room as much as I could.

I was overjoyed to work with the physical therapists daily. They had me walk in an orthopedic boot with a walker. They always brought me outside to walk around the beautiful fountain outside my room. After our sessions together I would stay outside for hours basking in the warm sun. I would dip my toes in the cold fountain water. I wanted to stay outside all day. The sun was my happy place.

One of the physicians in the facility was so dreamy. He had silver short cut hair and beautiful blue eyes. His skin was tan and I could see his tight muscles through his short sleeved white overcoat. He was a caring doctor. His visits brightened my day. When I was outside sitting in my wheelchair enjoying the sun he would stop by to say hi. He wanted to make sure I was getting the proper medications for my gastroparesis and neuropathy pain in my left leg. He also made sure that I was getting the help I needed from the nurses and nurses aids to go to the bathroom and to take a shower. But his main concern was that I wasn't eating and barely drinking. So he would have the nurses' aid bring me cottage cheese, fresh cantaloupe watermelon and ice the only thing I would eat.

Two weeks after admission to rehab I was vomiting and vomiting non-stop. I was burning up with a high fever. I passed out on my bed from excessive vomiting. The nurse discovered me the next morning while she was making her morning rounds to check up on me. I looked white as the sheet on my bed. She panicked and called 911.

The ambulance rushed me to the hospital with a 101 fever. My blood pressure was 85/50. My heart rate was 130. After my blood tests returned. The doctor entered the room. She said, "You have sepsis. You are going into renal failure. I am admitting you to the hospital and starting you on strong IV antibiotics."

I felt so sick and so weak. But with a bolus of IV fluids - 500 ml/ hr my kidneys slowly recovered.

A week later my labs were stable again. The doctor felt it was safe to send me back to the rehab facility to finish the final week of antibiotics.

The doctor said before I left the hospital, "You have never had sepsis before. Your health is definitely declining."

I thought to myself, "If I'm going to die then I'm going to die in the sun. Not laying in bed depressed withering away."

I spent the next week in 90 degree temp in the beautiful sunshine for hours outside my bedroom door. I was glowing a dark tan prepared to die alone in a rehab facility without my family and close friends. They would not allow visitors or for me to leave to visit loved ones because of the COVID boundaries in California.

Jared contacted me via text and told me: I've contacted your family. I just found out my wife has pancreatic cancer. We are pushing to sell the house now. You need to be around your family now that you are declining in health. You are quickly going to die. I can see it. Your family now needs to see and be with you in your final days.

I agreed to Jared's request. I cried when he told me the sad news of his wife's pancreatic cancer.

My brother Brian called me later that day and said, "Jared called us. He doesn't want you to stay alone at the house anymore now that you injured yourself. Mom and I are coming on Saturday to pick you up to take you home to live with me temporarily until we transfer you to a rehab center in Utah."

I agreed to the terms and spoke to Jared later that day. He said, "I will be there in a few days with your family. I'm happy they are coming to take care of you. Can Travis come be with you until we arrive? I don't want you to be alone?"

I replied, "Yes I want to see Travis before I go back to Utah."

Jared was happy I was going to be with Travis. When I called Travis he told me, "I'm leaving to go to San Francisco for the weekend for work. I wanted to meet your mom and Brian. But I won't be able to. Let's spend some time together before I leave. I can take you to the dollar store to get some things for your trip."

When I saw Travis walk up to my door 10 min later I gave him a hug. I didn't want to bring the rickety walker the rehab facility had given me to take home. I was wearing my orthopedic boot for my left leg. I trusted Travis with my life. He was all I needed for support. I latched his arm in mine. I hopped into his red car parked in the paved driveway out front. It felt so familiar and comfortable to be with my buddy. He had been my support emotionally, physically and spiritually the past eight months enduring the worst of my illness. He and Jared were my family. They were like my big brothers. I loved them both so dearly.

When Travis brought me home after shopping at the dollar store he made sure I was safe in my recliner chair. My walker was close by. I felt his warm embrace comforting me with his big arms around me. He said, "Have a good trip. I will miss you."

I replied, "Me too."

Travis walked to his car to drive home. A tear fell down my cheek. My buddy was leaving and I didn't know when I would see him again. The next few days felt like a hazy fog. Later that night I was not feeling well. But I slept like a baby in my own cozy bed. The next morning my mom and brother arrived early with Jared close behind them. I was so weak, unable to walk on my left leg. The rickety walker gave me no stability.

When Brian and my mom saw me they smiled, hugging me tight in their arms and said, "It's good to see you."

I nodded happily. My mom, Brian, and Jared were concerned about how immobile I was. I felt so feeble. Jared and Brian packed all my things up for me while I lay on my bed. I was dehydrated and malnourished. I had not eaten or drank more than bites of jello since I had returned home. I felt dizzy from the lack of fluids.

Within a few hours Jared and Brian had my things all packed up. The home and family I had lived with for two years I was now leaving. I looked inside the house one last time and stepped outside holding my walker. I embraced Jared in my arms with tears trickling down my face and said, "You are my family. No one has taken me in like you did and loved me as family."

Jared replied, "I love you too. You are the little sister I never had. Take care kiddo."

I replied, "My heart breaks for what your family is now going through with your sweet wife's cancer. You all will be in my prayers."

I hopped onto my good right leg. Brian took my left shoulder. He helped me into the brown Cadillac parked outside. I lay in the back of the car on the brown leather seats. I waved goodbye to my wonderful life in sunny California.

Chapter 23

When God Closes One Door He Opens A Window

"Gods Timing is never late, never early it takes patience and a lot of faith, but it's so worth it."

The ride home to Utah felt like a dream. I don't remember all the details of it. I was so sick- malnutrition and very dehydrated. I heard my mom and Brian talking. My mom said, "Son, you look tired. Do you want me to drive?"

Brian replied, "No mom I got this. You can't see clearly in the dark anymore."

I hadn't seen my family in two years. My mom still looked as radiant as always. But her old age of 77 was catching up with her. She had bad knees. She had a weak back. I was so happy I was finally seeing her again. I felt special that she and Brian had driven 700 miles to come pick me up. It was definitely a miracle I wasn't expecting.

I slept in the car on the way to Utah. I felt so weak. When we arrived at Brian's house 10 hours later it was morning. Brian helped me out of the car. My mom was close behind us. I hopped on my good leg into his house. He sat me down in the TV room on a few mattresses and said, "This is where you will be staying."

My mom walked over to me. She gave me a warm hug. I felt so loved in her arms. There is nothing like a mother's hug. She said, kissing me on the cheek, "Okay I'm heading back home to Roy. So glad you are here. Bye sweetie."

I waved goodbye to my mom. I lay on the bed in a foggy haze. Brian brought me water to drink. He was concerned how pale I was from my lack of nutrients and liquids. I felt the cold water go down my dry throat. But immediately I vomited it back up. I was shaking from dehydration. My heart rate was high, over 100. I felt like I was going to faint. Brian said to me, "Wow this is the worse I've seen you. I didn't know you were this bad."

He helped me into his red van. He rushed me to the ER. When we arrived at the ER the waiting room was packed with sick people waiting their turn to be called to go back to a room in the ER. The nurse at the registration desk noticed how pale I was. She immediately took my vitals. My heart rate was 130. She rushed me back to a room in the ER.

A kind nurse came in 5 min later to access my chest port and draw my blood. The doctor came to see me 20 min later. He said, "We need permission to release your medical records from the hospital in California where you had been receiving medical care for two years. Your labs show that you have an infection. We need a UA to check your urine and a CT scan to find out what infection it is?"

After 30 min of laying in terrible kidney pain I saw a friendly face walk in the room. He said, "From the results of your CT scan and urine culture you have a kidney infection. You have two small kidney stones on your left kidney. You are dehydrated and have low potassium. We are going to admit you to the hospital to give you IV antibiotics, IV fluids, IV nausea and IV pain medicine."

Time felt like it was standing still. I was curled up in bed in the fetal position writhing in kidney pain. A beautiful nurse with dark brown hair cascading down her back walked in 5 min later. She gave me the medications the doctor had ordered through my chest port. Slowly I could feel my body drifting off to sleep.

Sleep was where I went to escape. To feel pain free in my peaceful dreams. I saw a golden diamond sandy brown beach. The clouds hovering above me were ocean blue. A beautiful white angel dressed in white pants and a white shirt walked towards me. He was so handsome. He had dark brown hair and dark brown eyes. He looked so young. Not a flaw I could see. He had a light glowing around him. I ran to hug him. I felt a warmth of unconditional love flow through my body. It was my dad. He looked deep into my eyes and said, "Come home."

I woke up in terrible pain. I started to cry and contemplated, "I just had a wonderful dream of heaven. My dad is calling me home. How long to be pain free of this horrible disease that is slowly shutting down my body day by day."

I clumsily pressed the call light to request for more pain medicine from the nurse. 5 min later a sweet lady dressed in pink scrubs entered the room to give me pain medicine through my chest port. Immediately my pain disappeared. I felt an euphoric feeling. I slowly drifted off to sleep again.

A few days passed and the doctor came into my room and said firmly, "I want to send you home today. Your labs are looking better, and you can finish the rest of the antibiotics orally."

I told the doctor, "No, I can't do oral antibiotics with the gastroparesis. I can't keep it down. It makes me so sick. I just vomit it up on an empty stomach."

The doctor said, "Well I want to try to see if you can keep it down. The nurse will give you an oral tablet."

The doctor walked out of the room. A stunning woman dressed in dark blue scrubs gave me an oral antibiotic with water to drink. I felt nauseated immediately after she gave it to me. 20 min passed and I had not vomited up the antibiotic

The doctor discharged me to go home.

I called Brian to come pick me up at the hospital. He arrived 30 min later. The nurse wheeled me to his red van parked outside the emergency room. Within two hours of being discharged I was shaking. My heart was beating fast. I was burning up with a high fever and chills. I hadn't showered in two days. I was dripping in sweat. When we arrived home Brian said, "Let me help you take a shower. You may feel better."

Brian lifted me on his back. He walked up the gray carpeted stairs to the bathroom. He helped me onto the white shower chair seated in the bathtub. He exited the room while I took my clothes off on the shower chair. When I was finished undressing, I turned the silver knob. Water flowed into the white tub. I pulled the white shower knob. Water cascaded onto my sweaty body. It felt so good to be drenched in warm water. I could smell Johnson's baby shampoo as I washed my body. The white bubbles dripped down my skinny legs. I had lost most of my muscle on my left leg from my nasty fall a month ago. I lifted my head to feel the warm water on my face.

Suddenly I vomited straight acid. I had vomited up the oral antibiotic the doctor had given me just like I told him I would. My body shook like a rambling earthquake. I immediately turned off the tap water. I was fighting to breathe. I couldn't stop shaking. I yelled out to Brian, "Help me, Brian please."

I heard footsteps running up the stairs yelling, "Sis are you okay?"

My wonderful brother bound through the door rescuing me. He handed me my red, blue, white striped beach towel to cover up my body. I wrapped the towel around my chest. Brian took my trembling hand to help me step out of the tub on my good right leg. He helped me get dressed.

He was a gentleman and turned his head not to see my body. When I was fully dressed he lifted me up on his back trotting down the stairs. He laid me on my bed. I was still shaking. My chest hurt every breath I took. I said weakly, "I need to go back to the hospital. I vomited up the oral antibiotic the doctor gave me at the hospital."

Brian said kindly, "Okay let's go. You are pale. You look very sick. You haven't stopped shaking. Your speech has been really fast."

Brian rushed me to the ER in his red minivan. When we arrived at the ER the room was packed with sick people. At the registration desk the nurse immediately took me back to do my vitals. My heart rate was 140. The nurse said kindly,"

We are slammed tonight. We don't have any rooms right now. We will try to get you to a room as soon as we can."

She wheeled me back to the waiting room. Four hours later I felt I was going to pass out. I heard a sweet voice like an angel say, "Marci sorry for the wait. Let's get you into a room. You don't look so good."

She wheeled me into a room in the back of the ER. Immediately another nurse entered the room to help me change into a white gown. She accessed my chest port. She drew some blood. 15 min later the doctor came into my room. He said, "You definitely still have an infection. We need a UA to determine if

246

it's a kidney infection and if you have passed the kidney stone. The nurses need to do a straight catheter since you aren't peeing anymore to get an accurate reading."

Two nurses walked in 10 min later to put in the straight catheter. I wanted to die when the catheter was pushed up into my body. I tightened my leg to relieve the pressure. Finally 5 minutes later it was over. The doctor came in 15 min later and said concerning, "We found blood in your urine. You still have a kidney infection. Your kidney stones haven't passed yet. I'm admitting you to the hospital to put you on IV antibiotics and IV pain medicine. If we don't treat your kidney you could go septic again because now you are dealing with both medical issues back to back."

The next few days at the hospital my bladder and kidneys hurt when I would pee. The IV fluids were streaming through my chest port at 500 ml an hour causing me to pee every 30 min. Luckily the nurse gave me IV pain meds every 2 hours to endure passing the kidney stone. But the IV antibiotics made me feel so nauseated. The nurse gave me IV nausea meds every 6 hours to control the nausea. But my stomach felt like it was being turned inside out. The pain was horrific from the antibiotics streaming through my veins. I did not have the strength to get out of bed other than to void. I was shaking. I was so cold.

I was losing muscle tone from malnutrition. My weight had dropped ten more pounds since I had arrived in Utah. I had lost a total of 50 lbs in 28 months since I had been diagnosed with gastroparesis. The nurse's aides at the hospital were kind enough to bring me warm blankets to keep me toasty.

I stayed in the hospital on antibiotics for a few days until the doctor felt it was safe to discharge me. He had a social worker talk to me about finishing the rest of the five day antibiotics at an IV clinic at a local hospital in Provo. I told her frankly, "My medical insurance only covers out of state ER visits and hospital stays."

She replied, "The IV clinic covers two visits for free for low income patients like yourself. You will need to cover the rest. It's $500 a day for the IV antibiotic infusion. The doctor wants to discharge you today on that plan."

I told her firmly, "I can't afford to pay $3000 out of pocket. I haven't worked in 24 months because I've been so ill with gastroparesis,"

She said, "Well this is the plan. The doctor is discharging you today on oral strong pain medicine to pass the kidney stone and for the kidney infection.

I called Brian and shared with him the doctor's plan. We both agreed that going to the IV clinic would be a mistake to pay for their services out of pocket. Our plan was to go back to the ER when I was dehydrated again and had low potassium from vomiting. Then the doctor could reassess me if I needed further treatment.

Later that day I was in intense pain for 6 straight hours. It felt like I was in labor. I screamed out in agony, "Take me, take me now, kill me." I felt my lower abdomen muscle contract every hour, then every 30 minutes then every 10 minutes then every 5 minutes. With every life threatening contraction I breathed deeply ready for the next contraction. I screamed out during the painful contractions. I was so grateful I had pain medicine to take the edge off.

Brian had been by my side through it all. He said with empathy, "I had a kidney stone once it was so painful. I was in terrible pain for 6 straight hours like you. It's like you're giving birth to twin baby boys. Boys tend to be harder deliveries."

248

I just laughed when Brian shared his experience. Laughter is the best medicine. I had close friends and family say to me, "You stay so positive through all you have been through, still laughing and making jokes."

My reply was, "I've learned to laugh and not cry through my intense trials of life that broke me. It's okay to be a broken woman. Jesus taught me that. When I'm broken I'm more teachable. I'm more trusting of God's plan for me. Crying isn't going to make me feel better. Only laughter. I love to make people laugh. When my dad was alive, He said to me when he got sick. We are kindred spirits, because we are both the third oldest of the siblings. We get picked on by other siblings. We use humor to deal with it. We have a gift of making others laugh."

My dad was so right. Laughter gets me through.

Meanwhile, trying to pass the two kidney stones took everything out of me. I was in unbearable pain so I took a pain pill. I immediately felt loopy. I went off to dreamland. I awoke an hour later to a bright light at the foot of my bed. I saw an angel. It was my dad. I heard him say, "Are you ready for me to come and get you?"

I sat up in my bed to try to get a closer look at my dad. But he disappeared. I realized that I would be dying soon. I didn't know when. I didn't know how. But I knew it was soon. The more I was suffering in pain the more I was ready to go to the other side. I contemplated the joy I would feel crossing permanently beyond the veil to see my dad again. To feel the unconditional love I felt when I met the Savior in my two NE.

I fell asleep again with a smile on my face. I woke up the next morning. I tried to drink liquids. But I couldn't keep them down. I cried out in pain from the horrible vomiting, "I can't do this anymore. Please let me die. I want to be free of pain."

The next morning I decided I needed a break from my pathetic life. I was tired of wallowing in self-pity. My nephew Jordan had just had knee surgery a few days ago. I wanted to see how he was doing. I slowly scooted my butt up the stairs to his room. Each step felt like I was climbing a large mountain. My breathing was weak. I was panting like a dog when I finally reached the top of the stairs yelling to myself, "Victory."

Jordan came out of his room walking on crutches. He was standing firmly on his right leg. He smiled when he saw me reach the top of the stairs. He sat down next to me. I asked him, "How are you doing?"

He replied, "I'm super frustrated. My friends are all going on their LDS missions. Now that I had knee surgery I can't go at the time I wanted to go on my mission."

I was shocked by Jordan's reply. I said to Jordan, "Wow I didn't think anyone was dealing with a hard ache from their trials of life, but me. It's so nice to hear that you struggle. I never would have thought you felt his way."

I felt I should share with Jordan my recent NDE and the angelic visitations from my dad (Grandpa Z) As I shared these amazing heavenly experiences I asked Jordan, "Have you ever felt Grandpa Z since he passed on?"

His eyes lit up, "I can feel him now. He is standing beside you with his hand on your shoulder. He is here to help you endure to the end so you can be with him in heaven."

I was in complete shock by his reply and said, "Are you serious?

He replied, "Yes I feel him in the room with us."

I replied almost in tears, "He is always here for me. Why is the family in such denial of me dying?"

Jordan replied kindly, "Do you blame them? We lost Grandpa Z and it gutted us all. We don't want to lose you too."

I looked at my incredibly handsome nephew who had grown from a boy into a man. I loved being around him. He was so Christlike. He had a strong testimony of Jesus. He had a light about him that drew people into his goodness. He was just like his dad Brian. I was so impressed that my brother Brian had raised such a fine young man. Brian was my hero. He was so much like my dad. He knew how to calm me down when I was upset. He showered me with love taking care of me in his home.

But all good things must come to an end. The stay with Brian was only temporary until we could admit me in a 24-hour nursing home to care for me. The sad reality was I would be in a nursing home for the rest of my life. But I knew that I wouldn't be there long. The stages of dying were creeping into my life day by day. The doctors and nurses warned me that because of the chronic dehydration causing kidney infections and kidney stones that my kidneys would go into full renal failure. I would be labeled "terminal" when my kidneys were not able to recover. Then I could finally go to hospice.

My loved ones were all praying for a miracle for me to be healed. But I knew in my heart Heavenly Father wanted me home. I was ready to pass on to the other side. The next week I was in agony. I was severely dehydrated from excessive vomiting. I had been admitted to the hospital three times to try to pass the kidney stone and to heal my kidneys. But to no avail.

I remember the day so vividly when I awoke in the early morning projectile vomiting. I could not stop vomiting. My whole body was burning up like a hot furnace. I was pouring in sweat, so exhausted from vomiting. I passed out from severe weakness. I awoke in the late night and vomited more.

I heard Brian's car pull into the garage. When he opened the back door he gasped at my ghostly white appearance. He raced me to the ER. When the nurse took my vitals at the ER my blood pressure was 70/50 and heart rate was 130. She quickly took me back to a room in the ER. The rest of the night felt like a blur. I had a fever of 102'. I was trembling from severe dehydration. The doctor immediately came into my room. He was very concerned about my low blood pressure and high heart rate. He ordered IV fluids, IV nausea meds, blood work, a UA sample and an abdominal X- ray.

Thirty minutes later after all the tests had returned he said, concerned, "Your blood work came back. You have an infection. Your UA showed that you still have the kidney infection. The X- ray showed that you haven't passed the kidney stones. We are admitting you to the hospital."

The next five days in the hospital. I was in unbearable pain trying to pass the kidney stones and fight the kidney infection. The nurses were so kind and empathetic of my pain. But my blood pressure was still low 70/50 and my heart rate was still too high 130. I didn't meet the criteria for IV pain meds. I needed a stable systolic blood pressure over 100.

The doctor ordered a bolus of IV fluids to rehydrate me. I was in so much pain. I pleaded with the nurse who took care of me to give me some IV pain medicine. But the nurse replied sympathetically, "I'm so sorry but you don't meet the criteria for IV pain meds. Your blood pressure is too low. The IV pain meds could cause you to stop breathing."

It felt like the longest day waiting for my blood pressure to return to normal. It took 24 hours for my heart rate to go above 100. I was so overjoyed when I was able to receive IV pain meds every two hours to take the edge off the pain. My left ribs were so sore from projectile vomiting. My kidneys felt like multiple knives puncturing me. Stabbing me over and over again. Slowly I felt the IV fluids rehydrate me.

But I was so sick from the kidney infection and from the IV antibiotics the nurse gave me twice a day to treat it. It felt like my stomach was being ripped apart. The doctor who came to see me every day said, "We are going to keep you in the hospital until you pass the kidney stones and the kidney infection is gone. We are giving you strong IV pain meds, IV nausea meds and IV antibiotics twice a day to treat your kidneys."

I was in curdling pain for the next three days. I could feel the kidney stones in my urethra coming down the canal. Thankfully the IV fluids helped me to pass the kidney stones. When I passed them I instantly felt relief. I saw two small granules in the white hat the nurse's aides put on the toilet bowl to measure my urine output and to catch the kidney stones. Although my body was free of the kidney stones I still had the kidney infection. I had a cannula in my nose to help me breathe. The kidney infection took a toll on my respiratory system.

My mom FaceTime me later that day. I was happy to see her face. My mom was very concerned about how pale and sick I was. I told her gasping for air, breathing in oxygen in my nose, "I'm so ready to go. I felt dad the day before I went to the hospital. He was standing on the foot of my bed. He said, "Are you ready for me to come and get you?" I did not see his face. He was a silhouette of an angel. When I awoke to get a better look he had vanished. I knew he was ready to take me home to heaven soon."

My mom said, "Well don't die yet."

I said, "I won't there are still loved ones like my cousins I want to see again. I am having a cousin get together at Brian's on Saturday."

My mom replied, "That is so great."

I said, "Yes, once I see them, other loved ones like you, then I can go."

My mom replied, "Wow you are just at peace to go aren't you."

I replied, "Yes I have no quality of life. I live in the hospital now. The chronic dehydration is causing more kidney infections and kidney stones that can cause full renal failure. Please pray I can go to hospice."

My mom replied softly, "I don't want you to suffer anymore. I will pray that you can go to hospice."

I realized that my loving mother accepting me dying was the miracle I had been praying for. Finally my family was letting me go so I could pass on. My doctor came in early the next morning and told me, "Your labs look great. The kidney infection is gone. We can send you home today."

But when I tried to eat and drink again I vomited. I was dehydrated again because the doctor had stopped my IV fluids. After 4 pm the nurse gave me another dose of IV pain meds and discharged me. The nurse wheeled me outside the hospital to the shiny red van parked in the entrance way. Brian helped me into the red van and we drove home. I felt so weak. I was losing strength in my muscles. My left leg was atrophying more every day from my fall over 6 months ago. The bone was sticking out on the front of my leg from my loss of muscle. My ribs and back still hurt from the projectile vomiting. I hadn't slept more than two hours at a time in the hospital. The constant swarm of doctors, nurses, nurse's aides coming in to care for me all hours of the night made me so tired.

When Brian drove up to the driveway he helped me out of his van. He put his arm around me and hopping on one leg he walked me to my bed. He tucked me into my comfy covers. As soon as my head hit the pillow. I was fast asleep in a wonderful dream land. The next morning I awoke recalling a beautiful blessing Brian and my nephew Jordan gave me in the hospital the day before being discharged. "Enjoy your time in Utah with your family and friends. The desires of your heart will be fulfilled according to your faith."

I knew without a shadow of a doubt that the desires of my heart would be to pass on. But I was confident I would see loved ones like my cousins, my family and my dear friends before God called me home. I felt a rush of joy in my heart. I've shared my story. I've done all the Lord has asked me to do. Now I can go. God kept me broken to keep me at Jesus' feet. I've held onto the hem of his garment since. Soon I would be in heaven in my loving Savior's arms. I would see my wonderful dad. I imagined I would run into his arms on a crystal sandy beach just like in my dream. I now longed to be in heaven. To be flying up in the fluffy white clouds free of pain only to feel joy and peace.

My very talented close friend Justin who in the book his name is Travis. He wrote a beautiful song called "The Eternal Eye" that I wanted to share.

Through The Eternal Eye by Justin Laukat

Through the Eternal Eye
Brightly beaming through my soul Lighter than noon day sky
When life takes its toll

The light of Christ will brightly shine Radiating in my heart

When our hearts are intertwined

I'll strive to do my part

His throne before a sea of glass

His ever watchful eyes

And those who see the least of these See God moving in his majesty

Through the Eternal eye

He fills my mind with knowledge Challenging worldly ties

I'll battle through with courage

The light of Christ will brightly shine Radiating in my heart

When our hearts are intertwined

I'll strive to do my part

He guides us in our journey home With ever watchful eyes

And those who see the least of these See God working in his majesty

Chapter 24

I Am A Walking Miracle

"Miracles do happen" Marci Zollinger

April 2022

I heard my Uncle Clair's voice, "Marci, I am here representing your dad giving you a blessing, You will heal from this. You will go on a mission. You will get married. Then you will go. You will affect many lives through your faith and be a tool in the Lord's hands."

I felt my dad. He was standing next to me during the blessing. I heard sobbing. I recall seeing family members and dear friends flashing in my mind. I saw them weeping and mourning for their loss of me. It made me sad that I would lose them. Even though I was not aware of my physical surroundings in this glorious dimension I realized that maybe the Lord wanted me to pray one last time for him to heal me. I thought to myself, "What if I could be healed and get married in this life like the blessing said?"

But I was done. There was no gray anymore for my life. The Lord was either going to heal me or take me. To give me the gift to be married like he promised in my blessing. To be a mom or grandma. I wasn't going to pray for these miracles unless I knew without a shadow of a doubt it would happen.

I prayed one last prayer, "I'm ready to go. I want to go. I will continue to just let my body shut down. I haven't eaten or drank

257

anything in 4 days and will continue this course. So heal me or take me. If there is a possibility that I will be married in this life like my blessing said then I will come back. But I'm coming back on a huge mountain of faith. I will only come back if I can be blessed with these two miracles. You need to give me a reason to want to stay."

The spiritual dimension I was in I felt no pain. I could not respond to the voices I heard. I could not see or touch. I had left my body. I was in a realm where every fiber of my being wanted to stay. Once again my spirit was in glorious heaven. But my hearing was acute. The voices were pulling me back to the physical world like a whirlpool swirling me round and round. I was leaving this joyous dimension.

Like a bolt of lightning I was back in my body. I awoke in an unfamiliar bed with strangers all around me. The walls were bare white. The floors were dirty. The bed I slept in was tiny. I had my own bed covers wrapped around me to comfort me. I was scared of my surroundings. I called my brother Brian to come and get me. On the third ring he picked up the phone and said, "Hello."

I replied, "Bro I'm ready for you to pick me up."

Brian said, "What are you talking about sis. Mom and I picked you up from California to bring you to Utah to that nursing home you're in now. We had you in the hospital and you told the doctor that you were done. You told him you were going to stop eating and drinking. You had an infection in your chest port and you were going septic. You have been in hospice for a month now. Family has come to visit you. Levi flew out twice to see you. Cami's family came to see you. Chantelle and the girls came to see you. I came to see you several times with mom. They were crying that you were dying."

I replied, "I don't remember any of that except the crying I remember."

Brian replied, "They have had you pretty doped up. They have been giving morphine to you every hour. They have been giving you medication to keep you comfortable in hospice, to help you pass on."

I said, "I honestly don't remember anything you are telling me."

He said, "You haven't eaten or drank anything in a few days. You were septic. You were on your way out. Call me later and let me know how you are doing."

I said, "Okay I will."

I hung up the phone. I was sitting up in bed. A tray of food and water was sitting on my food table. I took a few bites of food waiting to vomit it up. I did not throw it up. I took another bite. I sipped on water. I kept it down. The rest of the day I was also able to keep lunch and dinner down too. I now felt strong enough to get out of bed. I placed both feet on the ground. My feet felt different to the touch. They weren't as wobbly. I used the dresser drawer to pull myself up. I took a few steps without my wheelchair. I could walk. I danced around the room in shock. The Lord had healed me. It is a miracle.

I called my brother Brian and said, "You won't believe it. You just won't believe it, I'm healed."

He said, "What do you mean you're healed? "

259

I said, "I could feel my body going. I prayed to the Lord to heal me or take me because I was done. I could no longer feel connected to my body. I was slipping into a coma. I woke up this morning. I was healed. I stopped vomiting. I could walk a few steps then walk with a walker."

Brian replied, "You are a walking miracle. I can't believe this. You were on your way out. Now you're healed."

Chapter 25

Christ's Perfect Love

"Come To the Table"

No one knows what their story in life will be, only God knows the ending. What I have learned in my life is that my life is not what I thought it would be. I had envisioned myself with a beautiful family and a happy healthy life. But God had other plans. He blessed me with the miracle but in his time and will. I have always tried to be a good person and help others. But God wanted me to reach higher. I made plans. God laughed at my plan. He said, "No my child this is who you will be. You won't be a mere flower but a magnificent mountain above the blue skies."

I perceive life like a long hike in the mountains. We are excited to begin our journey with our knapsack around our shoulders, water to drink and goody snacks to nibble on along the way. We are confident we can make it up the mountain. But then, obstacles stand in our way like severe heat, fatigue, wild animals and a loss of direction.

Suddenly, we feel lost and have veered off the path we mapped out as our destination. We feel scared and alone. We pray to God, "Please help me. I've lost my way."

Suddenly, we feel God's love to take another path. He says to us, "The path won't be easy. There will be bruises and scrapes along the way. At times you may feel like you are drowning, but if you ask me, I promise I will send others to help you along the way and rescue you. What I have for you is greater than what you see. I see great things in you. Trust me to bring you to greater heights than you ever dreamed you could reach"

Following God's plan is easier said than done. I've always had a difficult time trusting God's plan for me. When I trust in him I feel pain and suffering. I cry in agony from the unbearable path God leads me to. But he promised when I cry out for help, he will send others to rescue me- a close friend, family member or an angel from heaven, like my dad who has passed. After my visits to heaven it gave me a new perspective of life and people. In heaven I saw a huge beautiful yellow butterfly. The butterfly symbolizes hope. Since then I have seen the yellow butterfly hovering over me and felt my dad when I've been sad or lonely.

Now I'm walking on clouds. When God calls me home I can leave in peace feeling confident that I showed up for life. I fought blood, sweat and tears just to survive. I followed God's plan for me. I never gave up. Only God knows the end of my story. Whether I go in a few months or years to come. I've seen glorious heaven. I felt its love and joy. I live my life every day to be blessed to one day go to paradise. To be in that beautiful mansion with that sweet angel child I saw in heaven. To be with my wonderful father and my loving Savior, Jesus Christ. What a reunion that will be.

My beautiful loyal and kind friend Lori sent me this beautiful song when I was deadly ill for almost three long grueling years.

"Come To the Table" *by Sidewalk Prophets*

We all start on the outside
the outside looking in
This is where grace begins
We were hungry we were thirsty with nothing left to give

262

Oh the shape that we were in

And Just when all hope seemed lost Love opened the door for us

He said come to the table

Come join the sinners who have been redeemed

Take your place beside the Savior Sit down and be set free

Come to the table

Come meet this motley crew of misfits These liars and these thieves

There's no one unwelcome here

That sin and shame you brought with you

You can leave it at the door

And Let mercy draw you near

Come to the table

Come join the sinners who have been redeemed Take your place beside the Savior

Sit down and be set free

Come to the table

Come to the table

To the thief and to the doubter To the hero and the coward To the prisoner and the soldier To the young and to the older All who hunger all who thirst

All the last and all the first

All the paupers and the princes

All who've failed you've been forgiven

All who dream and all who suffer

All who loved and lost another

All the chained and all the free

All who follow all who lead

Anyone who's been let down

All the lost you have been found

263

All who have been labeled right or wrong To everyone who hears his song

Come to the table

Come join the sinners who have been redeemed Take your place beside the Savior

Sit down and be set free

Come to the table

Come to the table

Sit down and be set free

Come to the table

This physical dimension is not my home. I am here traveling like a tourist travels to Europe: Germany, Italy or Rome. But in the end their travels lead them back home to Florida. The place they call home. I am like that tourist. Jesus sent me to earth to get a body giving me a map of a plan to return home. I believe he told me, "We will be apart for a short time. But all your experiences will be for your good. When you are lost follow me and I will guide you to safety. I am the way the truth and the light follow me and you will return home to be with me. "

I don't know why the Lord sent me back from heaven when I was in hospice. But I'm realizing through his great miracles that others are moved by my miracle story. I have seen and felt the other side of the veil many times. Each time I visited heaven I felt and saw Jesus radiant light that surrounded me in his perfect love. A love that I have never felt in my existence on earth.

When the Savior calls me home I know that my earthly father who has passed will come to take me home to a glorious place indescribable to the human mind. A place where I will leave my body of clay, feel no more pain and rest from my earthly cares. Joy will feel my heart and soul to dwell in a spiritual dimension of pure light and love.

I'm Just Passing Through On My Way To Heaven. Heaven is my home.

BIBLIOGRAPHY

Tommy Walker "He Knows My Name"

Released 2000 Christian Gospel Worship Video with Lyrics. Absolute Label Services on Behalf of Integrity Music, Music EMT Music Publishing BMI - BroadCast Music Inc. Adoranda Brazil, Capitol CMG Publishing and 4 Music Right Societies YouTube https://youtu.bc/GXrAqE_tSmo Date of access October 13, 2020

Loren Thomas "Sometimes God Breaks You Just So He Can Fix You"

Her Way of Life. Herway.net
https://herway.net/life/sometimes-god-breaks-you-just-he-could-fix-you/

Date of Access April 23, 2020.

Billy Graham "My Home Is Heaven I'm Just Traveling Through This World" Brainy Quote - Famous Quotes. brainyquote.com
https://www.brainyquote.com/quotes/billy_graham_382921 Date of Access October 13, 2020

Anne Kennedy "Preventing Grace". And Then Jesus Said.
https://www.patheos.com/blogs/preventingrace/2019/07/23/and-then-Jesus-said/

Date of Access July 23, 2019

R.C Sproul "There Is Nothing In This Universe That We Need More Than Christ" R.C Sproul quotes
quotefancy.*com https://quotefancy.com/quote/1490338/R-C-Sproul-There-is-nothing-in-this-Universe-you-need-more-despartely-than-Christ*

Date of Access October 15, 2020

Wikipedia "Light Of The World" John 9:15
https://en.wikipedia.org/wiki/Light_of_the_World

Date of Access June 16, 2014

Sidewalk Prophets "Come To The Table" Official Lyric Video Album Something Different *https://youtu.be/DXXxLwxfo0U*

Date of Access 2015

Elder B. Eyring "Raise The Bar" YouTube *https://www2.byui.edu/Speeches/eyring_jan2005.htm* Date of Access October 10, 2020

Benson, Ezra T. "Life is Eternal." The Church of Jesus Christ of Latter-day Saints. *www.lds.org*. Date of Access August 4, 2019.

Curiano, Via. Motivational Quotes and Stories.

ww.inspiredtoreality.com. Date of Access August 4, 2019.

Freeman, Morgan. Everyday Power. www. everydaypower.com/morgan-freeman-quotes. Date of Access August 9, 2019.

Holland, Jeffrey R. "For a Wise Purpose." The Church of Jesus Christ of Latter-day Saints. www.lds.org. Date of Access August 5, 2019.

Holland, Jeffrey R. "Songs Sung and Unsung." The Church of Jesus Christ of Latter-day Saints. www. lds.org. Date of Access August 4, 2019.

Laughorn, Caroline. Pinterest. www.pinterest.es/pin/736268239062974441/?autologin=true. Date of Access August 9, 2019.

Lewis, C.S. Pureflix Insiders. www.insider.pure flix.com. Date of Access August 4, 2019.

Ma, Jack. Never Give Up: Jack Ma in His Own Words. Agate Publishing. February 2019.

Maybe, Stephanie. "Glorious." Wake Up Dreaming, Scott Wiley, August 1, 2012, track 6. Stephanie maybe, https://stephaniemabey.bandcamp.com/album/wake-up-dreaming.

Maraboli, Steve. Life, the Truth, and Being Free. A Better Today Publishing. November 2009.

Martin, Rachel Marie. The Brave Art of Motherhood. Waterbrooks, 2018.

McGraw, Philip. Calmer Choice. www.calmerchoice.org. Date of Access August 7, 2019.

Millard, Bart. "I Can Only Imagine." Almost There, INO Records, October 1999, track 5. Spotify, https://open.spotify.com/album/4BDftZAnppbkKAA4O4APzn.

Murray, Wendy. Facing Forward. Carol Stream. December 2002.

Phillips, Kim. Pinterest. *www.pinterest.com/pin/362328732517327034/?lp=true*. Date of Access August 9, 2019.

Robert, Sarah Jakes. Grace of God. *www.youtube.com/watch?v=bfdA6vXsvGY*. Date of Access August 9, 2019.

Uchtdorf, Dieter F. "Move Forward. The Church of Jesus Christ of Latter-day Saints. www.lds.org. Date of Access August 5, 2019. Uchtdorf, Dieter F. #nkmays. *www.hotsta.org/tag/nkmays*. Date of Access.

ABOUT THE AUTHOR

Marci Zollinger was born and raised in British Columbia, Canada. At 18 years of age she moved to Provo, Utah to attend Brigham Young University.

Marci has always been passionate about writing and was voted best writer amongst her fellow students in her English classes in school. Marci is a second time author and an advocate to end sex trafficking. She wrote her first book "Rescued In Heavens Eyes" She wrote her second book "Just Passing Through On My Way To Heaven" After her beautiful hospice experience when she almost died and was sent back from heaven for the third time she was inspired to combine both of her books together, to write this inspiring, true, miracle story.

Made in United States
Troutdale, OR
11/23/2024